Wayne Howell has covered the courts for the *Herald Sun* newspaper and the Australian Associated Press for about 12 of his 20 years in journalism. He reported on most of the stories in *Reasonable Doubt* at the time of the court trials. This is Wayne's third book. His very successful first book, *Eavesdropping on Evil*, tells the story of an extraordinary police bugging operation that caught two police killers. His second book, *Killer Excuses*, is a collection of the classic excuses killers use to avoid punishment.

REASONABLE DOUBT

Bizarre Tales of Death & Justice

Wayne Howell

The Five Mile Press

Published by
The Five Mile Press Pty Ltd
950 Stud Road, Rowville
Victoria 3178 Australia
Email: publishing@fivemile.com.au
Website: www.fivemile.com.au

Copyright © Wayne Howell, 2007
This anthology copyright © The Five Mile Press, 2007
All rights reserved

First published 2007
Reprinted 2007

Internal design by cthonic@bigpond.com
Cover design by Aimee Forde

Printed in Australia

National Library of Australia Cataloguing-in-Publication data

Howell, Wayne.
Reasonable Doubt: bizarre tales of death & justice.

ISBN 978 1 74178 451 0.

1. Crime - Case studies. 2. Criminal investigation. I. Title.

CONTENTS

Introduction	7
David Hookes: A Cricket Hero Dies	9
Gatto vs Veniamin: Defence Underworld-style	39
Sniper Wife	59
Mother-in-Law Nightmare	94
Being Al Pacino	125
Sleepwalk of Death	135
A Spiritual Death	149
Hypnotise Me	165
Warning Shot	178
Just Anger	211
Scare Tactics	239
Fatal Taunt	254
Bedsit Tragedy	264
One Body, Three Burials	273
Teaching a Toddler Who's Boss	292
Backyard Bonfire	318
Already Dead	326
Insanely Homesick	335

INTRODUCTION

Just because something's bizarre does not mean it's untrue: that's what the juries and judges who heard the extraordinary tales of killings and attempted killings in this book had to keep telling themselves. Confronted with odd, outlandish and blackly comic tales told by people fighting murder, attempted murder or manslaughter charges, juries and judges had to keep reminding themselves of the cliché that truth can be stranger than fiction. Incredible as some of these tales may have seemed, by law they had to accept them if they believed there was a reasonable chance they could be true; they could only convict if they were convinced the prosecution was right 'beyond all reasonable doubt'.

Why do people kill? How does it happen? Find out for yourself – the courts have made up their minds, now it's your turn. Read about:

- Underworld figure Mick Gatto, who said he shot Andrew 'Benji' Veniamin not to avenge a mate's murder, but because Benji had shot at him from a metre away – and missed.

- The pub bouncer who said he was only trying to defend himself when he fatally punched cricket hero David Hookes.

- The 'sniper wife' who ambushed her husband and shot him dead from 48 metres away but said it was self-defence because he would have killed her.

- The man who said he was sleepwalking when he got a gun out of a locked cabinet, shot his wife twice in the head, and returned the gun to the cabinet.

- The man who said when his wife told him her lover was 'meatier'

than him his whole body went hot and cold, he heard a loud pop …
and then realised he had bashed her to death with a hammer.

- The obsessed anti-abortionist who went to a family planning clinic
to commit a massacre but said his shooting of the clinic's security
guard was an accident.

- The husband and wife who said they watched a woman starve to
death and didn't call a doctor until it was too late because they believed she could live on just air and light.

- The man who said he killed his wife and frail mother-in-law to save
himself when they attacked him while he was sleeping.

- The man who said he accidentally shot his friend in his head while
acting out an Al Pacino cops 'n' crooks movie.

DAVID HOOKES
A Cricket Hero Dies

One of cricket's most famous matches of the modern era – the 1977 Centenary Test between Australia and England – was full of pomp and memories of 100 years of Test cricket. The Queen attended and dozens of former Test cricketers, decked out in their best suits, watched and reminisced about their glory days.

The first two days had moments dramatic enough to stop the 'old boys' yarns for a while: England fast bowler Bob Willis broke the jaw of Australian opener Rick McCosker with a fierce short ball, and the world's best fast bowler, Dennis Lillee, took six for 26 to skittle England for just 95 – 43 runs behind Australia's modest 138. But, as the pitch – and players' nerves – settled down, things became more sedate. Australia slowly built up a lead of about 200 and the 'oldies' got back to 'catching up'.

Then a blond, brash 21-year-old in his first Test changed all that.

In a match that was supposed to pay homage to cricket's past, David Hookes introduced its future.

With the fall of veteran Doug Walters' wicket shortly after lunch, Australia was five for 187. With McCosker uncertain to bat again (although he did, and made a vital 25 with his head swathed in bandages), the game was evenly poised; another wicket would have swung things England's way.

With Hookes on 36, England's captain – South African–born Tony Greig – decided to test Australia's new young hope with spin from both ends.

REASONABLE DOUBT

Hookes defended Greig's first two balls, but then decided enough was enough. So what that it was the 'Centenary Test' and all those big-shot legends were watching; so what that it was his first Test; so what that the bowler was the England captain: the 'offies' he was serving did not look that impressive; they looked hittable; in park cricket they would have been hittable – so Hookes hit them.

This is how – 18 years later to the *Herald Sun*'s Jon Anderson – Hookes described the five balls that changed his life, that turned him into a cricket legend who had lived out every cricket-mad youngster's dream.

Hookes: I didn't rate his [Greig's] off-spin all that highly and decided if the ball was up I'd hit it back over his head, which is what happened. I anticipated the next ball being quicker and glanced it to the fine-leg boundary while the third four came from a cover drive. The next was an on-drive through mid-wicket followed by another cover drive.

As Alf Batchelder put it in *The Centenary of Test Cricket*:

After each brilliant stroke, spectators expected the fireworks to cease. Each time such thoughts proved to be wrong, their excitement increased. The whole ground exploded when Hookes clipped the next ball to the mid-wicket fence. The left-hander was timing the ball so fluently that he appeared to caress it rather than hit it crudely like most mortals. His fifth boundary was so languid that it seemed it would roll only halfway to the fence, yet it carried a good 90 metres before dropping into the gutter ahead of the pursuing fieldsman ... Hookes drove Greig's final delivery, but Derek Randall fielded safely. The England skipper took his sweater from Max O'Connell [the umpire] with a smile of mock relief. Deep down he must have known he had little to smile about, for the onslaught had turned the tide Australia's way ... Suddenly, it all turned to disappointment. With no addition to his score, Hookes was caught at short leg off Underwood ... As Hookes

David Hookes: A Cricket Hero Dies

departed, the crowd rose, applauding not just his contribution to the score but some unforgettable moments of rare brilliance.

The old-timers' reminiscing party had been well and truly crashed. Nothing like it had been seen at the MCG for 50 years. In a quavering voice, radio commentator Colin McDonald declared: 'A star has been born.' The world's greatest batsman – Don Bradman – said it reminded him of the West Indian great Frank Woolley: 'For just five balls … I thought he had been reborn.' Greg Chappell, the Australian captain in that historic game, later said: 'It was Hookesy's youthful exuberance which allowed him to walk out there and play his natural game … The over against Tony Greig seemed to burst the mental chains which were holding everyone's batting and we started to realise this was a good batting wicket.' After the Hookes whirlwind, Australia's wicket-keeper Rod Marsh scored a century, helping his side set England a seemingly impossible 463 for victory. The fact that it got to within 45 runs – spookily the exact margin by which it lost the first Test in 1877 – was mainly thanks to an amazing 174 by jack-in-the-box batsman Derek Randall.

Hookes went on to be a key part of Kerry Packer's World Series Cricket rebellion against the cricket establishment. He played the part of the young, blond, blue-eyed swashbuckling hero who would appeal to women, as well as cricket-mad youngsters. In one game – in scoring 81 – he hit the great West Indian fast bowler Michael Holding for 22 in an over, and Joel Garner for 16 in an over, before missing an Andy Roberts bouncer that shattered his jaw.

Despite his talent – and (or maybe because of) his daring – Hookes played only 23 Tests and five World Series Cricket 'Tests'. He ended up with an average of 34.36 in Tests and 35.86 in WSC Tests. (He did, however, get the record for the most number of runs scored in Australia's interstate competition.) He only scored one Test century – an unbeaten 143 in Australia's first Test against Sri Lanka in 1983. Good as that innings was, Hookes didn't leave all his fireworks on the field. That night he lit strings of tom-thumb crackers and pushed them under his team-mates' doors. Eleven years later one of those team-mates – Graham Yallop – told the story: 'It was past midnight and we thought the Australian team was subject to a terrorist attack. Everyone dashed into the corridor in various states of undress, to see Hookesy doubled over with laughter, absolutely rapt at the success of it all.'

In 1995, Hookes – then an outspoken radio sports commentator – summed up his character to the *Herald Sun* as: 'Calm, not too flustered although I can be abrasive at times.' He said he read a book a week, the last being *The Clockers*, which he said was 'about drugs in New York'. Hookes said his most frightening experience was: 'Running with the bulls in Pamplona, which I have done seven times. When you're out on the street and suddenly realise that there is nowhere to go.' Was he worried about getting old? 'No, although I sometimes wonder what would I do at age 85 if I was left alone.'

Life is seldom as simple and wholesome as a 'Boy's Own' adventure story. Real-life heroes and heroines seldom follow the fairytale script. Even Hookesy's brief 'Boy's Own' Test debut was not unadulterated sporting heroics. Seconds after he was dismissed – even as the crowd rose to applaud him – their new hero was hardly acting the part … as he revealed 16 years later in his book, *Hookesy*.

Hookes: As I was walking off, Greig said: 'Piss off.' I half stopped and turned around, spat the dummy and said: 'At least I'm an Australian playing this game, not a fuckin' Pommie import.'

I shouldn't have said anything, of course, [but] I've never believed in telling batsmen where to go when they are out although it's done a lot. I don't mind a verbal battle when he's out there, but once he's out, let him get off in peace.

That little tirade by a young, disappointed batsman on 14 March 1977 was put right over a traditional after-game beer.

Hookes: The usual procedure and protocol in first-class matches is, or was, for the batting team to go into the fielding team's room for a

David Hookes: A Cricket Hero Dies

drink at the end of a day's play. So no-one was more surprised than me when I saw Tony Greig walking into our room, carrying a long-necked bottle of beer and two glasses.

'Mind if I sit down with you, son?' he asked. 'Please do,' I replied. And he said, 'Well played.' We shared a bottle of beer and talked about the game and he said something about what happens on the ground stays on the ground and I agreed.

It was a terrific gesture of Greigy's and one he didn't have to make.

David Hookes played his life like this: glorious shots followed by injudicious ones – on the cricket field and off. Some of his injudicious shots may have cut short a few innings, ended in him breaking his jaw, limited his Test career and gained him some notoriety as a commentator, but because they sprang from the same source as the glorious ones – his daring, his urge to entertain, his super self-confidence – they endeared Hookesy to a country that loves its larrikins. Hookes's injudicious shots were no worse than the ones most people play. It was just that most people didn't also play the glorious ones he did. It was those that kept him in the sometimes harsh public spotlight.

On 18 January 2004 – nearly 27 years after his put-things-right after-game beer with Tony Greig – Hookes was having another after-game beer following another of his triumphs: a dramatic win by the young Victorian cricket side he was coaching against his old South Australian team. The Victorian Bushrangers were on a high. They seemed to be taking on their coach's 'win from any position' motto. Six days earlier they had chased down a massive 452 runs against New South Wales. That day – in a one-day game against the South Australian 'Redbacks' – they had scored a more than handy 260 runs in 50 overs, only to find themselves staring at defeat with the Redbacks needing just over six runs an over with 10 overs left and seven wickets in hand. But, remarkably, they kept South Australia to 254 for 8. In the final over they captured the vital wicket of South Australia's captain and star batsman Darren Lehmann, then also a member of the Australian Test team. Lehmann wasn't impressed at being given out 'leg before wicket'. When asked if the bowler's pace had surprised him he sarcastically replied: 'If it was hitting the next set of stumps, it may well have, yeah.'

Still, despite his disappointment, after the game Lehmann happily accepted David Hookes's invitation to join him and some Victorian players for a beer ... or several. Hookes and Lehmann had been best mates for many years. They had played together for South Australia and had very similar attacking approaches to cricket. Lehmann had even been dubbed the 'new Hookes' by a South Australian newspaper. Hookes also invited another old mate and former team-mate, Wayne Phillips – the South Australian coach and former Australian batsman/wicket-keeper – as well as the team's physiotherapist Jon Porter. Instead of taking them to the Bushrangers' normal drinking hole, Hookes chose the 124-year-old Beaconsfield Hotel in inner-suburban bayside St Kilda.

The Bushrangers who joined their coach for drinks at the Beaconsfield with their opponents included fast bowlers Mick Lewis and Robert Cassell, assistant coach Greg Shipperd, and former fast bowler turned Cricket Victoria's cricket operation's general manager, Shaun Graf. The 'boys' were joined by Christine Padfield – Hookes's girlfriend of almost two years. (He had recently separated from his second wife, Robyn.) Ms Padfield's friend Tania Plumpton and Mick Lewis's then girlfriend Sue-Ann Hunter were also there.

They ensconced themselves in a corner with a good view of a television showing an Australia versus India day–night cricket match and happily whiled away the next few hours, Lehmann probably telling anyone who would listen that there was no way he should have been given out LBW.

About 11.30pm the bouncers walked through with the 'last drinks' call. A little while later they went through with the traditionally more insistent second call of 'last drinks'.

That's when things took an ugly turn towards tragedy.

That's also when it becomes difficult to piece together what happened. For the quarter of an hour or so after that second 'last drinks' call, the accounts of what happened by those who were there are frustratingly varied, even contradictory.

***

Sue-Anne Hunter, who was talking to Hookes, said that after the second 'last drinks' call a bouncer told Hookes: 'Tell the bitch to skol her drink.' She said Hookes replied: 'That's no way to speak to a lady and you shouldn't be asking such a young girl to skol her drink.'

Christine Padfield said she heard the bouncer tell Ms Hunter: 'Last drinks. Skol, skol, skol,' but didn't hear the word 'bitch'. She said Hookes replied: 'That's a pretty irresponsible thing to say. She'll finish her drink and then we will leave.' Ms Padfield said that was when 'without warning, the security grabbed David in a headlock' and marched him to the pub door. She said Wayne Phillips and Darren Lehmann tried in vain to free Hookes from the bouncer's grip and the bouncer pushed Hookes down the steps. 'He stumbled but managed to remain on his feet,' she said.

Tania Plumpton said the bouncer told Ms Hunter: 'Skol your drink, you bitch,' and Hookes had replied: 'Mate, that's no way to talk to a lady and you shouldn't be telling her to skol her drink.' She said Hookes was then put in a headlock, marched to the door and flung out.

Lehmann did not remember hearing a bouncer tell anyone to skol their drinks. He and Phillips denied trying to free Hookes from the bouncer.

That was just the first, confused, act of the tragedy.

The accounts of what happened in the moments after Hookes was thrown out of the Beaconsfield Hotel – about how and why a group of bouncers followed the cricket group about 70 metres down the adjacent Cowderoy Street – were also incredibly diverse.

There were the 'both sides were aggressive' accounts.

Wayne Phillips said there was a 'forceful language exchange' between the cricketing group and the bouncers. He agreed that Hookes was reluctant to leave, that he wanted to argue the toss and that he was acting aggressively all the way down the street in the middle of a 'rolling maul'. He also agreed that moments after being evicted Hookes had said something to the bouncers about closing the pub down and had threatened to give the pub a spray on his radio show.

Phillips: I think the security was saying: 'Why don't you just fuck off?' and David came back and said: 'Yeah? You're fucked, you mob' … I think there was just a continuation of the pushing and shoving where we trying to move David away. The security maintained a fairly close presence. It was all a bit rushed.

Darren Lehmann thought the bouncers were mostly the aggressors, but the cricketing group gave a little back. He said there was 'a lot of yelling between David and the security guards'.

Lehmann: It was a rush, a real rush to get out of there and get away from the pub and that's the way I was feeling and that's the way the group was feeling: to get away from the whole situation.

One Cowderoy Street resident, Joe Robilotta, said: 'There was a group of about 12 people just finger pointing and yelling and carrying on … It was happening so quickly … Someone grabbed someone and put them on to the ground in a headlock position and when they went to the ground, let him go and then everyone got up and started moving towards my property.' He said one of the bouncers screamed: 'You want to be smart … Now it's time to face the music.'

There were those who said the bouncers were the only aggressors.

Ms Plumpton said she yelled at the bouncers: 'Leave us alone. We want to go home.' She said she did not hear Hookes say anything to the bouncers moments after he was flung out, but a little while later a bouncer leant over her and 'said that David was a smartarse and that he was going to effing well kill him', and that Hookes had replied 'something along the lines of: "Oh, you're a tough boy."'

Shaun Graf said the cricketing group was not aggressive but bewildered by the bouncers' aggression. He could not remember Hookes swearing after – or while – he was being evicted. Graf said he also did not hear Hookes threatening to close down the hotel. He said Phillips was 'totally wrong' to describe what happened down Cowderoy Street after Hookes's

David Hookes: A Cricket Hero Dies

eviction as a 'rolling maul' of the cricket group and the bouncers. He also rejected a Cowderoy Street resident's description of it as a 'wild brawl'.

Young fast bowler Robert Cassell said: 'They [the bouncers] kept grabbing him [Hookes] and putting him on the ground and drag him a little bit and then ... he'd get up ... walk a few more metres and they'd attack him again and grab him and drag him to the ground.'

And there was the view that the only aggression came from the cricketing group.

One of the bouncers, Demetrius 'Jimmy' Demetriou, said that soon after Hookes was thrown out he [Hookes] had turned around and said: 'You're fucked. This place is fucked. Watch what I do to it tomorrow.'

> *Mr Demetriou*: It was very aggressiveness. [Down Cowderoy Street, at the corner] I've told them to keep the noise down and then David [Hookes] put his face into mine and said: 'You're fucked, watch it.' Like face to face ... There was a lot of yelling, threatening, abusive language. You can tell the tension, like it was there. I got scared. I am not saying I never get scared ... It was like they [the cricketing group] didn't want to leave. It was like they had unfinished business to do ... It was all aggressiveness. It was getting out of control.

* * *

One of the few things nobody disputed about this prolonged pub eviction was how it ended: a 21-year-old bouncer called Zdravko Micevic threw a left hook at Hookes, which hit him so hard he fell like a plank, fatally cracking his skull like an egg on the road.

The accounts of the circumstances surrounding that killer punch, however, were also very varied.

Christine Padfield said that after Hookes's T-shirt was ripped by one of the bouncers, she panicked and ran to get her car.

> *Ms Padfield*: I thought, hopefully I would be able to get David into the car ... I leant across and opened the door. At that point I was yelling for David to hop in the car ... He was just about to hop in

the car. He was then dragged around to the front of my car. Shaun [Graf] then managed to get him free again ... I wound down my window and it was at that point in time that I heard a loud thud and then when I looked around David was lying on the ground.

Ms Plumpton said that as she was trying to get Hookes in the car he looked at her and said: 'I am coming, Tan.'

Ms Plumpton: I pushed the front seat forward to get into the back seat and I heard quite a loud bang and I remember Christine saying: 'They effing well hit him.'

Wayne Phillips remembered: 'It was all a bit rushed ... We were trying to move David away and the next thing I saw him collapse in front of me.' He said that although he had been standing next to Hookes, he did not see why he collapsed. He said that Hookes had been acting aggressively down Cowderoy Street but that 'towards the end we'd had a bit of a win and he was quite quiet'.

Shaun Graf said he relaxed when Ms Padfield drove up with the car because he thought Hookes would be able to get in and away, but that he didn't get a chance.

Graf: I ran around to the other side of the car because the security were trying to ... stop him getting into the car ... One of the bouncers tried to pull him down to the ground. He [Hookes] lifted his hands up and said: 'Hey, I'm out of your pub,' and that's when he got hit. He basically had been pulled down into a crouching position. He tried to get up, to flex his hands ... and he said, 'I am out of your hotel,' and the next minute he got hit by the guy in the white shirt.

Cassell said Hookes had been trying to get into Ms Padfield's car just before the bouncer punched his face with a left-handed hook.

David Hookes: A Cricket Hero Dies

Cassell: I had a clear view of Hookesy … He was arguing with the bouncer who was standing sort of behind me. I was keeping an eye on him, he went to say something to that bouncer with the goatee beard and then – mid sort of sentence – he was hit.

He said he didn't notice Phillips; that Graf was 'far' from Hookes; and that Hookes and the man who hit him had not wrestled.

Lehmann said Hookes was 'hustled away from the car'.

Lehmann: People were still all around. There was lots of yelling going on and then I turned around, looked back and David's on the ground.

A nurse who was not part of the cricketing group, Leesa Rogerson, said: 'I just saw a man standing slightly away from the group, facing the group and then I saw him get punched … He was just standing to the side of the group, slightly back … Someone came – sort of jogged slightly – out of the group and punched him in the face somewhere and the man fell back on to the ground. He appeared to be unconscious straightaway … He just fell like a tree … just straight back … Because I'm a nurse, I went up to him.'

Mr Robilotta said that all of a sudden the group of people started coming towards his house 'yelling and screaming'. He said the 'guy in the white shirt [Hookes] … wasn't aggressive at all … was just standing there' with his arms by his side, saying something when 'all of a sudden the bouncer with the white long sleeves [Micevic] hit him and he fell to the ground'. He said Hookes and Micevic had 'walked to each other and it was like a face-off … they walked across and they confronted each other'.

***

Whatever the circumstances of that punch, there was no doubt this celebratory after-game beer had ended up with everything wrong, so wrong that nothing could be done to put it right.

20   REASONABLE DOUBT

Jon Porter: It's more of an audible memory … of feet scraping on the ground and then the sound of fist hitting flesh and then the sound of [long pause, he wipes a tear] the sound of a breaking bone … very loud. I immediately ran to the centre of the road. I saw David Hookes lying on the road and immediately tried to administer first aid … He was unconscious … He was flat on his back with his arms at his sides … There was a small amount of blood in the region of his nose and his mouth. His eyelids were open but unresponsive and he was unresponsive. I called out for someone to call for an ambulance and I can remember Darren Lehmann being on the phone, speaking to police or ambulance …

I thought I could hear a thready pulse there. A nurse introduced herself and I asked her to check. She said she could feel a thready pulse. I suspected, unfortunately, that his pulse had disappeared and he'd stopped breathing so I … was just about to commence CPR when the ambulance arrived.

Cassell: I was probably five metres away when Hookesy was hit … It was a left-hand hook sort of a punch … just on the cheek … He [Hookes] went quite stiff and just sort of fell backwards and hit his head on the ground … I went over [long pause] and held his head …

Graf: David was completely out. I was close enough to see his eyes. He was completely out cold as he hit the deck.

Four months later, Christine Padfield told ABC television's *Australian Story* about the night the man she called her 'soul mate' died.

Ms Padfield: I think I went into shock. He was bleeding from his nose and I was just rubbing his back and speaking to him to make sure he was OK. He was kind of making these little noises every now and then.

Tania Plumpton told the program: 'I remember slapping his face and saying: "C'mon, David, wake up, wake up." And I just remember the ambulance saying, "We've got a pulse," and I thought everything was going to be all right.'

Ms Padfield: Not long after we had turned up at the hospital, Robyn arrived probably about five minutes after us. So it was hard. It was hard not being able to go and see him and be there for him because the family wouldn't allow that. I did feel, um … very shut out.

***

About 24 hours later the Hookes family agreed to his life support being turned off. They also fulfilled Hookes's wishes and donated his organs, which helped improve the lives of 10 people, including two children. In the week after Hookes's death, after it was widely reported that he had donated his organs, the Australian Organ Donor Register had calls from nearly 1200 people – triple its weekly average.

David Hookes's death triggered an extraordinary response in Australia and from cricket fans around the world. The acting prime minister, John Anderson, said: 'I know I would speak for all Australians when I extend that sympathy to them [the Hookes family].' The Australian cricket captain, Ricky Ponting, said: 'It's hit everybody pretty hard. All we can do as a team is say our hearts go out to David, his family, friends and everyone involved with cricket in Victoria and South Australia.' Ponting's predecessor, Steve Waugh, said he had felt 'physically very sick' when he heard about Hookes's death.

A few days after his best mate's violent death, Lehmann faced a press conference hiding tearful eyes behind dark glasses. Asked if cricket still meant the same thing to him as it did a few days earlier, Lehmann's reply was: 'No.'

Lehmann: He was the first bloke I'd ring if I was having any problems, whether it be cricket-wise or personal. He was always there, just a phone call away. It's just hard to fathom that you can't ring him any more or see him … He was a great friend – first and foremost – a childhood hero, the greatest influence on my career. He is the one

REASONABLE DOUBT

I admired from day one until the end and I am going to miss him a bloody lot.

At Australia's first international cricket match after Hookes's death – against India – players wore black armbands, flags were at half-mast and, of course, the giant electronic scoreboard replayed his five fours in a row in the Centenary Test. The youngest, most daring player in that famous game had been the first to die. One fan's banner was: 'David Hookes, the world of cricket won't forget you.' Another was simply: 'Thanks.' Fans flooded newspaper death notices, letters pages and websites with their thoughts and memories.

There was also, however, a disturbing and frighteningly nasty side to this mourning.

The Micevic home was besieged with hate mail and death threats. Mr Micevic's lawyer, Brian Rolfe, said 'the most offensive and outrageous hate mail' had been sent to his client, to his legal firm and even to people who just happened to have the same surname as his client. Some of the mail – including a threat to burn down his house with him and his family in it – was so vicious Mr Micevic and his family were forced to flee their home in west suburban St Albans. A couple of weeks later the abandoned house was set alight. Victorian Premier Steve Bracks appealed for calm: 'My message to those people who feel angry and aggrieved about this issue is to leave it to the Victoria Police and leave it to the courts. They will deal with this matter with the full force of the law. There is no place for individual action. This is not the Victoria that I've grown up in and this is not the Victoria we expect and I know that 99.9 per cent of Victorians will be with me on this.'

On the day Hookes was pronounced dead (wrote Christian Ryan on the website, www.cricinfo.com), a Sydney train was scrawled with: 'Middle Eastern people are ruining our country, raping our children and killing David Hookes.'

On Christmas Eve 2004, the 124-year-old Beaconsfield Hotel closed. In almost a year since Hookes's death, business had dropped away. Staff had been abused and even spat on by Hookes's fans. Some patrons would taunt staff by referring to Hookes's death when they were asked to leave or told they had had enough to drink. The hotel also faced a civil law suit from Hookes's widow, Robyn, over his death.

Finally, on 22 August 2005 – 19 months after the punch that fatally felled Hookes – Mr Micevic's manslaughter trial started in the Victorian Supreme Court.

***

Mr Micevic did not deny killing David Hookes but he pleaded not guilty to his manslaughter, claiming he had punched Hookes only to defend himself. Unlike most defendants, Mr Micevic, then 23, chose to go into the witness box to tell his story.

He told the jury that he had won the Australian junior welterweight boxing title when he was 16, but that he had finished boxing when he was 18 and, anyway, his boxing ability had nothing to do with the night he fatally felled David Hookes.

> *Prosecutor Ray Elston SC*: You are trained to throw punches. You know how to throw a punch, don't you?
> *Mr Micevic*: Yes, but this was a different situation: it wasn't a boxing ring.

He said he didn't mind cricket, but was not a big fan and hadn't recognised any of the cricketing group that night at the Beaconsfield. Mr Micevic denied that he had used the words 'skol' or 'bitch' that night to Hookes or Sue-Anne Hunter. He said he did not use those words at work: 'It's not very professional.'

> *Mr Micevic*: I asked them to finish their drinks again and make their way out and the gentleman [Hookes] just swore at me saying, 'Fuck you,' and I told him, 'There is no need for that.' Then he said, 'Do you want me to repeat myself?' and then he repeated it about three times. That's when I asked him to leave the venue and he wouldn't so I restrained him and pushed him outside ... He [Hookes] was

getting really aggressive and he was trying to release the hold and he was trying to elbow me … There was a female that jumped on me outside the hotel from behind, by my neck, and she was pulled off by another security guard and his [Hookes's] mates were just trying to release the hold …

They [the cricketing group outside the pub] were being very abusive to us. They didn't seem to want to leave … We just told them to 'fuck off and go home'. I remember a lady telling us she was going to sue us … We were pushing them and they were pushing back. It was very loud, very loud. I was a bit worried because we were outnumbered …

As the scuffle was happening that's when he [Hookes] hit me in the stomach twice. He grabbed me by the shirt and pulled me down … [The punches] winded me … My head was basically down towards his, on his chest and that's when I was worried of getting pulled down to the ground and I threw a punch back …

It happened very quickly – a second … I was scared of falling on to the ground and not being able to protect myself or being kicked as I was on the ground.

He said after he punched Hookes he wanted to see if he was OK but 'I wasn't allowed because his friends kept pushing us away and telling us to "fuck off".'

Under cross-examination by Mr Elston, Mr Micevic denied the cricketing group's behaviour had infuriated him; that there had been no need to follow the group down the street; or that the bouncers had impeded the cricketing group's departure. He said that after complaints from neighbours the Beaconsfield Hotel managers had instructed bouncers to move customers away from the area to reduce the noise. He also stuck to his denial that he had told anyone to 'skol'.

Mr Elston: I suggest to you that you said words to the effect of 'Skol the drink' or 'Skol your drink, bitch'.
Mr Micevic: No, I didn't.

Mr Elston: So, for absolutely no reason apparent to you, this man swears at you?

Mr Micevic: That's right …:

Mr Elston: I suggest to you that all the way down Cowderoy Street people in the group were saying things along the lines of: 'Let us go, please. Let us go. We're leaving.'

Mr Micevic: No, they didn't seem to want to leave …

Mr Elston: I suggest to you that the punch you threw was a very, very forceful punch.

Mr Micevic: I couldn't tell because it happened pretty quickly. I just threw it back. I didn't know if it was very hard. I may have hit him hard. I don't know … It was just an instinct. I just … I was worried and scared. I was under pressure. I didn't think where I was going to hit him. I could've hit him on the shoulder but it was just unfortunate that it hit him in the head …

Mr Elston: I suggest to you what you were doing was targeting David Hookes and you went for him.

Mr Micevic: No, it was not how it worked.

Mr Elston: You were angry because of what he had said to you.

Mr Micevic: No.

Mr Elston: I suggest to you the man you ejected and the man you followed was ultimately the man you physically confronted and struck. I suggest you did that because you were angry with him.

Mr Micevic: No, it wasn't my fault.

Mr Elston: I suggest to you, you were so angry with him, you belted him in the face as hard as you could, out of payback.

Mr Micevic: No, that's not how it happened.

Mr Elston: I suggest to you that he never touched you at all in the entire journey down Cowderoy Street and the only contact was when you belted him as hard as you could.

Mr Micevic: No, I don't agree with that.

Mr Micevic had told his story, but his defence team had to get over a few hurdles before a jury would accept it or at least accept that it was reasonably possible that it was true. They included the public's generally low opinion of bouncers and its very high opinion of David Hookes, as well as the evidence – diverse and muddled as it was – of witnesses who said Mr Micevic had been the attacker.

Defence barrister Terry Forrest QC tackled head-on the possible problem for his client of the 'Hookes legend'; the possibility that some members of the jury would be Hookes's fans ready to punish the man who had killed him.

Mr Forrest: That young man [pointing to Mr Micevic in the dock] has been demonised by some members of the press. David Hookes has been sanctified by them. Neither of these images is real.

He said, given how much alcohol Hookes had drunk that night (a patholo-gist found Hookes had a blood-alcohol level of .12 to .14 – almost three times the legal driving limit), it was not hard to believe that he swore at Mr Micevic for no apparent reason.

Mr Forrest: David Hookes was in a mood. We submit he dealt with this 21-year-old security officer with arrogance and disdain: 'Fuck you. You heard me. Fuck you. How many times do I have to repeat myself? Fuck you' … Don't think I am trying to vilify the cricketing group or David Hookes. All of us do silly things … A lot of us at the Bar table do silly things. We drink too much. We say too much. We have bad nights. That doesn't mean we are bad people and it doesn't mean we won't get up to be decent people in the morning. The trag-edy of this situation is that that didn't happen for David Hookes …

We don't forget David Hookes. What happened 1½ years ago was a tragedy. A man in the prime of his distinguished and celebrated life died. He didn't deserve to die. No-one intended for him to die and it was a tragedy. Don't compound that tragedy by giving Zdravko Micevic less than justice.

David Hookes: A Cricket Hero Dies

To try to counter the cliché that bouncers are steroid-hyped, ego-driven bullies itching for a fight, the defence produced evidence that Mr Micevic was anything but. A long-term family friend and neighbour, Nernad Dimitrijebic, said that he was known as a 'real nice boy … a shy boy'. His boss at the concreting job he had been doing since he was released on bail soon after David Hookes's death said he was known as 'a very humble, quiet, honest guy'. The head of the security guard agency for which Mr Micevic worked at the time Hookes died, Peter Clare, gave the man known to his workmates as Vic or Strav a glowing reference.

> *Mr Clare*: Role model, extremely tolerant with patrons … All patrons enjoyed him, his company and so forth … I used him as a role model to anyone new … He was the perfect employee … He had fantastic tolerance and patience.

Still, there was the evidence of the witnesses. People had sworn they saw Mr Micevic punch David Hookes: after confronting face-to-face a passive Hookes who had his arms by his sides (Mr Robilotta); after jogging a couple of metres up to him (Ms Rogerson); as Hookes was being held down in a crouching position after Hookes had put his hands up and said: 'I'm out of your pub' (Graf); and while Hookes, his hands down by his sides, was arguing with another bouncer (Cassell).

Mr Forrest tackled the cricketing group's evidence by saying their loyalty to David Hookes made them unreliably biased witnesses; even 'mischievous revisionists of history' intent on 'preserving reputation and honour rather than telling what really happened'.

> *Mr Forrest*: We submit that by and large the evidence given by the cricketing group has been selective; has been designed to place before you a rose-coloured version of what occurred. This is not a sports disciplinary tribunal, it's not an advanced class in spin doctoring: it's a court of law where people take the oath and are expected to tell the truth. That's the only way justice can function properly.

28 REASONABLE DOUBT

He accused Ms Hunter – who had said that because of the alcohol she had drunk that day and night she only remembered Mr Micevic telling Hookes: 'Tell the bitch to skol her drink', Hookes retorting that he shouldn't say that to a young woman and seeing Hookes on the road – of having a 'convenient case of amnesia'. Mr Forrest even accused Hookes's deputy coach Greg Shipperd of lying to the court. Mr Shipperd had said he saw nothing of Hookes's eviction because he was talking to former West Coast Eagles player Peter Melesso inside the pub. Mr Melesso, however, told the court he had left the pub about 11.20pm – about 15 minutes before the eviction. In his cross-examination of Mr Shipperd, Mr Forrest's junior counsel, Damian Sheales, was direct.

Mr Sheales: I put it to you that you were pushed out of the hotel with the rest of the cricketing group … I put it to you that is the truth of the matter and your assertion to the contrary is a complete lie.
Mr Shipperd: That's not correct.
Mr Sheales: I put it to you that the reason you are lying is because you know the truth does you and your group no credit at all.
Mr Shipperd: That's not true.

Mr Forrest tackled Shaun Graf.

Mr Forrest: Mr Graf, during this entire evening, you don't see one aggressive act from the cricketing group or hear one aggressive word. Is that your position?
Mr Graf: Correct.
Mr Forrest: There was considerable noise, anger and aggression, I suggest, being demonstrated by the cricketing group as they were on the footpath outside the hotel.
Mr Graf: I would say bewilderment.
Mr Forrest: Bewilderment? OK, and bewilderment. Did that encompass David Hookes saying: 'You're fucked'?
Mr Graf: I didn't hear that.

David Hookes: A Cricket Hero Dies

Mr Forrest: Did he say it in a bewildered way?

Mr Graf: He was saying: 'We are out of your hotel. We're going.'

Mr Forrest: He wasn't saying: 'Your hotel's fucked. You're gone'?

Mr Graf: Never heard it.

Mr Forrest: Mr Phillips was part of the group?

Mr Graf: Yeah.

Mr Forrest: A sober and sensible man?

Mr Graf: Every time I have been with him, he has been.

Mr Forrest: He has told us David Hookes ... was making threats about the viability of the hotel. Did you hear anything to that effect?

Mr Graf: Look, that's his statement. I certainly didn't hear that.

Mr Forrest: I suggest to you Mr Graf that you are not being entirely frank with us.

Mr Graf: Mate, I can tell you, I swore on the Bible and ... I am telling the truth.

Mr Forrest: Did you hear Mr Hookes swear?

Mr Graf: I can't recall ...

Mr Forrest: Mr Graf ... are you only prepared to remember what you believe is favourable to the cricketing group?

Mr Graf: Totally incorrect ...

Mr Forrest: If evidence is given here that ... in Cowderoy Street there was a wild brawl. You just didn't see that?

Mr Graf: No.

Mr Forrest: Security people were saying, I suggest, things to the effect of: 'Go. Fuck off. Get out of here.'

Mr Graf: No.

Mr Forrest: You can recall what they weren't saying, but you can't recall what the cricketers were saying?

Mr Graf: Yes ...

Mr Forrest: There was pushing and shoving: a physical struggle between the cricketers group and security in the vicinity of that car at about the time that Mr Hookes was felled. Isn't that the case?

30   **REASONABLE DOUBT**

Mr Graf: No.

Mr Forrest: If Mr Phillips tells us that's what's going on, that's just completely contrary to your recollection?

Mr Graf: That's his statement.

Mr Forrest: I am asking you to comment upon it. Do you think that that is wrong?

Mr Graf: I say that is wrong …

Mr Forrest: You say that the security officer had a hold of Mr Hookes immediately before he was hit?

Mr Graf: He [Hookes] was being dragged down.

Mr Forrest: Are you sure it wasn't a security officer who had been dragged down by Mr Hookes?

Mr Graf: Totally incorrect.

Mr Forrest: Mr Hookes threw two punches.

Mr Graf: No punches were thrown by David Hookes …

Mr Forrest: Mr Hookes threw two punches and one came back from the security officer. That's what happened.

Mr Graf: Totally incorrect.

Mr Forrest's attack on Robert Cassell's evidence homed in on his sobriety at the time.

Mr Forrest: Mr Hookes was fighting with this man before he punched him, wasn't he?

Cassell: He was arguing with the bouncer.

Mr Forrest: He was fighting with that man in the white top before the man in the white top punched him, wasn't he?

Cassell: No.

Mr Forrest: You were 20 at the time?

Cassell: Yes.

Mr Forrest: You had a stubby after cricket and five hours of drinking?

Cassell: I had 10 pots, yes.

Mr Forrest: Ten pots and a stubby are going to have some effect, aren't they, Mr Cassell?

Cassell: Yes.

Mr Forrest: Ten pots is a fair bit for a young fella, with a stubby on top, isn't it?

Cassell: I wouldn't say it's a fair bit for me …

Mr Forrest: It's important to be accurate here. You've told us that all the way down Cowderoy Street, every couple of metres, Mr Hookes was grabbed in a headlock and forced to the ground. With respect, sir, that is obviously a considerable exaggeration?

Cassell: OK. So for the first 20 metres or so … then they attacked Hookesy and dragged him to the ground a few times.

Mr Forrest suggested to the jury that Wayne Phillips was the only member of the cricketing group who had been 'by and large an honest witness'; the only one to 'tell it as it was'; to 'take his oath seriously'; to admit Hookes was aggressive during his eviction from the pub and down Cowderoy Street.

But, even if the jury rejected most of the cricketing group's evidence as biased, the defence still had to deal with the evidence of Leesa Rogerson – that Mr Micevic had 'sort of jogged up' to Hookes and hit him. Mr Forrest tried to cast doubt on this by getting Ms Rogerson to acknowledge she needed glasses for driving, but she hadn't been wearing them the night Hookes was punched.

Mr Forrest: I am suggesting to you that you cannot exclude the proposition that Mr Hookes punched Mr Micevic twice in the very short time before that punch.

Ms Rogerson: No.

Mr Forrest's cross-examination of Joe Robilotta was much more dramatic. It was vital for the defence that his claim that Mr Micevic had punched Hookes after confronting him face to face was discredited.

REASONABLE DOUBT

Mr Forrest: Mr Robilotta, you made yourself available to a number of media outlets in the 24 to 36 hours after this episode. That's correct, isn't it?

Mr Robilotta: That's correct …

Mr Forrest: Mr Micevic, for whom I appear, told police shortly after this incident occurred that Mr Hookes had struck him twice to the chest immediately before he threw the left hook. I suggest to you that's in fact what occurred. What do you say to that?

Mr Robilotta: Mr Hookes was just standing there, no clenched fists, no aggressive nature whatsoever.

Mr Forrest: There was, I suggest, considerable physical activity … pushing, shoving, struggling, shouting?

Mr Robilotta: Not at that particular moment.

Mr Forrest: Everything went calm, did it?

Mr Robilotta: They walked to each other and it was like a face-off … They walked across and then confronted each other and that's what happened.

During a short break, Justice Philip Cummins asked why at the start of Mr Robilotta's evidence, and after 'a look' by a defence lawyer, a man had walked into the court and sat in the press benches close to Mr Robilotta. He was told the man was television reporter Charles Slade and that the reason he had come to court would be obvious during cross-examination.

After the break Mr Forrest started trying to discredit Mr Robilotta's evidence.

Mr Forrest: Mr Robilotta, I suggest you have an axe to grind against the security industry.

Mr Robilotta: No, not at all …

Mr Forrest: You have gone on record in the media as describing them [bouncers] as ego-driven, haven't you?

Mr Robilotta: Occasionally there is some, yes.

Mr Forrest: On this night you exaggerated what you say you saw, to the media, for your own self-gratification, I suggest to you.

Mr Robilotta: Like I said … anyone's death is not something to boast about, so I don't know where you are coming from with that angle.

Mr Forrest: It's not something to use as a vehicle for self-promotion either, is it?

Mr Robilotta: I don't need self-promotion.

Mr Forrest: When you gave your media interviews, you said that 'Hookesy' – as you called him – was confronted by three bouncers immediately prior to being hit. Didn't you?

Mr Robilotta: That's correct.

Mr Forrest: That's different to what you say to us today, isn't it? You say he was confronted by two bouncers …

Mr Robilotta: It was a long time ago. I can't remember.

Mr Forrest also challenged Mr Robilotta's claim that he knew Mr Micevic was a bouncer because he saw his security officer tag tucked into the back of his shirt. He asked him if he would still be so sure he saw the tag tucked into Mr Micevic's shirt if he was told other witnesses said it had been torn off by one of the cricketing group in the hotel and that it was later found in the hotel.

Mr Robilotta: Nothing affects the observation I have made … I don't appreciate being disrespected by yourself and labelled as a grandstander and things like that, that's not nice because I have worked very hard in the industry to get to a level where I am at.

Mr Forrest: You went on *Today Tonight*?

Mr Robilotta: Yes, at 7.30 in the morning after two hours' sleep.

Mr Forrest: You said on *Today Tonight*, 'It was sort of like an ego thing for the bouncer to do, to give him a good whack.' You said that didn't you?

Mr Robilotta: That's right.

Mr Forrest: You said: 'Because I work in the industry, I know what

REASONABLE DOUBT

these bouncers are like and I just know the type of ego it was about. And when they were walking off it was sort of "Yeah, right, mate" and then they gave him [Mr Micevic] a bit of a footy tap on the bum.'

Mr Robilotta: That's correct, yes.

Mr Forrest: You were prepared not only to offer them the benefit of your astute observations, you were prepared to psychoanalyse the participants?

Mr Robilotta: Being a bar owner, you understand what these security people sometimes get up to and we are left with the public liability and the suing and all this stuff so you have got to be aware of what's going on …

Mr Forrest: You dealt with a man at Channel 9 called Charles Slade?

Mr Robilotta: That's right.

Mr Forrest: That's Mr Slade who just walked through the door?

Mr Robilotta: That's correct.

Mr Forrest: You rang him, sir, and you asked him whether there would be a spot available for you as a contestant on the reality show on Channel 9 called *The Block*, didn't you?

Mr Robilotta: I can't remember.

Mr Forrest: You were prepared, I suggest, to try to turn this tragedy into a vehicle for self-promotion.

Mr Robilotta: As I was saying to you before: a death of anyone is not a … I don't need to promote myself. I have told you I have worked in this industry for 15 years and have gained the respect through a lot of people in the industry and you're out to, I don't know … You're doing your job very well. Yes, you are.

Mr Forrest: Don't worry about that. Don't worry about the speech. Save us the speeches.

Mr Robilotta: I feel sorry for both parties and I am just giving evidence of what I saw.

Mr Forrest: You rang Mr Slade the day after this occurred and tried to get on to *The Block* as a contestant, didn't you?

Mr Robilotta: Can't remember. It's a long time ago.

David Hookes: A Cricket Hero Dies

Mr Forrest: You said to him you had a pregnant wife? Was it the case that you had a pregnant wife?

Mr Robilotta: No, I've never been married.

***

In his closing address, the prosecutor acknowledged the jury was faced with a 'diversity of recollections' of how David Hookes died, but he said the traumatic experience they were trying to remember made cool-headed recollection very difficult.

Mr Elston: For those in the cricketing group … their lives changed forever when they heard the truly sickening sound of David Hookes's head hitting the ground in Cowderoy Street and it was obvious from that point on that David Hookes was in true peril to survive.

He said Mr Micevic's claim that Hookes had sworn at him for no reason was 'a little bizarre' given that it had been a pleasant evening, and Hookes had been happy after his Bushrangers' big win. He said it was likely that Mr Micevic's anger towards Hookes had been further fuelled by Hookes's threats to their jobs.

Mr Elston: The cricketing group were only loud, we say, because of the aggressive presence of the security. If the security had simply gone back to the hotel, then it's all over. It's pretty much like taking oxygen from fire.

It ended up, as you heard Mr Robilotta describe it: the accused and Mr Hookes facing off or face to face.

The prosecution case is that the accused, having finally caught up with David Hookes, simply delivered his punch deliberately and accurately at the face of David Hookes in essence by way of payback for what had gone on in the hotel and at the front as perceived by the accused … That punch … was delivered by an angry young man, who had pursued David Hookes the best part of 100 metres.

***

REASONABLE DOUBT

Mr Forrest, in his closing address, asked the jury why, if Mr Micevic had been angry and wanting payback, he had punched Mr Hookes with his nonfavoured left hand. He suggested: 'Because he threw a defensive punch, not an attacking punch.'

He said the altercation between the cricketing group and the bouncers down Cowderoy Street had been violent enough for two local residents to call the police.

> *Mr Forrest*: It's violent and it's dangerous and in this situation, we submit, this young man was intimidated and outnumbered and was acting in self-defence.

***

So the six men and six women on the jury had to pick their way through a labyrinth of evidence; they had to decide whom they believed and whether they were convinced beyond a reasonable doubt that Mr Micevic had not been genuinely trying to defend himself when he punched David Hookes. On the fifth day of their deliberations a question they asked Justice Cummins seemed to indicate how hard they were finding their task.

> *Jury*: If I as a juror feel that there is equal value and credible evidence supporting conflicting perspectives, does that mean reasonable doubt?

The judge said they could find Mr Micevic guilty only if they accepted the prosecution case 'beyond a reasonable doubt'. They should acquit Mr Micevic, he said, even if they thought that the prosecution case was slightly more likely to be true than the defence case.

> *Justice Cummins*: If there is equally valid and credible evidence either way? What do you do? The answer is you acquit the accused. That is the answer.

Seven hours later, at 5.45pm on 12 September 2005, the jury did exactly that. As the forewoman announced 'Not guilty' a female juror wept; Mrs

David Hookes: A Cricket Hero Dies

Hookes sat still, looking drained; and Mr Micevic's mother, sitting immediately behind them, gasped and then started quietly weeping. In the dock, Mr Micevic betrayed no emotion. As the courtroom emptied Mrs Hookes and her two children stayed in their seats. In the court's courtyard, Mr Micevic smiled and smoked a cigarette with family and supporters. He gave his lawyer a big, happy 'Thank you, mate' hug.

On the court steps – surrounded by a forest of television cameras and flashing cameras – Mr Micevic told one reporter: 'Mate, I feel like a million bucks.' Asked if he had thought he would go to jail, he said: 'It was always at the back of my mind but I hoped the truth would come out and I would get the right result.' In his celebrations Mr Micevic didn't forget the family of the man he had killed: 'I haven't had a chance to say this before, but I'd like to express my condolences to the Hookes family. I'm sorry this ever had to happen. It's just unfortunate. I wish them all the best in the future. I'm very relieved. I'm just glad it's all over. I can get on with my life.'

Hookes's half-brother Terry Cranage fought tears as he spoke to the media.

Mr Cranage: We are bitterly disappointed at the verdict, obviously. There are no winners through this process – only losers. Nothing will bring David back but, because he touched so many people in so many ways, in so many walks of life, he will never be forgotten by his multitude of fans and admirers. We must now move on … without David, as difficult as this may be.

But the Hookes family wasn't ready to 'move on' just yet. It continued its fight in the civil courts. Mrs Hookes continued suing Mr Micevic, the agency that employed him as a bouncer and the former Beaconsfield Hotel for her husband's death. Mr Micevic's defence to that claim was that he had 'at all times acted in self-defence'.

***

In a slightly bizarre postscript, six months later Mr Micevic was again on the front page of the *Herald Sun*. This time it was because he was helping the Australian boxing team prepare for the Commonwealth Games. Aussie 81kg gold medal hope Ben McEachran told the paper: 'He's a talented boxer who would beat a lot of good fighters and he gave me some great sparring.' Mr Micevic told reporter Grantlee Kieza: 'Things have settled down in my life and the attacks on my home have stopped. I'm working as a concreter now and I won't be going back to working as a bouncer – it's a horrible job ... People recognise me in the street all the time but, thankfully, most of them are very supportive. They know what happened was just an accident. I did not mean for anything bad to happen like that and I honestly wish it was me who died instead of him.'

GATTO VS VENIAMIN
Defence Underworld-style

It could be a scene out of an Australian version of *The Godfather* or *The Sopranos*. It is 2.30pm, 23 March 2004 in Melbourne's little Italy – inner-suburban Carlton. A silver Mercedes screeches to a halt and double-parks outside the La Porcella restaurant. Out of it jumps a short (168cm), shaven-headed, heavily tattooed 28-year-old man in white thongs, baseball cap, three-quarter-length tracksuit pants and a muscle-revealing white T-shirt. He slams the door of his flash $200,000 'borrowed' car and swaggers into La Porcella. Inside, at a long table, is a large group of mostly Italian Australian men; regulars finishing off one of their famously long, leisurely pasta lunches. At the head of the table in his usual seat – where he can see everyone arrive and no-one can sneak up on him – is a large man with a helmet of greying hair wearing a dark pinstriped suit, a blue-and-white striped shirt and a pink–red floral tie.

The man disturbing the lunch is Andrew 'Benji' Veniamin, a psycho-pathic thug who once had to be restrained from storming into a police station and shooting as many police as he could. Their crime? They had searched his mother's house and found a .38 calibre revolver. Veniamin is suspected of killing four of at least 21 gangsters in Melbourne's five-year-old underworld war. Two of his suspected victims were his former friends – Dino Dibra and Paul 'PK' Kallipolitis. Dibra, especially, had revelled in his gangster persona, once fronting up to a court hearing into charges of attempting to murder two nightclub bouncers in a shiny silver track-suit and chunky gold chains. As a teenager his bedroom walls had been covered in gangster movie posters. A few months before he was gunned down outside his West Sunshine home at the age of 25 in October 2000, Dibra explained his fascination with gangsters to a *Herald Sun* reporter: 'Mate, I've just watched *Reservoir Dogs* too many times.' Veniamin is on the dole, has two girlfriends, three mobile phones and 44 unpaid speeding fines. His favourite guns are .38 calibre revolvers 'because they don't jam'.

The man holding the lunch – the man Benji has come to see – is Dominic 'Mick' Gatto, a 48-year-old former heavyweight boxer, No 2 in Victoria. He's a building industry 'mediator' who boasts he looks after 'all their union problems'. He also regularly carries a gun – a .25 pistol he bought from a gangster called Lewis Moran about three years earlier. (Eight days later, Moran was to become the 23rd victim in the underworld war, gunned down while having a beer with his mates in his favourite Brunswick pub.) Mr Gatto lives in a large house in outer-eastern East Doncaster, but so regularly makes the haul down the freeway to Carlton to lunch at La Porcella – two, three times a week, sometimes more – that it's dubbed Gatto's Office.

This very odd couple have known each other for three years – since Mr Gatto took the hot-headed Veniamin under his wing.

Mr Gatto: He was forever getting himself into trouble at nightclubs and what have you and I was always sort of getting involved, sort of patching things up.

In the dozens of phone calls that police eavesdropped on in the eight months before this meeting at La Porcella, the pair had called each other 'buddy' and 'mate'. 'Hello buddy, it's the Little Bloke, mate,' Veniamin was overheard saying. 'What's going on, champ?' the Big Bloke replied. Another time Mr Gatto asked Veniamin: 'What's cookin' good lookin'?'

But about four months earlier – on 13 December 2003 – their friendship was severely tested. On that day the underworld war claimed its biggest victim – 62-year-old Graham 'The Munster' Kinniburgh. The

Gatto vs Veniamin: Defence Underworld-style 41

retired master safebreaker was an old-school 'gentleman' crime figure. Some say he modelled himself on Marlon Brando's Don Corleone in *The Godfather*. But, unlike Brando's character, Kinniburgh's death was far from peaceful. He was shot dead in the driveway of his home in the well-heeled leafy suburb of Kew. A very close friend, Mick Gatto helped carry Kinniburgh's coffin and put a death notice in the *Herald Sun*: 'This has left a void in my life that can't be replaced ... I love you "Pa" and I will never forget you.'

Veniamin had an alibi putting him far from Kinniburgh when he was shot, but many – even the big bloke who got him out of his nightclub 'troubles' – still suspected him.

> *Mr Gatto*: I was a little bit wary. I wasn't sure ... I was led to believe that he could have been responsible for Graham's death ... There was rumours just circulating around the town and that was one of the pretty strong ones ... but, I mean, I had no proof or anything ... I did keep in touch with him just so I could keep tabs on him and, you know, just see what he was up to ... There was no reason, that I could think of, why anyone would want to hurt Graham and me being such a close friend of his ... I thought I might be the next to go and there was all them rumours anyway. Not right after he died but a couple of days later. There were rumours that were getting around, you know: you're next ... I wanted to know what he [Veniamin] was doing and where he was going and, you know. A couple of his friends from the western suburbs who are friends of mine, I used to ask them all the time: 'What's he up to, that bloke?' 'Where's he been?' 'What's he doin'?' You know, I just wanted to know. It was just intelligence. I just really wanted to know because I believed that he could have been waiting about to cause me harm.

Mr Gatto said that when he and Veniamin went for a walk in Carlton about a week after Kinniburgh's shooting, Veniamin strongly denied being the killer.

Mr Gatto: He was just reassuring me that it wasn't him and had nothing to do with him and he believed it was the police that done it because it looked so professional and we were just sort of going through the motions.

But Mr Gatto was not completely 'reassured'.

Mr Gatto: Well, you know, he was a tricky little bloke but, I mean, I wasn't sure. I wasn't sure but I did have some doubt, yes.

About 10 days after Kinniburgh's death, Mr Gatto and Veniamin joined a group of rival underworld factions for peace talks in the relative safety of the crowded, glitzy, closely monitored Crown Casino. Police lipreaders read Mr Gatto telling Veniamin and others: 'I'll be careful with you. You be careful with me. I believe you. You believe me. Now we're even. That's a warning. It's not my war.'

When police warned Gatto that he was in danger and asked him about Veniamin being a friend, he told them: 'You don't know what's in a man's heart.'

Mr Gatto: I kept hearing that I was a target. I was going to be next, to be the next killed and kept getting told by different police and a couple of police: 'Be careful.'

***

So, on 23 March 2004 when Benji saunters into his 'office' Mr Gatto is a little nervous. He is also surprised, even though moments before he had spoken to Veniamin on the phone telling him where he was, to 'keep in touch' and he was 'welcome any time'. He hadn't expected Veniamin to take up what he said as an invitation quite so quickly.

Mr Gatto calls out: 'Hello stranger,' and Benji walks up and sits next to him. They chat about stuff. Veniamin tells his 'Big Bloke' some good news. Just a couple of hours earlier, he had heard a magistrate refuse to let police take a DNA sample from one of Veniamin's mates, a mate who's

Gatto vs Veniamin: Defence Underworld-style   43

accused of murdering an amphetamines dealer/hot-dog seller. They also talk about police raiding a kebab shop. 'Like there was nothing of any significance,' Mr Gatto was later to say of the conversation.

After a while, Veniamin gets bored with this small talk. He wants to get down to business. He kicks his 'buddy' Mick's foot under the table and jerks his head to the side. Mick asks: 'Do you want to have a chat?' Veniamin says: 'Yes, I do.' Mick pushes his chair back, gets up, gives his mobile phone to one of the men at the table and the pair walk to the back of the restaurant. Later Mr Gatto was to say: 'I thought that we were going to go outside but actually he pointed into the kitchen and I said: "Wherever you want to go." '

They end up in a narrow passage, squeezing between cartons of canned tomatoes. It is an Italian restaurant, after all.

Veniamin turns to the topic on his mind: underworld scuttlebutt that he helped kill The Munster.

Mr Gatto: He [Veniamin] turned around and he was just looking at me and I said: 'What's doing mate?' and he said: 'I'm sick of hearing all this shit,' and I said: 'What do you mean?' and he said: 'I'm still hearing that you think that I am responsible for your mate,' and I said: 'Well, I have to be honest with you, mate, that's what I keep hearing. That's what people keep saying' ... We were just talking and he said: 'Well, I have told you. I wouldn't interfere with you. You're a mate' ... and I said: 'Dino Dibra and PK were your mates and you fuckin' killed them,' and he turned around and he said: 'Well, they deserved it. They were dogs.' Or something like that and at that point I turned around and I said: 'Look, Andrew. I think it's better if you stay out of our company. I really don't believe that you can be trusted. I'd rather you not come around near us at all.' ... He just said: 'I'm sorry to hear that' ... and I was looking at him in the eyes and his face went all funny and he sort of stepped back and he said: 'We had to kill Graham. We had to kill fuckin' Graham.' He said: 'Fuck him. Fuck you' ...

I have never seen anyone sort of change so quick. He just went from one extreme to another and I couldn't believe it …

I never seen where he got it from but he pulled a gun out and that's when I lunged at him … I grabbed his arm with my hand and the gun went off past my head … I actually thought it hit me. It was just the loudest thing I have ever heard in my life … It was like a bomb going off in that room … I had hold of his hand with both my hands and I sort of pushed it towards him … He had his hand on the trigger and I just forced his hands, squeezed his hands to force him to pull the trigger …

[It took] a few seconds. I remember nearly falling on the ground, on top of him. He sort of pulled me off balance … The gun was going off. It was just: Bang! Bang! … I have to be honest. I thought I was a dead duck anyway. I thought I was gone …

I just pulled the gun out of his hand … out of the grip of his hand and I ran out of the hallway, out of the corridor into the restaurant …

He was laying there still gurgling, making funny noises … He was spluttering and coughing blood … I had the .38 in my hand by my side. All my friends were sitting there at the table. I don't know what they were doing but Michael [Moussa 'Michael' Choucair] the owner of the restaurant run down and we met each other … I had my left hand on my right ear and, you know, I couldn't hear properly and I just didn't know what was going on …

As we met each other, he [Mr Choucair] said: 'What happened?' and I said: 'He just tried to fuckin' kill me like he killed Graham.' I said: 'Am I all right?' and at that point I put the gun in my pants and said: 'Is my ear all right because I think he hit me' or something and he said: 'It looks a bit red but I think you're all right.'

We stepped back into the kitchen and because I was so fat, I had such a big stomach, the gun nearly fell out. Anyway, I grabbed it and I gave it to him. I said: 'You'd better take that.' I gave him the gun and he went and wrapped it in a towel or something …

Gatto vs Veniamin: Defence Underworld-style   45

Mr Gatto said he then gave his .25 pistol to Brian Patrick 'Mickey' Finn – 'a real good old bloke ... He's known me since I was a kid ... just a real nice old man'.

> *Mr Gatto*: Brian Finn walked over to me and he said: 'I have got to get out of here' or 'I'm going' and I said: 'Do me a favour, get rid of that for me,' and I gave him the gun and he put it in his pocket ... and he just left ... Michael asked me: 'What'll I do?' and I said: 'You'd better ring the police and ring an ambulance.' And then I turned around and grabbed my phone off Ronnie [one of his friends] and I said: 'You wouldn't believe what happened. He just tried to fuckin' kill me, this bloke ... like he tried to kill Graham.'

Mr Gatto remembered telling police outside La Porcella's – as Benji's still-warm body oozed blood on to the tomato boxes – 'something like "He tried to shoot me and he finished off second best."'

Detective Senior Constable Damien Jackson said Mr Gatto told police at the scene: 'There's a man out the back who shot Graham – said he shot Graham – and was going to do me. I grabbed the gun off him and he came off worse.'

> *Mr Gatto*: Just didn't know where I was. I was in a state of shock. I mean I couldn't believe I was still alive. You know, it was just my life flashed before me. The whole world was jus' over, you know. I thought I was a dead duck.

Why didn't he pull out his gun when Veniamin pulled his?

> *Mr Gatto*: I would have been a statistic if I had done that. If I had tried to pull it out of my pocket, he would have shot me straight in the head. I mean I never had time. It was just that quick. I never had a chance to go for my pocket. If I hadn't of lunged at him and grabbed his arm, mate, I wouldn't be here today to tell the story. I'd be a statistic.

Why did he give his gun to Mickey Finn?

Mr Gatto: I didn't want to be arrested with it … for having a loaded gun on me.

Why didn't he give his gun to the police?

Mr Gatto: I seriously believed that once they had done all their checks and whatever then they would release me. They would have realised that what I was telling them was the truth and I didn't want to be arrested for having a loaded firearm.

As to whether he murdered Andrew Veniamin, Mr Gatto's reply was succinct.

Mr Gatto: Christ! No way known. What I done is stopped him from murdering me … He died because he just pulled a gun at me. He went ballistic. He tried to kill me and I stopped him doing that and he got shot rather than me. Thank God he did.

Less than half an hour after double-parking his $200,000 Mercedes outside the restaurant at the corner of Faraday and Rathdowne streets, Veniamin was dead. He had been shot twice in his neck and once in the head. Five shots had been fired in the struggle.

Soon afterwards, despite his confidence that police would believe his excuse for killing Veniamin – that he had been trying to save his own life – Mr Gatto was charged with murder.

***

In April 2005 Mr Gatto started another fight for his life; a fight not to spend the rest of his life in jail as a convicted murderer.

Most of the time Mr Gatto let his defence team of lawyers, including one of the state's top QCs, Robert Richter, do all the fighting talk. But, unlike most defendants, this former boxer was never going to just watch.

Gatto vs Veniamin: Defence Underworld-style 47

Most defence lawyers advise their clients against giving evidence. They don't want a clever prosecutor tying their client in knots, making them lose their temper, making them look guilty. Mr Gatto, however, decided to take on prosecutor Geoff Horgan SC.

Right on the bell, the prosecutor charged out of his corner and took a big swing.

Mr Horgan: Can I suggest at the outset … that the account you have given about this shooting in that passageway at La Porcella restaurant on 23 March last year is a complete fiction; a tissue of lies from start to finish.

Mr Gatto: I can't help what you believe. I can only tell you the truth …

Mr Horgan: You say you managed to control the gun that he had in his hand to cause him to shoot himself three times?

Mr Gatto: That's what happened. Yes.

Mr Horgan: Is that your evidence?

Mr Gatto: That's a million per cent …

Mr Horgan: You believed that this man was a successful executioner?

Mr Gatto: Yes, I did.

Mr Horgan: You believed Veniamin had murdered six or eight people?

Mr Gatto: Yes.

Mr Horgan: But he couldn't – you say to this jury – manage to pull a gun out of his pants in that narrow passage and shoot a target your size?

Mr Gatto: Mr Horgan, if he wanted to kill me. I would have, I would have been like a lamb going to slaughter, if he wanted to kill me … It was just a spur of the moment thing, what happened … He only tried to kill me after I told him that he wasn't welcome there any more and he wasn't trusted … He just changed completely. He just lost it.

Mr Horgan: You say that this six-times executioner was not able to shoot … you as a target.

Mr Gatto: Thank God. Thank God, is all I can say.

The prosecutor tackled Mr Gatto's claim that he feared Veniamin was out to kill him.

Mr Horgan: You would refer to each other as 'buddy'?

Mr Gatto: I refer to the prison guards as 'buddy' and 'champ' also ...

Mr Horgan: A man you kissed on two occasions we see on the video. [The security video from the 'peace conference' at Crown Casino is shown.]

Mr Gatto: It's just a European thing. I do it with everyone. I'd do it with Robert Richter [his acting-startled barrister] if I had an opportunity ...

Mr Horgan: On the 23rd of March 2004 you suspected Veniamin was responsible for Graham Kinniburgh's death?

Mr Gatto: On the 23rd of March I wasn't sure that Veniamin had killed Graham.

Mr Horgan: As at 23 March 2004 you loathed Andrew Veniamin didn't you?

Mr Gatto: Well, when you put it that way: yes, you're probably right ... I believe that he killed Graham. Yes, I did loathe him. Yes ... He [Veniamin] was a Dr Jekyll and Mr Hyde ...

Mr Horgan: When did Veniamin admit to you that he had killed Dino Dibra and Paul Kallipolitis?

Mr Gatto: He admitted that to me at my birthday ... I said, 'I've got to be careful of you' or something like that or 'I've got to watch you' and he said: 'What do you mean, mate? You're a mate of mine. What are you talking about?' I said: 'Well, you killed PK and Dino and they were your mates too. You grew up with them.' He said: 'Mick, they were dogs. I'm dirty I never put another clip into them.'

Mick Gatto's claim that Veniamin, amongst those tomato boxes, in the back of La Porcella, admitted killing Graham Kinniburgh, was then tackled. The prosecutor pointed out that Veniamin's alibi meant that this was one murder he hadn't committed.

Mr Horgan: I am putting to you, after you shot him, you wanted to put into his mouth words that would justify shooting him …

Mr Gatto: Well you're wrong there. You're so wrong.

Mr Horgan: It's absurd for Veniamin to have said he had killed Kinniburgh … Let's be clear about this: I am saying to you that as of 23 March 2004, you did not know that Andrew Veniamin could *not* have killed Graham Kinniburgh but you were looking for a justification, for an excuse, for your murder of him and you invented words for him and you just got it wrong because you didn't know that he had been excluded from that murder.

Mr Gatto: No … I grabbed his hand and the gun went off.

Mr Horgan: Mr Gatto, you are just making this up.

Mr Gatto: … You are trying to railroad me … The truth is the truth … Mr Horgan, for the last 14 months I wake up in a cold sweat every night reliving exactly what took place that day …

Mr Horgan: You thought that when police had the forensic evidence, they'd let you go?

Mr Gatto: Yes, I still believe if it was anyone else in my place, they'd get a key to the city. It's just unfortunate it's me … I mean they put a man on the moon 30 years ago, [I thought] that they would establish very quickly that what I was saying was true … It's a freak of a thing that I never got hit by a bullet or a ricochet bullet … He was trying to kill me. What do you expect me to do? Just stand there and let him do it? …

Mr Horgan: Is it revenge at that stage [when Veniamin is down]?

Mr Gatto: It's not revenge at that stage …

Mr Horgan: Before you left the passageway, was he in his death throes? Was he moving?

Mr Gatto: He was laying there still gurgling, making funny noises … He was coughing. Coughing and spluttering.

Mr Horgan: Why did you take the gun out of his hand?

Mr Gatto: I didn't know whether he was stunned. I didn't know the extent of his injuries … It's a survival instinct to take the gun off him ... I remember the first shot. I remember after that a sequence of shots, but I don't remember them in order ... It was like a bomb going off in that room. I'm just trying to explain it to you.

The prosecutor then asked Mr Gatto to explain how he got Veniamin's blood on the lower part of his pants.

Mr Horgan: Doesn't it mean, Mr Gatto, that ... you have fired that shot into the wall deliberately after killing Mr Veniamin and in doing so you have knelt in blood and fired backwards to set up your defence?

Mr Gatto: [Checking] So, I have got down on the ground?

Mr Horgan: Yes, and fired backwards into the wall deliberately.

Mr Gatto: Please! You people! I'm sorry to say it but yous are all off your head.

Mr Horgan: The point is you got saturated blood just below the knee.

Mr Gatto: That's right.

Mr Horgan: And the only way you can get saturated blood just below the knee, I suggest to you, Mr Gatto, is if you have actually knelt in a pool of blood on the floor.

Mr Gatto: Well that's not what Rebecca Hayes [a defence forensic expert] said ... I don't know how it happened.

Mr Horgan: You can't, to this jury now, offer any explanation?

Mr Gatto: Well, I did. I said I think at that time I stumbled ... that [he] coughed on me or whatever ... I mean I just can't believe the nonsense that yous are trying to create in this trial. I mean the truth is what I have said and forensics proves it. Now you are trying to twist everything to make it look like I killed him, lured him there and killed him. I mean it's ridiculous – what you are going on about – completely ridiculous.

Mr Horgan: Well, that's your view.

Mr Gatto: My view is the truth.

Mr Horgan: You were saying that once you killed Veniamin you have done the world a favour. That's your point isn't it? …

Mr Gatto: That wasn't my point at all … I've got as much regret about what happened as anyone else has. I am not happy about what happened. I'm not happy about what my family's been put through …

Mr Horgan: Andrew Veniamin, the man you're afraid might kill you at any moment, and you just walk out the back with him. You don't pat him down. You don't search him thoroughly. You just casually walk out the back with him?

Mr Gatto: Well, we are a different breed to the police that you mix with, Mr Horgan. We don't do things that way. There was no issue with him and me at that point, that I knew of anyway. It was all suspicions, innuendos, rumours come from all sides.

Mr Horgan: He posed a risk to your life at any moment and you were prepared to go out the back with him to a hidden place?

Mr Gatto: That's right. He was there on his own. I was comfortable doing that.

Mr Horgan: And he could kill you at any moment being the unpredictable man that he was?

Mr Gatto: So be it … If he had have got me, well, then I would have been a statistic and it would have been him you'd be cross-examining.

Mr Gatto denied that his friends at that La Porcella lunch refused to make statements to police immediately after the shooting on his orders because he was orchestrating their evidence.

Mr Gatto: That's the way they are. They don't make statements. They don't sign statements … that's the way they have been brought up, not to tell on people, not to make statements.

Finally, after nearly two days, the cross-examination ended.

Mr Horgan: I suggest to you, Mr Gatto, that about a quarter to three on 23 March 2004 you invited Andrew Veniamin to that restaurant?

Mr Gatto: Yes?

Mr Horgan: You led the way out the back.

Mr Gatto: I never led the way. I'm not 100 per cent what happened but I'm pretty sure it was him.

Mr Horgan: And you murdered him in that back passageway, about that time.

Mr Gatto: Well, we all know that's not right.

Mr Horgan: And your story of self-defence is total rubbish.

Mr Gatto: Well, that's your side of the story and you have got to stick with that. Our side is supported by every conceivable method.

***

The prosecutor continued his attack on Mr Gatto's self-defence excuse by accusing 72-year-old Prahran pensioner Brian Patrick 'Mickey' Finn of perjury, of lying under oath to try to save a man he had known for 30 years.

Mr Finn told the court that he was at the La Porcella lunch on 23 March 2004 and that a few minutes after Mick Gatto and Andrew Veniamin walked out to the back of the restaurant he heard, 'Bang! Bang! Bang!'

Mr Finn: I thought it was a motorcar backfiring and then everyone stopped at their table and then after a while – I don't know how long, a minute or so, two minutes – when I looked around … there was Mick, standing there, Mick Gatto … He stood there and was all ashen-faced and then he just spoke and he said: 'Fair dinkum that bastard in there tried to kill me. Fair dinkum.' That's all he said. Similar to that, I don't know exactly word for word …

I got up from my chair and I said to Ronnie Bongetti, 'I'll see you later, Ronnie.' Then I went down the staircase and I passed Mick and Mick said, 'Here, take this, Brian,' and he handed me a small gun and I took it and walked out of the café and went home …

I just took it home, wiped it clean with a towel, with a tea towel because my fingerprints were on it, and then I wrapped it up and

Gatto vs Veniamin: Defence Underworld-style   53

put it in the bathroom wrapped up and a few weeks later I moved it from the bathroom and put it elsewhere – in the loungeroom. I used to move it around here and there sometimes.

The prosecution strongly attacked this evidence. Its theory was that if the jurors accepted that Mr Gatto handed over a .25 pistol right after the shooting, they were more likely to accept that the gun that killed Benji Veniamin – a .38 revolver – had belonged to Veniamin. They would be more likely to accept that Veniamin had somehow managed to secretly carry in a .38 Smith and Wesson revolver to the back of La Porcella, even though he had been wearing a relatively tight-fitting T-shirt, three-quarter-length tracksuit pants and boxer shorts.

The problem for the defence in getting the jury to believe Mr Finn's story was that he had only come forward with it about eight months after the shooting – during Mr Gatto's pre-trial committal hearing. Also, none of those at that rudely interrupted La Porcella lunch had told police about Mr Finn being there.

The prosecutor went straight on the attack.

Mr Horgan: Mr Finn, I suggest to you that you weren't at that restaurant at the time of the shooting on 23 March 2004 …
Mr Finn: I have one daughter. May she be struck dead if I wasn't in that restaurant on that day.

He said that a few weeks after the shooting he told one of his mates about Mick Gatto giving him his gun shortly after shooting Veniamin.

Mr Finn: He said, 'What are you going to do about it, Brian?' and I said, 'Oh just I'm just going to say nothing at all' … Later on in November [2004] … the people were saying that the gun used in the shooting belonged to Mick and I knew that I had the gun that he gave me and Normie and I talked it over and he said, 'It's in the benefit of Mick,' seeing that I had his gun that I should go to the legal

54   REASONABLE DOUBT

people now and tell them that I had his gun … so that's the reason I came forward.

Mr Horgan: Why didn't you go to the police with this important, relevant information about what happened on 23 March?

Mr Finn: Well, sir, if you was in my place why would you go to the police? You would go to Mick's legal people, wouldn't you?

Mr Horgan: No, I wouldn't. Why wouldn't you go to the police?

Mr Finn: I think it's natural that anyone would go to the people that are defending your mate. That's why I went to them …

Mr Horgan: Why didn't you come forward at the time?

Mr Finn: The reason I didn't come forward was because I thought if I tell the police or the legal people Mick Gatto gave me a gun, that wouldn't look very good for Mick Gatto, would it? I thought: I won't come forward. So I didn't mention it at all.

Mr Finn – with Gatto smiling and raising his glass of water at him, something Justice Philip Cummins quickly stopped – explained why he hadn't been forthcoming with police.

Mr Finn: The police both called me a liar from the word go, and when a person is called a liar right from the word go without even meeting people, it doesn't give you much initiative to discuss much with them at all, does it, sir? You call me a liar before you even met me?

Mr Horgan: Mr Finn. Yes, I think it is a pack of lies. If you haven't understood me up till now, let me make it quite clear: I think you are committing perjury.

Justice Philip Cummins: Mr Finn … why did it take you eight months after the killing to come forward?

Mr Finn: Because, sir, after the months went by I got the mail from Normie … that the police and the other people were saying the .38 belonged to Mick Gatto and I knew in my own heart he gave me a pistol when I left the restaurant and I knew that that was his gun and the .38 must have been, you know, the other fella's and that's why I

Gatto vs Veniamin: Defence Underworld-style   55

came forward after all those months, otherwise that's it.

Justice Cummins: You knew a life had been taken?

Mr Finn: I did, sir.

Mr Horgan: But you didn't come forward.

Mr Finn: I didn't come forward.

Mr Horgan: You told police, 'No-one knew I had it.' You agree that was a lie?

Mr Finn: Yes, but I wasn't under oath then, sir. They said I was a liar so why tell them everything … They are calling me a liar. Why can't I give them one back?

Mr Horgan: Why take the weapon?

Mr Finn: It was a split-second decision, I just took it … I didn't think anything.

Mr Horgan: Why didn't you come forward?

Mr Finn: Well, when I had the gun with me and I thought: if I come forward and tell the police that I have a gun Mick Gatto gave me that would make it look worse for him and that's the reason I didn't come forward, and then later on …

Mr Horgan: You thought it might look worse for him?

Mr Finn: Yes.

Mr Horgan: What you're saying to this jury is: 'I was only going to do what I thought would help Mick Gatto?'

Mr Finn: That's right …

Justice Cummins: Mr Gatto, don't wave at the witness. Thank you.

In re-examination, Mr Finn told Mr Richter that he had not seen Mr Gatto since the day of Veniamin's death and denied he would commit perjury for Mr Gatto.

Mr Finn: I wouldn't commit perjury for anybody.

✳✳✳

In summing up his case, Mr Horgan said Mr Gatto was a 'constant liar … a perjurer, a demonstrable perjurer'. He claimed there had been an 'orchestrated perjury' to protect him and Mr Finn was a part of it. He said the reason why none of those at Mr Gatto's table told police that Mr Finn had been there was because he hadn't been.

Mr Horgan: Brian Finn … was not there on 23 March 2004 at all. He's an invention … Andrew Veniamin wasn't much of a fellow, was he? Not a nice piece of work … He may have been a multiple murderer … But does it mean you say: 'Well, because it's Andrew Veniamin it doesn't matter much'? Of course you don't, because we live in a civilised society where the law protects the very good people and the people in the middle and the very bad people in exactly the same way. We don't live in a jungle.

We don't – as Mr Gatto seems to think – think … anyone who killed Andrew Veniamin should have been given the keys to the city … that's despicable, that's not this society.

He said Mr Gatto murdered Veniamin as revenge for the death of Graham Kinniburgh and as a pre-emptive strike because he feared for his life.

Mr Horgan: Veniamin gets shot three times fatally. The prosecution says all of this demonstrates a deliberate and sustained attempt to murder.

He claimed the gun that killed Veniamin was Mr Gatto's; that it was ridiculous to suggest that Veniamin, in the middle of the day, while being constantly watched by police, would have been able to hide a .38 revolver under his T-shirt and tracksuit pants.

Mr Horgan: If Dominic Gatto's version of events were correct Dominic Gatto would be a dead man. It takes but a second, a fraction of a second [with a gun that you haven't seen produced] for Veniamin to have pulled the trigger and killed Dominic Gatto.

Gatto vs Veniamin: Defence Underworld-style 57

Mr Richter, on the other hand, told the jury Veniamin had given up his right to life by pulling a gun on Mr Gatto at the back of the La Porcella restaurant.

> *Mr Richter*: If ... you think it is reasonably possible that Veniamin produced that gun at the restaurant, then you will acquit him [Gatto]. If he [Veniamin] drew it, then in the agony of those moments in that hallway his life was forfeit, not because he is an outlaw but because by doing that the law says Dominic Gatto had the right to defend himself unto death if he felt it was reasonably necessary to do what he did ...
>
> Veniamin had snapped. He was going to kill Gatto then and there and he pulled the gun on him and Gatto fought for his life for the first time and now he's fighting for his life for the second time.

***

On 15 June 2005, after a seven-week trial and almost 15 months after Veniamin's violent death, it took the jury eight hours to agree on a verdict.

When Mr Gatto was brought in to hear whether he would be branded a cold-blooded mob-style executioner or a man who had miraculously avoided becoming a gang war 'statistic', he blew a kiss to his many supporters in the public gallery.

Before the jury was brought in, Justice Cummins asked the packed, tense court: 'Do your best not to express your emotion before the jury leaves the court.' He might as well have been talking to a soccer crowd at a big match. Upon hearing the words 'Not guilty', the courtroom erupted. Fists punched the air. Women shrieked and squealed with delight. Men cheered. Amid all the mayhem, Mr Gatto bowed to the jury. He put his big ex-boxer's fist over his heart and bowed. Then – just as he threatened he would during the trial – he planted a great big 'it's a European-thing' kiss on Mr Richter's hairy cheek.

On the steps of the court, with his wife Cheryle by his side and some of his many supporters behind him, Mr Gatto told a massive media scrum:

'This is the lucky country. Thank God for the legal system. Thank God for the jury.'

The celebrations at Mr Gatto's home went well into the night.

But it seems in the so-called underworld there are seldom completely happy endings. One of those celebrating with Mr Gatto was former lawyer Mario Condello, who was on bail after being charged with being part of a gangland murder plot. Condello told the *Herald Sun* there was 'never any doubt' of his friend's innocence. He then said he had to leave, explaining: 'I've got to go because I have a curfew.'

On the day after Mr Gatto's acquittal, the *Herald Sun* reported one of Veniamin's mates as saying: 'It's not all over. There are still scores to be settled.'

On 6 February 2006, 53-year-old Condello was gunned down in the driveway of his luxury Brighton home. Once again, Mr Gatto had to help carry a mate's coffin.

SNIPER WIFE

My full name is Claire Margaret MacDonald and I am 38 years old. My date of birth is the 18th of June, 1966. I am a trained primary school teacher; however, I am now doing home duties looking after my family.

My husband is Warren John MacDonald and we have been married for 17 years. We have lived at 600 Acheron Road, Acheron for 15 years ... We have five children together. They are: John, who is the eldest and he is almost 10; Jillian, who is 8; Jennifer, who is almost seven; Jacqueline, who is five; and Douglas, who is two and a half.

Warren works as a surveyor on the Eildon Dam reconstruction ... I last taught at Alexandra Primary in the middle of 1997 but I have done a bit of emergency teaching since then ... We have 106 acres ... Warren and I have built this house from scratch; just the two of us.

That was the start of the police statement Claire MacDonald made just hours after her husband was shot dead; after six bullets had been fired at Warren MacDonald when he walked up to try to start an old Land Rover on their 'Breakaway Mountain' property, almost 100km north-east of Melbourne. Two bullets slammed into his back. One hit his head. One scorched its way through the collar of his jacket and slammed into the Land Rover's rear-vision mirror. One hit his chest. One missed. While under fire and severely wounded, Warren MacDonald had staggered behind and then into the Land Rover in a futile effort to dodge the remorseless attack on him. As well as screaming in pain, he had called out: 'Where are you?' but his attacker hadn't told him. Mr MacDonald was gunned down

60　　　　**REASONABLE DOUBT**

on 30 September 2004 – 11 days after his 40th birthday and just a couple of days after he and his family had returned from a holiday. Moments later, his wife was by her fatally wounded husband's side, tearfully calling an ambulance. She put a change mat under his head and a jacket over his bloodied body. A few hours later, Claire MacDonald talked to police about her nightmare:

On 19th September 2004, the whole family went for a holiday to Kangaroo Island, in South Australia … We got back home two days ago about 4.30pm on Tuesday 28 September. Yesterday, Warren started back at work … I started unpacking … My son, Douglas, had picked up conjunctivitis so I took him to the doctor about 10.15am. I went to … the supermarket and then to the chemist and then went to see Patty Brown to let her know we were home. She is a very good friend. I got home with the kids about 1.30pm.

We had visited friends in Adelaide and they had given me cuttings of lavender and some cacti … The children helped me to put six of them in pots. We did not have enough pots for the rest of them.

I started preparing tea about 5pm. Warren arrived home about 5.50pm. Warren spent some time at the computer while I was cooking dinner. We had tea about 7pm because Warren had been showing the kids photos from the trip on the computer. At 7.30pm the children normally go to bed but they stayed up a bit longer as *The Dukes of Hazzard* was on TV. The kids were in bed by 8.30pm.

About 15 minutes to 20 minutes later, Warren took either his laptop or a memory stick out to the car so he would not forget it in the morning. I was doing the dishes and Warren called me out because it was such a moonlit night … He said, 'Let's go for a walk.' He decided to take his .22 rifle in case we saw a rabbit … We walked up the track past the sheds for about another two or three hundred metres. As we came up around the corner we could see a light about 50 metres away … I think the light was coming from a treed area at the edge of the clearing. We heard a couple of shots about a few seconds apart; maybe 15 seconds apart.

Warren told me to be very quiet and we would try to get closer to see who was there and what was going on. We crept along a pile of metal so that we weren't seen. As we were getting to the treed area, we could see a man sitting on the ground. He had a torch in his left hand. The torch that he had was half the size of what police use and would take a D-cell battery. The torch was a dark colour. I could see that he had a dark-coloured or black backpack. It was like a day pack and it had a bed roll on top of it. Like something he might sleep in. I did not really see much of him until he stood up. The pack was strapped to his back.

Warren yelled at him and said: 'What are you doing?' That was when the guy stood up. Warren got angry and was yelling and swearing … he went ballistic … He told the man: 'This is private property. You should not be here. Who do you think you are?' He went on for about five minutes. Warren does not tolerate people who just walk on to other people's property. The other guy started getting angry and started yelling back. He said he was only trying to get a couple of rabbits because he was hungry and he was not doing anybody any harm.

The guy was a bit taller than Warren, so about 185cm … The moon was out but it was dark. He had dark pants … He had like a polar fleece windcheater on with like half a zip. He had a dark-coloured beanie … He was scrawny to medium. He was an Australian but I didn't see his complexion … He looked like he had not shaved for a couple of days. He had quite a thick stubble. He would have been a bit older than us – maybe in his 40s … I didn't see the firearm. It might have been on the ground.

I moved away; I don't like yelling … I was getting a bit frightened. Warren was shielding me from him a bit. The last thing I remember Warren saying to him was the direction of the nearest fence and if he did not leave, he would call the police.

The other guy started going through the fence and I heard him say: 'OK, I'm going … Watch your back, mate. There's no need to get upset' – or something like that.

We stood there for a few minutes to make sure he was gone and we went back to the house.

The whole time Warren was just holding his rifle down by his side. He never threatened this guy with the rifle at all. The guy walked to our right to the fence and disappeared down the hill through the trees. He would have been heading in the direction of the rental property which is in Yellowbox Road. There is someone there now renting … and I think they drive a blue Commodore. Not a really old one and not a new one.

We didn't notify the police at all. I think Warren felt he had scared him away and that would be the end of it.

I can't remember the man picking up or carrying a rifle. Warren was obscuring my vision at times, so I can't be sure. We didn't go and search the treed area where the man had been. I don't think Warren saw him as a threat. I haven't seen this man before. Warren thought the same as me that the man was just a wanderer.

We went to bed about 10.30 to 10.45 after doing a few things.

On Thursday 30 September 2004 [today], Warren went to work as usual about 6.15am. Before Warren left, he told me to keep my eyes open and be careful.

I did some washing and cleaning after breakfast. It was about 11am before the kids were ready to go and we drove into Alexandra. I dropped some cub information to the group leader … Greg Kleinitz. He wasn't home so I dropped the information just inside the flywire door … I went to the post office and posted some letters. Warren rang about 11.10am and asked me to … [organise] a hands-free kit into my car … He asked me how I was going and how things were going. It was just normal chitchat … I got home at about 12.15pm. I made lunches for the kids. After that I was down in the cellar packing away some of the camping gear. I had done what I needed to do, so I decided to find some extra pots to plant some more cuttings. I remembered that we had some pots up near the pile of rubbish near the cleared area. I was pretty tired so I decided to take the little Land Rover for a run up there because it had not been started for a while ...

The girls were playing Leggo and Douglas was playing with his car. John was watching TV and playing with Douglas.

I drove up the track and I turned it around to face the way I had just come. At that point the car just stalled. I tried to start it a couple of times. I stopped then because I thought that I would flood the car or drain the battery. I went over to the pile of rubbish and found two pots and put them on a tree stump ...

I walked back to the house ... and checked the children were all OK ... That must have been about 2.30pm. I rang the library to renew a book John had that was overdue. I could not get through and rang Telstra to see if there was a problem and spent about three-quarters of an hour on the phone with them.

About 4pm, I took some mince out the freezer to make dinner. I started to cook the dinner. I started making the spaghetti sauce. I did some more unpacking and later went up to the top tank to check the water supply about 5.15pm because I remember thinking Warren would be home soon. I walked back to the cleared area to give the car another try and start it up. I told John where I was going and asked him to tell Dad where I was and what happened. I told John I had my phone with me if he needed me.

I walked up to the cleared area and stopped for a few minutes because there were some kangaroos there. I went to the toilet over in the treed area. At this time, I heard a shot coming from the direction [of a neighbour's property] ... I heard a second shot, which seemed to come from behind me ... It was so windy it could have been the first shot bouncing around in the wind.

I did not see anyone there. I thought everything was fine because the kangaroos were there and when I arrived there they were scared away. The kangaroos would not have been there if someone was in the trees, so I wasn't really concerned. I walked to the car and tried to start it but it would not start ...

I tried a couple of times and then I saw Warren walking up the track about 6.15pm. Warren had his .22 rifle with him – the one with the scope on it. I don't know why Warren had it. He is such an over-cautious person.

I explained to Warren what had happened … I was at the front of the car when he got into it. We tried a couple of times to start it. He sat in the driver's seat and tried to start it. He told me he would need some jumper cables and to bring my car up. Warren said: 'Before you go, do you want a bit of nookie up in the bush?' We ended up in amongst the pile of rubbish for a few, maybe five or ten minutes kissing and cuddling … I told Warren that I should go and check on the kids and go and get the jumper leads.

Warren had the bonnet up and was checking the leads when I left. While he did this, I jogged back to the house … After that I did not see him. I went inside to see if the kids were OK. I turned the dinner off. I got the keys to the white Land Rover as the good set of jumper leads are in that car … I chattered to the kids for a while … I told John I would only be a few minutes … I got into my car and drove back up the track … It was about 6.30pm. I was only in the house for a few minutes …

I got to the corner where the old Land Rover was and as I got around the corner, I could see Warren lying on the ground … I saw him lying there face down … It was like he had fallen out of the car. I drove right up to the car and went over to Warren … Warren was basically lying on his stomach and I grabbed him by the left shoulder and shook him and called his name. It was then that I saw the blood. The first blood I saw was on his face. Then a bit on his back and quite a bit on his left leg … I shook him but didn't get any response … I raced to my car and got my mobile phone and called Triple 0 and asked for an ambulance and told them that I think my husband had been shot. There was a spot of blood on his jumper maybe the size of a 10-cent piece. Warren had an orange jumper on and the blood had come through. I saw lots of blood but I did not see any other spots, just the one. I assumed he may have been shot because of that spot and all the other blood.

I had my hand on his back and I thought I could feel his chest rising. I tried to roll him over but he was too heavy and I could not do it. I thought it best to leave him in the position he was in. I was talking to the ambulance officer and he told me to make sure his airway was clear and to get something to prop his head. I raced to the back of the car and got a jacket, a picnic rug and a change mat to prop his head and keep him warm …

I was getting pretty distraught and crying and I was not sure what to do and I was praying that the ambulance would get there soon. I was talking to Warren all the time – trying to get some kind of response. I did not really notice any other injuries. I used my hand to open his airway.

It was starting to get dark and I went and put the headlights on in my car. I didn't know what to do.

I did not notice anyone else around me at the time I got there. I didn't hear anyone and I didn't see anyone. I didn't hear any shots fired. I was back at the house and the telly was on. I didn't hear anything.

I was worried about the kids and rang John and told him that daddy had been hurt and that an ambulance was on the way and just not to worry if he saw an ambulance going past. I asked him to look after the kids. I had to explain it a few times to John because he thought I was having a joke and I went back to Warren after that and cried.

I saw some headlights and was worried about someone not seeing them, so I walked back to the corner and got halfway when the police and ambulance arrived …

I think the magazine in Warren's rifle is a five-shot magazine. The rifle is a .22 bolt action … I don't know how many firearms Warren has, but there is a lot. I could not say when was the last time

I fired any of the firearms. I haven't fired any recently … I haven't fired any guns … Not for ages.

I am not aware of anyone who would want to do this to Warren. I don't think Warren would have any enemies. He would tell me if he had a problem with anyone at work but nothing that would escalate to this.

Warren and I have had our arguments like any other couple may have but nothing would cause me to do this. I certainly did not shoot Warren and I would not hurt a fly.

***

Claire MacDonald signed her police statement as 'true and correct' and 'in the belief that a person making a false statement in the circumstances is liable to the penalties of perjury' at 7.12pm on 1 October 2004. Shortly afterwards she spoke to Senior Constable Fiona Stevens – the policewoman who had been asked to interrogate the MacDonald children over their father's death.

Senior Constable Stevens: She [Ms MacDonald] had become teary and she broke down at one stage and I touched her arm and reassured her and settled her down. Then we spoke a little further and then she actually reached over and touched me and broke down again …

I just said to her if she was in a position to reduce the trauma to the children then as a mother she needed to consider that and put the children first. She then replied to me: 'I haven't told them everything', and I asked her to explain to me what she meant by that. She said: 'I didn't tell them about the way he treated me and the children.' Then she went on to tell me of some emotional abuse and excessive discipline of the children by the father and that's when she first broke down and cried uncontrollably and that's when I touched her on the arm and comforted her and she actually settled down …

She regained her composure and I checked: 'Is there anything you can think of to lessen the traumatic process?' and she said: 'Yes'

Sniper Wife   67

and I asked her: 'What?' and she said: 'To tell the whole truth.' And I said: 'What is that?' And she said: 'I'll tell about the abuse and the effect it's had.' And I said: 'Anything else?' and that's when she took hold of my hand and broke down again and I actually moved beside her and was comforting her. And, at that time, I asked her if there was anything she wanted to tell the investigators and that's when she said: 'Yes, that I killed Warren.' And I asked her to repeat it so that I was very, very clear about what she was saying to me and she said: *'I did it. I shot Warren. I killed him'* ...

So I advised her that that was probably the hardest part: that she'd said that and now because of what she'd told me, I was obliged to tell her something very important and asked her to listen carefully. She said: 'Yes', and then I gave Claire MacDonald the caution and read her her rights.

***

So, two hours after signing her police statement, Ms MacDonald was once again being interviewed by investigating police. This time she told a *very* different story of how her husband – the man she started dating when they were in the same final-year class at Aquinas College in Melbourne's east suburban Ringwood – came to be shot dead on their Breakaway Mountain property.

This time she admitted using her children to lure their father to his death. She told them to tell him to come up the hill to help her start the 1956 roofless Land Rover, which had stalled – but it hadn't. She had then put on her husband's army camouflage clothes and hat, and grabbed one of their 200 or so guns – a .22 bolt-action rifle with a long-distance sight. She wrapped it in a green towel just in case she bumped into one of the children on her way out. This quietly spoken mum and respected primary school teacher then hid in a clump of trees about 48 metres from the old Land Rover – her ambush bait. Then she waited and waited; for nearly two hours she lay in her sniper's nest waiting for her prey. When he finally walked into her trap – wearing his orange fluorescent surveyor's shirt and polar fleece top – she fired a shot into his back. She kept firing, emptying

68   **REASONABLE DOUBT**

a five-bullet cartridge. When her husband staggered into the driver's seat, she put a sixth bullet in her gun and fired. Warren MacDonald then slumped forward and toppled out of the car.

So much for 'I wouldn't hurt a fly'. So much for a mysterious, scrawny, unshaven wanderer with a fleecy halfway-zipped windcheater who might have exacted a fearsome revenge after being shooed away for trying to shoot some rabbits. So much for 'kissing and cuddling'; for 'a little bit of nookie' with her husband. So much for not knowing of anyone who would want to kill Warren. It turned out Claire MacDonald had known better than anybody, someone who desperately – *desperately* – wanted him dead.

> *Detective*: Claire, is it true that you made a Triple 0 phone call to the ambulance from your property at 600 Acheron Road, Acheron last night, being Thursday 30 September?
>
> *Ms MacDonald*: Yes.
>
> *Detective*: OK. Can you tell me what led up to you making that phone call?
>
> *Ms MacDonald*: I had just had enough of the way that I had been treated and my children were being treated. And, because of the threats that he made to me, I decided that Warren didn't deserve to live any more. I thought if I drove one of the Land Rovers up to the cleared area behind our sheds under the pretence that Warren needed to come up and get it started again, then I could hide and shoot him.
>
> *Detective*: Can you tell me what happened?
>
> *Ms MacDonald*: I fabricated a story and said to the children that I was going to get pot cuttings so they wouldn't be anywhere near ... I said I wouldn't be long and that I had my mobile phone with me if John needed to ring me ... I think I went up there about half past four ...
>
> *Detective*: What time was Warren due home?
>
> *Ms MacDonald*: Any time after about 20 past five ...

Detective: Did he in fact arrive home?

Ms MacDonald: He did and it was about a quarter past six.

Detective: And where were you when Warren arrived home?

Ms MacDonald: I was hiding in the trees in the cleared area ... up past the sheds ... There's lots of metal rubbish and things that were supposedly going to be useful but never ever quite got there.

Detective: What happened when you were hiding there?

Ms MacDonald: Warren walked up to the car and looked around and I had the thought in my head that I had to do it. If I didn't do it now, I would be the one that was dead ... He came around the front of the car and he turned around. And I had his back in the sights and I just fired and he let out a cry ... 'Where are you?' and just cries of pain ... I think he probably knew I was up here somewhere and he was probably feeling guilty that he had pushed me to this ...

And then I fired again but I don't know where that one went ... He moved around to the other side of the car, I think, maybe, to give himself something to hide behind ... He was crying out in pain [she breaks down weeping] ... I was pretty panicked. I actually couldn't believe that I had carried it through and I just thought to myself: 'I don't care what happens, I'll never have to be in bed with you again' ... He walked around to the other side of the car and I wasn't sure that I had gotten him ... I couldn't go back. I had to just keep going until he was dead. I think I emptied the cartridge ... I remember thinking he was about to drive away and I couldn't let him live and so I got out the extra one I had in my pocket ... I put that in the magazine and fired again and he slumped forward onto the steering wheel and then fell out of the car ... I waited a few minutes and he wasn't moving ... I was still frightened, so I actually crept through the fence and tried to get close to the car to see what had happened ...

Detective [on the video re-enactment in the 'sniper's nest' treed area]: Can you just show us where you were?

Ms MacDonald: Yeah, I was kneeling down about here and I had my elbow here and the barrel was resting between these two branches … because I was shaking and I just wasn't sure whether I was gonna do what I was gonna do [crying].

Detective: OK, was it to steady the rifle?

Ms MacDonald: Yeah … He didn't deserve to live. He was hurting my children and he didn't deserve to live and I just wanted him out of my life, out of my children's lives.

Detective: Did it ever cross your mind to stop shooting because he was only injured and crying out and there was a chance he could have survived?

Ms MacDonald: No, I knew that while he was alive, it would have been worse. He would have set out to get me.

Detective: So you then made a decision to keep on shooting?

Ms MacDonald: Yep.

Detective: With what intention?

Ms MacDonald: Just so he wouldn't survive.

She said she had to deliberately load each of the bullets she fired at her husband.

Detective: Have you used that firearm in the past?

Ms MacDonald: Yep …

Detective: Are you a member of any clubs, firearm clubs?

Ms MacDonald: The Shooters Association – which is so wrong, I know but – and the Antique and Historical Collectors Guild.

Detective: Have you ever shot in competitions?

Ms MacDonald: Yep.

Detective: Have you ever won any awards?

Ms MacDonald: One. I came second in my competition in Taggerty years and years ago but any competitions after that were really just for fun over at Seymour Black Powder Club …

Detective: And what made you take the firearm up to where you were?

Ms MacDonald: I just didn't want to have any physical contact with him. I didn't want to be close to him. And I thought: 'If I use the gun that had the sight on it, that would do it' … and I would not have to confront him.

Detective: When you shot Warren, how far away were you from him?

Ms MacDonald: Twenty or 30 metres.

Detective: What were you hiding behind?

Ms MacDonald: A fallen tree …

Detective: How many shots hit him?

Ms MacDonald: I think maybe one to his back, one to his head and I must have got him in his leg, I think. I don't know. One hit the mirror …

Detective: … Did you continue to train the sights on his back?

Ms MacDonald: He was moving around. He had moved around to the other side of the car …

Detective: What was your intention when you were firing the rounds at him?

Ms MacDonald: Just to make sure he didn't get up again.

Detective: Was it your intention to kill him?

Ms MacDonald: Yeah.

Detective: OK. When you finished firing the sixth shot, what did you do then?

Ms MacDonald: I just waited a couple of minutes and then I crept through the hedge, just around the fence, sorry, and walked along the other side of the fence to see if he really was dead.

Detective: And was he moving?

Ms MacDonald: No.

Detective: Did you physically go over and speak to him or touch him to see if he was alive or deceased?

Ms MacDonald: No. I was too scared … I went back to the house. I went in through the back door. Took off the shirt and hat that I was wearing and the towel that I had taken up there …

Detective: Before you walked over there what did you do with the rifle?

Ms MacDonald: I just left it lying on the ground there.

Detective: Why did you leave it there?

Ms MacDonald: I was just so confused and I thought that if I could make people think someone else had done it, then I wouldn't need to worry about what happened to it …

Detective: Were you wearing anything on your hands?

Ms MacDonald: Yeah, just rubber disposable gloves.

She said that the camouflage shirt, hat and the green towel were all still unwashed in the laundry basket but she had burnt the rubber gloves in the living-room fireplace – 'just to get rid of them'.

Detective: What did you do from then, after you've burnt the gloves? …

Ms MacDonald: Then I said to the kids that I had come back to get the jumper leads in my car. And I checked on tea and made sure everyone was OK. And then I said to John to look after them and Mummy would be back soon. Then I got the keys to the light Land Rover 110, which had a good set of jumper leads in it. So, I got the keys to that vehicle and got the jumper leads out just so that if any-one – just to make the story believable, I suppose … I put them [the leads] in the Land Rover Discovery … I drove it up to where the other Land Rover was, up near Warren.

And I walked over to him and put my hand on his back and told him how much I hated him for making me do this. And I spoke like that for about five minutes. I just told him how much I hated him. And then I got my phone out and rang Triple 0 …

I just said I thought my husband had been shot and I need an ambulance and … then they put me through to an ambulance operator who asked me to go and make sure his airways were clear.

Detective: And did you do that?

Ms MacDonald: I did. Of course, I knew it wasn't going to do anything …

Detective: Were you confident that he was dead already?

Ms MacDonald: I didn't think he was breathing, but I didn't want to touch him. I didn't want to feel for a pulse or anything.

Detective: Did the ambulance operator give you any instructions?

Ms MacDonald: Just told me to, maybe, prop his head up … 'Just try and make him comfortable.' I went back to the Discovery and got out a nappy change mat and a jacket and a picnic rug and I put the change mat under his head and covered him with the jacket and the picnic rug, just to make it look like I was keeping him warm …

I went to where he was lying and I think I might have lifted his leg down from the car, that was hooked on the car and I put the little jacket over his shoulders. I didn't want to touch him and so I used his hair to lift his head up to put the change mat under his head and then I covered him with the picnic rug … And just told him how much I hated him [she breaks down crying] and how I couldn't believe he had pushed me to do this … I just couldn't do it any more and I couldn't see the children being treated the way they were and I thought: they're so young and they just didn't deserve to be treated the way they were. I just knelt there for ages – it seemed like ages – just crying and wishing that there had been some other way of dealing with it.

Detective: And what did you do after that?

Ms MacDonald: I switched the headlights on the car because it was getting dark … and I knelt back down beside him and, again, I just cried and told him that I wished he hadn't made me do it, which seemed to help me so I was not angry any more.

Detective: And did you contact the children again?

Ms MacDonald: Yeah, I rang John because I was worried that they would get a fright when the ambulance drove past. I said to John that Daddy had been hurt and that an ambulance was coming and not to worry if he saw one going past. He said, you know, 'Don't play jokes, Mum' … he said: 'You're joking, aren't you?' I had to tell him about three times that I wasn't joking. I said: 'Just keep everyone inside and look after everybody.'

Ms MacDonald apologised for lying about the scrawny wanderer.

Detective: Did you meet someone that was shooting or spotlighting in the paddock?

Ms MacDonald: No, but we did hear shooting and see a spotlight ...

Detective: The man you described as being quite tall with a backpack ... ?

Ms MacDonald: Made it all up ... [Crying] Sorry.

Detective: Do you want to tell us the background circumstances that led up to what happened on Thursday night, being the shooting of Warren?

Ms MacDonald: I think the single thing that sticks out most ... From very early on in our marriage ... five or six years into our marriage ... it was a case of I just had to do what I was told ... It was just even stupid things like he didn't like me wearing make-up. He didn't like me cutting my hair. He didn't like me having half a teaspoon of sugar in my tea. Everything had to be done his way. I was just there to, really, be a slave, just to do what he wanted to do ...

The alarm would go off at quarter to six. I would switch it off. I would get out of bed. I would make sure the fire was going. I would make his breakfast. I would make his lunch. I would make sure he had clothes to wear. Then I would wake him up ...

He would humiliate me in front of people. He would make me take his boots off ... and then say to people: 'Why have a dog and bark too?'

I had to constantly provide him with drinks every night. It was my job to make sure that he had a glass of drink and it was always full. It was just always his way, everything.

He was always telling me how filthy I was and how I couldn't keep any house that we had clean. I just wasn't good at anything ... I think I'm such a placid person that I believed that I loved him and I just wanted to make his life happy and do whatever I could for him.

Detective: Have you sought any counselling in relation to the way that you say he's treated you?

Ms MacDonald: No.

Detective: Have you confided in friends or relatives?

Ms MacDonald: I had probably – just in the last 12 months – confided in Patty Brown … I just had to tell somebody … Like he was a cub leader and two of my children are cubs – John and Jillian. One day, we were all going to cubs and we had to go to the chemist first and because the chemist was taking too long to make the script up and he was going to be late, he said to me: 'I'm going. You can walk up.' He left me to walk from the main street of Alexandra to the other end of town just because he was in a bad mood for some reason. I think that was the first thing I told Patty …

Detective: Can you think of any course of conduct that you could have taken other than shooting Warren to get out of the bad situation that you found yourself in?

Ms MacDonald: On I don't know how many occasions, when we'd had disagreements usually about my having milk at the table when it should have been in the fridge; or not having the floor vacuumed; or not having the dishes done; or not having his shirt ironed; or not having the kids' fingernails trimmed; or something so stupid, he would just tell me what an arsehole I was and how I was making his life a misery and everything was my fault and that I should have been back at work earning money, instead of just taking every cent that he put in … He was constantly telling me how I didn't have the right to say what things would get done or what things would get bought because I wasn't bringing any new money into the family and that I should have been – in the seven years that I was at home doing nothing – I should have been able to work from home, or do something to provide the family with more income …

Detective: Has he ever been physically aggressive with you?

Ms MacDonald: Yes … Sometimes, if, maybe, I had not paid a bill or something stupid, he would get really angry with me and would say things like: 'I could just punch you in the face,' and he would bring his fist so close to my face or he would grab me by the scruff of the neck and – I haven't told anybody this – he would always push me so hard on the chest … If ever we had an argument and the question of not living together came up, he would say if I ever left him that he would just put a bullet in my head and bury me somewhere and tell everybody that I had run away.

Detective: Did you take that threat seriously?

Ms MacDonald: Absolutely.

Detective: How often would he make that threat?

Ms MacDonald: At least half a dozen times that I can remember …

Detective: Did you ever make any attempt to leave home?

Ms MacDonald: No, I was too scared.

Detective: What did you think would happen if you did try to leave him?

Ms MacDonald: He would find me wherever I went and he would hurt me …

Detective: Apart from shooting Warren, what other options were available to you? For example, could you have collected up all the kids while Warren was at work and gone and stayed with a relative, or gone to the police station and told them what happened?

Ms MacDonald: I was just too frightened. I knew that he would just see it as all my fault.

Detective: Did those options enter your mind at all?

Ms MacDonald: They did, but I just dismissed them. I thought of just running away altogether and then I thought: 'That's not fair. This is the kids' home. They shouldn't have to leave. They shouldn't have to be put through being just scared and moved around' …

Detective: Are you aware of refuges available to people that may wish to leave a particular situation and disappear?

Ms MacDonald: Yeah.

Detective: Did you consider any of these options?

Ms MacDonald: I just knew – the way he talked and the way he acted towards me – he would not rest. The way he treated the children, he absolutely adored them and he would not have allowed me to take them away from him.

Her husband may have adored his children but Ms MacDonald said the children were 'absolutely terrified' of their father.

Ms MacDonald: Whenever he was due home, everyone instantly went on eggshells and there was not allowed to be any toys within sight, it was just: 'Quick, clean up before Dad gets home.'

A few months ago, Warren, John and Jillian had gone down to check the dam, which is below the house, in the army Land Rover and when they came back John and Jillian went straight to bed and Warren said to me: 'John slammed the door, the little shit-for-brains.' I thought: 'Oh, here we go.' And then I went up to see John and just to talk quietly to him without Warren knowing I was talking to him [getting upset] and he said to me that he just tried to close the door and Warren grabbed him by the scruff of his shirt and kicked him three times on the bottom for slamming the door. Another incident was when we were playing football and John [she weeps] had gone to kick the ball when one of the girls had reached for it and, to teach him a lesson, Warren kicked John's hands to remind him he shouldn't kick a ball that's near someone else's hands …

They were all absolutely terrified of him … If he wasn't around or he had to stay at work late or had to work on a Saturday, the kids thought it was the best thing: that they could be themselves and not have to worry about anything. [breaks down crying] …

Detective: Did he ever injure any of the children?

Ms MacDonald: John suffered lots of bruises.

Detective: Were they ever viewed by a doctor?

Ms MacDonald: No.

Detective: Were you afraid to take the children to a doctor?

Ms MacDonald: Absolutely …

REASONABLE DOUBT

She said John had been Warren's 'whipping boy ... someone smaller than him that he could exercise power over'. He hadn't been as violent towards his daughters but would regularly spank them and John with a long, flat 'smacking stick' kept on the top shelf in the lounge cupboard.

> *Ms Macdonald*: He used to ask me to get it down and hand it to him and he would make the children come over into this area and he would say: 'Now bend over and touch your toes,' and they were so scared 'cause they knew what was going to happen and he used to say: 'No, move a bit. I can't get a good enough swing,' and he would hit them ... he would smack them on the bottom ... He would make me smack them and then say: 'No, that wasn't hard enough, do it again.'
>
> *Detective*: And did you do that?
>
> *Ms MacDonald*: Well, I had to otherwise he would have done it harder ...
>
> *Detective*: How is the children's relationship with their father?
>
> *Ms MacDonald*: I know John hates him.
>
> *Detective*: Would he admit that?
>
> *Ms MacDonald*: He has admitted it to me ...
>
> *Detective*: Have you ever sought an intervention order against Warren?
>
> *Ms MacDonald*: I was too scared to.

She said that there were over 200 guns in the house but that most of them were 'collectables' and that Warren had never threatened her with a gun.

> *Detective*: Is there any reason that you chose a firearm to kill Warren?
>
> *Ms MacDonald*: I just thought: I wouldn't have to have any contact with him; I wouldn't have to touch him; I wouldn't have to struggle; I wouldn't have to be near him.
>
> *Detective*: How long had you thought about killing Warren?

Ms MacDonald: Wednesday night … Seriously. I probably thought quite often how much happier we would all be if just was not in the picture …

Detective: What was different on Wednesday night that made you come to that decision?

Ms MacDonald: I had gone down to our cellar, which is absolutely jam-packed full of stuff because the house is not finished and we don't have anywhere to store anything, And again that's my fault – I don't know how. Down in the cellar is where I keep boxes of potatoes … and I had gone down to pack away some camping stuff, I think, from the holiday and was taking too long and he came down to see what I was doing and straightaway he said: 'What's in these boxes?' I said: 'Potatoes.' He said: 'What's this box?' and there were four boxes on a covered coffee table and he started yelling how I couldn't even store potatoes properly and how they were all shot and I was poisoning him by feeding him potatoes that had been shot … and he started throwing the boxes of potatoes around and there was just stuff everywhere.

He even said he had been bringing scrap paper home from work [starting to cry] and I had it stored down there and I didn't even store that properly [breaks down crying].

I had some artificial flowers that were on the top shelf and he said: 'What are these? Who bought these?' and … I said my mum bought them … he just threw them on the floor and stomped all over them because it was something of mine.

Detective: Was that before or after you went for your walk on Wednesday night?

Ms MacDonald: That was after … just before we went to bed about 10 o'clock.

Detective: That was when you decided to take some sort of action?

Ms MacDonald: He actually threatened to punch me again because I was, you know, I was so slack and 'What do you do all day?' and I couldn't even throw a box of potatoes out and he started yelling at me and telling me what an arsehole I was … He was poking me on my arm telling me how useless I was and I was just a shit-for-brains and a moron and didn't have a brain … He told me that I would have to clean it up tomorrow. 'Get rid of the potatoes,' he said … It went on for about 10 minutes … and he looked at me with such anger and said: 'I could just punch you in the face,' and then I started yelling back at him – which I don't usually do – because I'd just had enough and he just walked out.

Detective: What did you say to him, when you yelled back?

Ms MacDonald: I don't know – how … he didn't appreciate anything I did and I spent my whole life revolving around looking after him and his moods and just never got anything back …

Detective: And what was his reaction to you standing up for yourself?

Ms MacDonald: He didn't like me yelling back at him and he just put his fingers in his ears … He just kicked the wall and said: 'Get out … Get upstairs.' We went to bed and he said: 'Right, I want anal sex.' This was his way of paying me back for doing the wrong thing because he knew I didn't like it and he knew it hurt. It was just his way of getting back at me.

Detective: And did that actually take place?

Ms MacDonald: Yeah.

Detective: And did you consent to that?

Ms MacDonald: I suppose I did but … it was always a case of I just wanted to get it over and done with because if I ever refused, he would tell me what a cold, frigid bitch I was and how he wished that he had been with more women. It was just easier to get it over and done with.

Detective: Was he aware that you weren't happy about what was happening?

Ms MacDonald: Yep. He was very much aware of the fact that he never seemed to make me happy. He was never able to do anything for me – I just couldn't – and that was another point that was my fault because it's all in your brain and you should be able to have an orgasm and every second night he would have to have sex – every second night. It was very rare that we would go more than two days without him demanding sex ... I hated it.

Detective: Did you ever tell him: 'No', that you didn't want to have sex?

Ms MacDonald: Quite often.

Detective: What was his reaction to that?

Ms MacDonald: Just be: I'm a cold, frigid bitch and 'I don't know why I married you,' and 'I should just go out and pay somebody' ...

If I was too tired or I wasn't well or even if I had my period, or anything, he would just say: 'Just lie there. I just need to empty out.' He wouldn't care whether I wanted to or not ... if I suggested that I didn't want to, he would start calling me names and say I was a frigid bitch ... His favourite term was 'the Ice Queen of Acheron', he used to call me if I said 'No' or didn't want it.

Detective: And the kids [who all slept in the same room as their parents because the unfinished home only had one bedroom], did they sleep through all this?

Ms MacDonald: They did, and that was another reason: I thought if I make a scene or if I make a noise or anything they would wake up and see what was going on [crying].

Detective: So you were afraid for them, were you?

Ms MacDonald: Very much ...

Detective: Did he ever physically force himself upon you sexually?

Ms MacDonald: Yes ... He was actually constantly looking at pornographic images on the internet and he was seated at the computer of a night-time, every night, and he would be on the computer and he would get himself excited by what he was watching and then he would say: 'Look, this girl can do it. Why can't you?' referring to blow jobs and I just hated it and my teeth always got in the way and so he would hit me on my head and felt and tapped my teeth and I'd say to him: 'I can't help it. I can't do it.' And he would say: 'What a load of frog shit,' or 'You're just an arsehole,' or something like that.

Ms MacDonald said that after the potato tantrum in the cellar and the punishment sex afterwards, she lay in bed planning to kill her husband.

> *Ms MacDonald*: I just thought if I could make it look like someone else had done it, then he would be dead and we could all just move and lead a normal life.
>
> *Detective*: When you were lying in bed thinking about this, tell me the thoughts that were going through your mind as to how you thought you might be able to do this and get away with it.
>
> *Ms MacDonald*: I suppose the only thing I really thought of was wearing gloves, so that there would be no powder residue and my fingerprints would not be directly on the gun.

She said she decided to take the old Land Rover up – ostensibly to get the pots so that her children did not see their father shot.

> *Ms MacDonald*: I thought that if I took the car up there, so it was away from the children, under the pretence of getting some of these pots, then Warren needed to come up … I could just lie and wait for him.
>
> *Detective*: Was the intention of killing him once you got into that position?
>
> *Ms MacDonald*: I still didn't know until probably he was walking up the track that I was actually going to go through with it …
>
> *Detective*: Is it correct that you've changed your mind, and now want to tell the truth about what occurred? What was it that changed your mind to do that?
>
> *Ms MacDonald*: Fear, I think … It was going to be so much worse for the children and I just don't want to put them through any more.

***

At Claire MacDonald's trial in the Supreme Court of Victoria in February and March 2006, the defence's main argument was that she was not guilty of murder because she had acted in self-defence: if she hadn't shot her husband he would have killed or seriously injured her. Its fallback was

Sniper Wife

that she was only guilty of manslaughter: she had been provoked into temporarily losing self-control.

The trial heard that Warren MacDonald had been a dedicated and able surveyor. Workmate Roger Mottram said that Warren had been proud of his children and had photographs of them around his office. He said that he had been a 'very hard worker' but that it wasn't all about work. At times 'he was very jovial, boisterous', and he 'liked to play the odd joke or two'. Under cross-examination, it turned out he hadn't appreciated all of Warren's 'jokes'.

Mr Mottram: He came to work one day with a computer memory stick. He asked me to open it for him … It came up with rather explicit pornography and I had quite a lot of trouble turning it off quickly … He [Warren] thought it was funny.

Nobody was denying that at home Warren MacDonald was a disciplinarian. The dead man's retired police officer father, John MacDonald, told the court his son had been fascinated with cars and guns since childhood. He said Warren had collected about a dozen Land Rovers. He said Warren had been dedicated to his work as a surveyor and had worked on freeways and on the Australian Grand Prix track at Melbourne's Albert Park. He said his son had always been available for him but agreed that at home, Warren was strict.

John MacDonald: With the family, Warren was the boss … He ran the show. Nobody told him what to do or how to do it. He did it himself, his way and you wouldn't cross him … He was a very proud father. He was always wanting to show his children off … but very much a disciplinarian. If the children did something amiss, they were punished by way of physical exercise … normally push-ups, that type of thing.

Patricia Brown – Claire MacDonald's closest friend – agreed.

Ms Brown: The children were wonderful children and very well behaved but, you know, if I sort of gave them a biscuit to eat, they had to all line up in a row and they weren't allowed to move until they had eaten the biscuit … And if they did something wrong, they were made to get down on the floor or on the ground and do push-ups – even the two-year-old, which I thought was a bit harsh.

A former teacher colleague and friend of Claire's, Leanne Mits, remembered the MacDonalds coming to her place for lunch and eight-year-old John doing something to annoy his father.

Ms Mits: Warren pointed a finger and in a strong military voice demanded that John 'Drop' in the kitchen and 'Do 10'. John dropped and did 10 push-ups, and stood up at attention waiting for his dad to dismiss him.

Farewells were also done with military precision.

Ms Mits: He would say: 'Claire, we're leaving. Get the children in the car.' They would be gone in five minutes.

John MacDonald told his daughter-in-law's murder trial that his dead son insisted his wife do *all* the work in the house. If he wanted a drink, Claire would have to get it. Ms Brown agreed.

Ms Brown: One particular incident which really upset me was at his birthday party … Claire was running around trying to look after the five children … I arrived a little late and everybody else had eaten and Claire hadn't eaten as she was jumping up and down, jumping up and down … and Warren just indicated to her by saying: 'Get me a drink,' like this. And I thought: 'Well, that's a bit rude. She's trying to look after the children. Her dinner's on the table getting cold and he expects her to run after him.' And I must admit, I got a bit angry and said to her: 'Look, for goodness sake, I will get the drink for him' – you know, I had eaten – and then I said something like: 'Tip it on his head,' which wasn't the right thing to say but I was angry because he was treating her in such a manner.

Another friend of Claire's – Lynne Orchard – remembered going to lunch at Warren and Claire's.

> *Ms Orchard*: Claire was just about to sit down to eat her lunch and Warren decided he wanted beetroot in his sandwich and that he wasn't going to eat it without it. So she had to go down to the cellar … Because they buy in bulk, not everything is labelled and the first tin she opened was baked beans. He told her she was stupid and to go and get another tin and he wasn't going to be home the following day but all she and the children were allowed to eat were these baked beans. They were not to go to waste and that was all they were allowed to eat the following day.

Another friend of Claire's – Anne Hail – said that Warren was constantly telling his wife she was 'dumb' or a 'stupid woman' or 'Bitch!' or 'Whore!'. She had been particularly appalled at how he treated her while she was in labour with their first child. She said the labour had gone incredibly quickly and the MacDonalds had dropped around at her house because she was going to be Claire's support, before making the long trip to the hospital.

> *Ms Hail*: Claire was throwing up in my sink – as often happens as you progress through labour – and Warren was out of his tree because he hadn't had dinner and Claire hadn't prepared the dinner and it was time to eat.
>
> *Defence barrister*: So she's going into labour – vomiting – and he's worried about the fact that he hasn't had his dinner?
>
> *Ms Hail*: That's true.

She said at the hospital, while his wife was in labour, Warren went to get himself some fish and chips and that he was gone for most of the labour, but not all …

> *Ms Hail*: He happened to be there when Claire was crying and upset … He got up off the chair that he was sitting on at the end of the delivery room bed, took her by the shoulders and gave her a good shake and said to her to pull herself together and to get on with the job of delivering his child. I thought I should have slapped him, but I didn't.

She said that as well as guns and Land Rovers, Warren also had a large collection of war-related books, magazines, videos and DVDs. Ms Hail also remembered how Warren MacDonald had once killed a general conversation about married people breaking up.

> *Ms Hail*: Warren stopped the conversation at that point and incredibly aggressively said to Claire: 'If you ever leave me, I will track you down and kill you.' I was frightened and I didn't know what to say. She [Claire] didn't know what to say and the conversation pretty much ended there.

She said Warren had insisted Claire learn to shoot. She said he had believed it was 'important for her because she was out on the property often on her own with the kids, she should know how to shoot snakes'.

The MacDonalds – as Claire told police – had built their dream home 'from scratch' themselves. To do so, for two years, the growing family lived a nightmare primitive life in the windowless cellar. Even when she was heavily pregnant, Warren MacDonald insisted his wife help out building the house. She was his brickie's labourer – fetching the bricks and mixing the cement.

> *Ms Brown*: She would be wheeling the wheelbarrow of bricks and Warren would be saying: 'Hurry up, Claire. Hurry up!' He'd be laying the bricks and shouting out: 'I need more mud. Hurry up!'

Ms Brown agreed that Claire was a 'fairly gentle soul' – quiet and quite timid. She said that she had said her husband could be aggressive but she would 'never really run him down'. Ms Brown said she noted that Claire looked exhausted on the day she returned from the Kangaroo Island holiday.

Ms Brown: I asked her: 'Claire, Are you OK?' and she said: 'Not really,' and I said: 'Well, you should feel great, you've just had a holiday.' She said: 'It was a nightmare ... It was just terrible ... Warren had us up in early hours of the morning, just when it got light and I had to get the children ready – dressed and fed – and then he would take us on a long hike.' And I said: 'But that's ridiculous' – the baby was only two – and she said: 'I know. It was a nightmare.'

She said the baby would get upset and was crying and Warren would then become upset with the baby and then she'd have to carry the baby. It's the most that Claire's ever opened up to me.

I said: 'What are you going to do?' and she said: 'Well, I have got to do something because when it's affecting my children I have to do something and I said: 'What will you do?' and she said: 'Well, I will leave him,' and I said to her: 'Well, you have to be careful and make sure you leave when he's at work because you know he gets very angry and there are guns on the property.' She said: 'I know.' I said: 'How will you manage?' She told me that she had rung Centrelink to find out what sort of monetary allowance she would be getting and she said: 'I think I could manage on that,' and I said: 'Well, please don't leave unless he's at work and if things get really tough and you've got to get out in a hurry ... just come to me.' She said: 'I will,' but I didn't believe she would have wanted to involve me because that's the sort of person she is ...

She's very gentle, a wonderful mother and very private. Claire always seemed to be sort of anxious and trying to please and being careful of what she said in front of Warren. It was very different when she was on her own: she was much more relaxed.

Psychiatrist Daniel Sullivan told the trial Claire MacDonald was a classic case of 'learned helplessness' – where abused women get so conditioned to their lot they feel they can't leave even very unpleasant or threatening relationships. He said the term dated back to a 1960s experiment on dogs. Psychologists found that after a while dogs subjected to electrical shocks in a place they could not escape did not even try to escape when they could.

***

Prosecutor Ray Elston SC rejected Mrs MacDonald's claim that she had killed her husband in self-defence.

> *Mr Elston*: In a situation of an unhappy marriage, where there had been disharmony for quite some time, the accused determined to finalise the matter, and in a cold-blooded, determined and carefully calculated way executed her husband … The actions of the accused, I say to you, were not done in any way … to defend herself from the actual or threatened violence of her husband … Did the episode in the cellar justify his execution? Did the unhappy marriage justify his execution? … What happened … was simply somebody inflicting the ultimate punishment on somebody who has imposed upon her and her children a lifestyle which is just unacceptable …
>
> She had never been bashed or injured by him. She'd never left him … She told police: 'He just didn't deserve to live.' That's not self-defence, ladies and gentlemen, that's simply retribution for a sad and unhappy marriage and murder is not the solution to that situation. That's merely retaliation for the past.

He denied it was a case of a woman who had learned helplessness, who felt she had no other way of getting out of a horrible marriage, finally snapping. He pointed out that Ms MacDonald had supportive friends and had contacted Centrelink to investigate what help she could get if she left the marriage. He said she was an intelligent woman – a qualified teacher – who had the wherewithal to leave her husband. He also said that she had plenty of opportunities to leave when Warren MacDonald was working his long hours. He said when police had asked her whether she had considered the option of leaving her husband, Ms MacDonald said she had, but that she had dismissed it because it was unfair that her children should have to leave their home.

> *Mr Elston*: What you have when you watch that video [of police interviewing Ms MacDonald] is somebody who has determined to end a life which is causing her misery. As tragic as you may think it is, it's a confession to murder ... She determined she wanted her husband out of her life, out of their children's lives because as she said: 'He just didn't deserve to live any more.' Those are her words ...
>
> You can understand that attitude, but that's not a justification for killing someone: 'I thought of the options but I dismissed them because I think I can get away with it'; 'It's just not fair on the kids to make them move around so I will kill him, point the finger at somebody else, I will get away with it and we can get on with our lives' ...
>
> This is not a woman who over the years had become utterly helpless ... She had *not* extricated herself from this relationship and she *has* got five children but, on balance, in a civilised community there are a number of options that exist for people who have friends, who have workplaces to go to, who have a community to live in.
>
> She was anything but helpless, but has simply made the wrong decision to extricate herself from a marriage. At the end of the day for her, here was a continuation of a life she had come to loathe and a husband she loathed, and she determined to finish that.

The prosecutor also denied that when she killed her husband, Ms MacDonald could have been provoked by her husband's actions into temporarily losing her self-control.

> *Mr Elston*: She was not paralysed with fear. She chose a path which punished her husband for their life together and adopted a solution

which ensured that their life was terminated, their marriage life was terminated. The result of that is there is no ... self-defence; there is no provocation and loss of self-control: what you have is murder.

She spends the day ... planning the killing of her husband ... Two have hit him in the back; one in the face; one in the chest; one has gone whizzing past through the collar of the jacket and into the rear-vision mirror: that's five on target, which is not bad shooting, you might think. The sixth is manually loaded. All of this is consistent with a clear, purposive, steady resolve to shoot him to death.

Thereafter follows the bogus call to Triple 0 with the pretended concern for the husband and the pretence of helping the executed husband ... It's clear she has determined to lie and point the finger at some transient ...

'Warren didn't deserve to live any more' – that's what she said. 'Warren didn't deserve to live any more': judge, jury and executioner.

Ms MacDonald's barrister, James Montgomery, denied that his client's marriage was just an unhappy marriage that should have or could have ended up in the Family Court with some typical argie-bargie over the children by warring parents – instead of with the husband being gunned down by his camouflaged wife from a sniper's nest.

Mr Montgomery: What was it that caused Claire MacDonald to shoot her husband that day apart from any other day? ... Was it to get her out of a sad and unhappy marriage, according to the prosecution? Was that it? Was it a sad and unhappy marriage and should it have ended up in the Family Court? Or was it a marriage where the husband was a sadist, a rapist who dominated and controlled his wife and children through fear?

What sort of marriage is it where a husband exacts punishment, metes it out by anally raping his wife ... It doesn't matter who the woman is, if you have sex with her without consent, that's rape. If you have it in circumstances where you are using it as a form of punishment, that's an aggravating feature.

Sniper Wife

On the night before the shooting down in that cellar ... in an unprecedented form of action ... he's thrown things around like potatoes and boxes and flowers from her mother ... He's poking her in the chest saying: 'I'll punish you', 'I will punch you'. He's kicking the wall: 'Get upstairs and take your punishment.'

Now, apparently, that wouldn't ... cause a person to lose self-control, according to the prosecution. It wouldn't cause Claire MacDonald to think this was a ... threat to her safety, a real threat to her health, that some really serious injury was forthcoming?

What options does she have? Take the gun out and shoot him while he is asleep in front of the children? I don't think so. She can't leave because she knows ... he said in front of other people, he'll hunt her down and shoot her and bury her. How does she deal with it? She's threatened and out of control and that's how she shoots her husband.

Let's put in context what the prosecution said to you ad nauseam that she said to police: 'He didn't deserve to live.' What in fact she said when she first brought this up was: 'And *because of the threats that he made to me*, I decided that Warren didn't deserve to live any more.'

And she is asked: 'What happened while you were hiding there?' – this is in the bushes – and she says: 'Warren walked up to the car and looked around and I had the thought in my head that I had to do it – I just – if *I didn't do it now, I would be the one that would be dead.*'

What you have here is a woman who has been abused physically, sexually, psychologically by her husband, culminating in the incident in the cellar which produced in her the fear of a continuing threat and also causes her to lose self-control. What option does she have? 'Let's go to a counsellor'? Can you imagine Warren MacDonald going to a counsellor? What was she to do? Punch him back and try to strangle him?

How does a woman who is physically unequal with the man cope with that threat? Theirs is a house full of guns, you would not be surprised that instead of embarking on an unequal physical struggle, she would think of a gun. There is a gun culture up there ...

REASONABLE DOUBT

The prosecution says: but there was all that planning. Well, let's think about the planning. She takes a gun that you can assume would be immediately traced back to that house. Pathetically, she puts on rubber gloves and burns them afterwards while at the same time leaving at the scene the most incriminating item of all – the rifle – in the position in which it was used. It's not much of a murder plan.

The story she told was clearly implausible. It was a story borne out of panic, confusion, fear and a desire to avoid the fact that it was her who shot her husband – not that she murdered him …

This is a very tragic thing that has occurred. This was a very tragic marriage relationship up there on Breakaway Mountain. When a woman, after being threatened by a husband who is out of control and then raped by him, feels so threatened and out of control that she shoots him and kills him, how could you be satisfied beyond a reasonable doubt that that is murder …

If you are not satisfied beyond a reasonable doubt that she was not acting in self-defence, you have to acquit her …

After she fired the shots, she was screaming at him: 'Why did you make me do this? … The prosecutor has spoken to you about a civilised society. A civilised society is not reflected by the behaviour of Warren MacDonald in his marriage. That's not the way civilised people behave …

When you add all that up [Warren MacDonald's reign of fear over his wife and children] and you consider the expert evidence [that Claire MacDonald had learned helplessness] and you consider what happened the night before [in the cellar and then in bed while their children slept in the same room] … a civilised society – which you represent – would not convict her of murder but would acquit her.

***

On 3 March 2006, the verdict of the seven women and five men on the jury was announced – 17 months after Warren MacDonald was gunned down and a day and a half after they started deliberating. Was Claire MacDonald guilty or not guilty of murdering her husband? 'Not guilty.'

Was she guilty or not guilty of her husband's manslaughter? 'Not guilty.' As the verdicts were announced, Ms MacDonald gasped and then broke down weeping; one of the women on the jury wiped away tears.

Justice Geoffrey Nettle: Mrs MacDonald, you have been found not guilty: you are free to go.

Outside, as she walked down the street pursued by reporters, a pale and still-teary Ms MacDonald told them: 'I just want to go home.'

MOTHER-IN-LAW NIGHTMARE

Everything was happy – even beautiful – in the Spina household in the hours before Maria Spina woke up her husband of 28 years … by punching his head 'very hard'. That shock punch from that stocky (166cm, 118kg) woman slammed into Nicola Spina as he slept in his bed about 2am on Sunday 21 October 2001. Another and another quickly followed.

Spina: One, two. Bang, bong.

Maria Spina, 49, then shoved, scratched and pulled the hair of her barely awake 55-year-old husband. When he hit back, she called for her mother's help. Giovanna Persico was 73 years old, hard of hearing, just 162cm tall and 76kg, but she enthusiastically joined in the bizarre bedroom battle. Mother and daughter punched, bit and scratched Nicola Spina. They broke his glasses and chased him – in his T-shirt and underpants – around the room. The nightmarish awakening took a terrifying turn when the women urged each other in Italian to: 'Finish him off!' That's when Spina fought for his life, lashing out at his attackers in a 'Mad Max' kind of mood.

Spina: I hear, 'bong, bang, bang, boom' and then they say: 'Help, help.' Mother-in-law come … My wife, she call for help – she really want to fix me up. Pulling, scratching and I don't know where to look in the dark. I don't know what to do … Scratch me, pull me, bash me … 15 minutes … 'Oh God, God!' … I heard them yelling:

'Ah, we're going to get you this time!' One, two. Bang, bong, pushing ... I don't know what they done. They bite me - both of them ... They're yelling: 'We'll do it now. That's it. Finish him off.' You know, in the Italian language. When I hear that – they push here, punching there – and: Jesus! Now, I'm going to die now.

So, I manage to jump out of bed ... and then they were chasing me around here (pointing to a drawing of the bedroom) ... So, I start pushing them against the wall ... Oh, I push so hard ... into the brick ... I smash her against the double brick wall. I was like a jumping in the moon ... Both at the same time, I pushed them against the wall – very hard.

He said his wife's head was probably cut so badly because it was 'banged on the wall many times ... maybe her head hit the corner'.

The women's heads were smashed. Their blood was sprayed and smeared on the wall.

Detective Peter Trichias: Was there a lot of blood on the walls?
Spina: A lot of blood, yes.

In the bedroom battle, Giovanna Persico – 'a 75-year-old who couldn't do a very heavy punch ... the most she can do is a slap or a scratch' – went down first.

Spina: My mother-in-law, she quick collapse, but I kept going with my wife.

Suddenly, it was quiet: the threat was over.

Det Trichias: How did it stop?
Spina: I throw them both on the ground. Then I look at myself: 'What I done?' Why? I don't want to be in this situation ... I'm just looking. Thinking: 'Why this to me? ...

Det Trichias: Did you do anything else to them while they were on the ground?

Spina: Well, to tell you honestly the truth, I put 'em in the garage and I clean up all the blood ... from the walls ... I put 'em in the garage. Cover up their heads [with plastic bags] that blood not go everywhere, and that's it.

Det Trichias: When you moved them from the room to the garage, were they dead then or were they alive? Do you know?

Spina: Dead. Dead.

Det Trichias: Did you check to see whether they were alive?

Spina: Dead. Dead. I was so weak ...

Det Trichias: How long did you leave them on the floor before you moved them?

Spina: Until I recover a bit. I went to drink cold water, you know. I was feeling so battered. You know. I couldn't even speak ... I was so weak, so tired. It was so confusion. What I do? You know? I went to drink a glass of water and then another one and then another one and I sat down and I think: 'Why? Why this? I can't understand why. Can't understand why this happen to my house.' ...

Det Trichias: Do you know how long, even approximately, before you moved them?

Spina: It was one minuto – it was like two years for me ... When you frightened, it's terrible. Terrible.

He told police that he had cleaned the blood from the walls and carpet with water and some Spree detergent. He had a shower and washed the T-shirt and underpants he had been wearing when he was so terrifyingly awoken and hung them on the backyard clothes line.

There had been no warning, no hint an attack like this was imminent. About 6.30am on Saturday 20 October 2001, Spina had gone to his factory job at an engineering company. Maria hadn't felt well and she had asked him to collect her mother from her Oakleigh home. He had done as she asked, bringing Giovanna Persico over to their house about 11am and the three of them had had a pleasant afternoon. It hadn't always been like that.

> *Det Trichias*: What was your marriage like?
> *Spina*: Beautiful.
> *Det Trichias*: Have you had any problems at all lately?
> *Spina*: Who doesn't have a problem these days? I hit [Maria] a long time ago ... we have arguments every night but it's normal. A hit or a punch in the teeth: that's what I want to tell her who I am.
> *Det Trichias*: How come the argument leads to hitting her?
> *Spina*: I am the man ...
> *Det Trichias*: Has your wife ever hit you in the past?
> *Spina*: Yes ... when you least expect it, she comes from behind and goes [hits his hands], that's how she is. Me different: I just give her a bump.

Maria's family, Spina said, had not made things easy. He had 'a feeling' his wife had left him for 30 days in 1981 because 'someone pump her up behind my back ... I don't know – family, family'.

> *Spina*: Faustino [Maria's oldest brother] – the one who rung you ... he's the one cause the problem. He's always too close to my wife ... Look, between husband and wife – other people should stay out ... We were happy. I don't know. Someone put their nose in my business. I don't know why ... I been forced to do this, what happened.

For Spina, his wife's family was just 'too big'. But in the hours before that fight, Spina, his wife and her mother had got on very well.

> *Det Trichias*: Was there any problem with your mother-in-law or wife that day?
> *Spina*: Beautiful.
> *Det Trichias*: Did you have any argument with your wife ...

Spina: No, it was beautiful.

Det Trichias: … or mother-in-law?

Spina: Beautiful … We had a meal. Everything together. Happy. No problem … We watch TV … After the Tattslotto numbers come out, I said: 'It would be nice' and I went to bed … and they remain to watching TV, both of them …

I went to bed. Went to sleep. I wake again. There's still the TV on … They're yappin' yappin' in the kitchen … I go to sleep again …

It was one, two o'clock. I didn't look at the time. I have a punch on my head …

He agreed to police videoing him at his home as he showed them how he killed his wife and mother-in-law.

Spina: You can make a movie. I don't care … I was like Mad Max – that mood … When you sleeping and – punch! You don't know where you are. God! … It's like movie.

As the two women's bodies lay in the garage, Spina spent Sunday 21 October cleaning up the blood and generally tidying up his house. About 2pm on Monday 22 October 2001, the day after killing his wife and mother-in-law – with their battered bodies still on the garage floor – Spina phoned Faustino and asked him to come around to fix an answering machine.

Spina: I wanted to tell him … what happened.

Det Trichias: What's happened when he's come over?

Spina: I didn't know what to do … First of all I offered him a drink. He wouldn't drink it. I had a beer. Then I come back and say: 'When your sister and mother come back, I am going to kill them, both of them 'cause I am here waiting for the dinner to be ready' … I still have no guts to tell him … I wanted to tell him what's happened to his sister and the mother – didn't have the guts.

Mother-in-Law Nightmare

Spina challenged the two policemen interviewing him.

> *Spina*: If you were in my position, what you tell to the brother? ... You have the guts? What could happen then, if you tell him: 'This, in my house.' You tell him?

He admitted holding a gun, but not to planning to shoot Faustino.

> *Spina*: I was so crazy still ... I had a gun then ... a double-barrel shotgun. I was going to use it for myself, after what I done.

Spina agreed that he had used rags to tie a cut-off plastic milk bottle to the gun's barrel but said he did not know why: 'I was so confused.' He admitted ordering Faustino to stay but insisted he had not touched him with the gun. He had wanted Faustino to stay but not because he wanted to kill or even punish the man he blamed for ruining his marriage.

> *Spina*: I wish he could stay all night to keep me company ... He wanted to go, but I was so confused, I just said: 'You stay here.' I knew why I want him there: make sure nothing happen to me.

He agreed that he had threatened Faustino, but only because he was afraid of what Faustino might do if he saw the bloodied bodies of his mother and sister in the garage.

> *Det Trichias*: Did you threaten him at all when he was at the house?
>
> *Spina*: Yeah. Yeah ... I said to him: 'You lie on the ground. Pretend you're dead. So they [his wife and mother-in-law] don't scream on me any more. They don't fight me any more.' He knows they fight ... He was laughing. I said: 'All right, lie on the couch. Stop laughing now.'
>
> *Det Trichias*: Were you laughing?

Spina: No, I was not laughing. I know what I done. He didn't know. I know. So, he was laughing, I was not.

Det Trichias: When you were talking to him and you had a gun, were you pointing the gun at him?

Spina: Yes. He's a big man, mate. I was scared he jumping on me but I didn't do nothing to him. When he left, we shake hands … He say: 'You my best man. I know that you my brother-in-law.' I know that, but he didn't know what had happened …

I was trying to keep him calm … All the time I keep saying: 'Sit down' … I don't want him jump on me … I didn't feel safe … I was frightened if he jump on me and then opens the garage door: what happens? …

I don't want him to know, otherwise he could have grabbed me. I could have shot him. I tell him: he kill me now. He get me on the spot or grab me and bash me against the fence – that's it. So I didn't tell, until you people catch me – and I'm alive … So here I am – he's there. He's all right – I'm all right.

For four hours – from 3.40pm – Spina forced Faustino to keep him company. He let him regularly try to phone his mother. Why not? She wasn't going to answer. About 7.30pm, Faustino appeared to dial Triple 0 for police and emergency services on his mobile phone. Spina didn't object; indeed, the pair laughed about it. When Faustino finally left, Spina shook his hand. It was all just craziness.

Just after midnight on Tuesday 23 October 2001 – nearly 48 hours after he had killed the women lying in his garage – Spina decided it was time to bury them. He decided to take them to the Springvale Cemetery just a couple of minutes' drive away. He put a large black plastic sheet on the floor of the boot of his Toyota Landcruiser and heaved the head-bagged bodies on to it. Just after 1am, he threw their handbags, a purse and a pair of blood-stained workman gloves in with them, covered them with a plastic curtain, and drove out.

Mother-in-Law Nightmare

Det Trichias: Did you have a plan of what you were going to do when you go to the cemetery?

Spina: I don't know. Maybe sit down and cry.

Moments after he drove out of his home in Police Road in eastern suburban Mulgrave, a police car stopped him.

***

That was the story Spina told police of how he came to be driving out of his home in the dead of night with the battered bodies of his wife and mother-in-law: he had killed them while fighting for his life. That was his story of his afternoon pointing a double-barrelled shotgun at his brother-in-law: it was just craziness; a crazy way of getting someone to make sure he didn't commit suicide, an aborted attempt at confessing.

Spina was keen to show police his injuries.

Spina: You want to see all the bruises ... Look at my eyes. Look at my face. Look at all the scratches here and here. Punches. They bite me. I don't know which. Both of them were doing this ... You better take a photograph because it will disappear ... Here, have a look at my hair – missing.

He also repeatedly gave his excuse for killing the women.

Spina: I lost my head ... to defend myself ... I want it: self-defence ... I don't know what I was doing. I was asleep. They punching my head and I act at once ... I don't mean to kill her – ever. I don't want to kill her, not even a cat.

He appeared calm, unemotional, even stoic.

Spina: What can I say? What's done is done ... What can I say? It's happened ... I've been forced to do this.

REASONABLE DOUBT

He answered a lot of questions but police still didn't believe him. There were too many questions not answered to their satisfaction.

1. If Spina hadn't used any kind of weapon to kill the women:
   - Why was he carrying in the boot of his car – with the two dead women – two pieces of rope with blood matching Giovanna Persico's DNA?
   - Why did the bruises on Mrs Persico's neck look like they had been caused by a rope?
   - Why was a bloodstain found on a billiard cue racked in the billiard room?
   - Why did a blood-spatter expert find that although some of the blood spatter could have been caused by a head hitting the wall, it was more likely to have been caused by 'multiple blows ... from an object hitting a bloodied surface' and that that 'bloodied surface' was likely to have been 30cm to 50cm away from the wall and could have been a bloodied head?

2. If he had been driving out to the Springvale Cemetery to bury the women he had accidentally killed while defending himself:
   - Why did he not have a spade? Did he just forget the spade? Was it just more crazy thinking or was he planning to dump the bodies somewhere safe, just as a cunning murderer would?
   - Why was he carrying the bloody rope and a pair of his shoes with Giovanna Persico's blood on them? Was that just his mixed-up thinking and panic, or was he trying to get rid of evidence of two murders?

3. If he had been attacked so viciously that he had to kill to defend himself, why were his injuries so minor? Spina had only superficial wounds on his face, forearms, hands and chest. There was no sign of injury to either side of his head or of any hair having been pulled

out. Was it that his injuries had healed before he was examined? Were the injuries superficial because he had been lying on his bed when he was attacked and then managed to dodge most of the women's blows, or were they just the sorts of minor injuries two women fighting for their lives would have caused?

4. If he had been woken up by being punched in the head and had then furiously defended himself in a frenzied fight, why were his spectacles broken on his face? When did he put them on? During a pause in the fracas he forgot to tell police about, or was he lying about being asleep?

The trickiest questions for Spina to answer, however, were posed by two silent witnesses – the bodies of the dead women. The main one was that the pathologist found both women had to have been strangled for at least 15 seconds – Spina had not even mentioned strangling them, just bashing them against the wall. Because of her thick neck, the pathologist believed it might even have taken at least 30 to 40 seconds to strangle Maria Spina. Then there were the neck bruises, particularly on Mrs Persico, which looked like they had been caused by a rope. The pathologist also believed that Maria Spina's head had been hit with a blunt object, possibly a billiard cue, an 'absolute minimum' of eight times.

Police not only rejected Spina's self-defence claim, but they also didn't believe he had killed them when he said he did.

After talking to Maria's brothers Faustino and Joseph, to her favourite niece Joanne Persico, and to Spina's workmates, police suspected a much more horrific scenario: that over four days Spina had tried to rid himself of those he most hated and envied – his wife, two of her brothers and their mother.

It had been, police believed, a bizarrely bloody long weekend of horror ... and blackly comic bungling.

What police suspected happened at the Spina home from Friday 19 October 2001 to Tuesday 23 October 2001

Friday 19 October: Spina bashes and strangles his wife – probably during an argument over her taking $5000 out of their bank account. He then calls Joseph Persico and tries to lure him to come over by asking him to check on his pizza oven. Mr Persico says he will come over the next afternoon.

Saturday 20 October: Spina picks up Giovanna Persico from her home – possibly by force: uncharacteristically, she leaves her gates and doors unlocked. When he gets her to his home, Spina bashes and strangles the mother-in-law he considers belittles him and interferes in his marriage. At 6.30pm, Joseph Persico and his daughter arrive but Spina changes his mind about killing Joseph and doesn't answer the door. Maybe he hasn't finished cleaning up after killing Mrs Persico, or maybe he baulks at killing Joseph because his daughter is with him.

Monday 22 October: Spina lures another Persico he considers pesky to his home. He holds Faustino Persico at gunpoint for four hours but can't get up the nerve to kill him and lets him go about 7.30pm, after Faustino manages to call the police on his mobile phone.

Tuesday, October 23: Just after midnight, Spina tries to get rid of the bodies of his wife and mother-in-law but police catch him driving out of his home.

Joanne Persico's story

Police suspected that Maria Spina was killed on Friday 19 October because on that day she did not phone to say 'Happy 14th birthday' to her goddaughter and favourite niece – Faustino's daughter, Joanne Persico.

Joanne: Aunty Grace [the Persicos' name for Maria] … was like another mother to me and I was just like a daughter to her …

I saw her every two weeks and she would call me two or three times a week … but she would hang up at four o'clock because Nick would come home … She would say: 'Giovanna, that's my name in Italian, I'm sorry, I have to go. He is home' … She made me feel really special and like I was just this person that she gave all her love to … She would never forget my birthday. Like, the least she would do would be to telephone me to say: 'Happy birthday'.

I even remember my 12th birthday. She sent a surprise bunch of 12 roses to my house and she kept calling me that day saying: 'Are you going to be home' … Like – yeah! – I'm going to be home. She would never have forgotten.

Joanne said when her Aunty Grace didn't call on her birthday she thought it was 'really strange' but did not 'make a big deal out of it' because she and her aunt had planned to go birthday present shopping at Chadstone Shopping Centre the next day …

Joanne: I thought she had probably got tied up with something.

But the next day, her aunt not only failed to take her niece birthday present shopping, she didn't even phone to say why. It was all very baffling for Joanne because it had been her Aunt Grace who had suggested the shopping trip in the first place – on Tuesday that week. Her Aunt Grace had confirmed the trip the next day and had checked the details on the Thursday … but then nothing.

Prosecutor: Did you hear from her at all that day [Saturday 20 October 2001]?
Joanne: [Long pause. She blinks away tears.] No, I didn't.
Prosecutor: Did you ring your Aunt Maria's home to find out: 'Where is my present? When are we going?'
Joanne: No, because I never rang my aunty at her house because Nick would direct the phone to his mobile and he would answer and I didn't like speaking to him, so I didn't call.

Joseph Persico's story

Nicola Spina's relationship with his wife's family, according to Joseph Persico, had never been very good but it had deteriorated after Spina's widowed mother died in 1992. After that Spina seemed to become even more envious of the Persico family.

> *Joseph*: He withdrew into himself. He just concentrated on doing work and making money. It seemed to be money was his only purpose in life … They [Nicola and Maria] were quite well off …
>
> He didn't particularly like to associate with my family or our family, in general.

He said he had only once seen Spina threaten Maria – on Father's Day 2000 when they were at his place.

> *Joseph*: We were sitting at the table – my wife and my daughter were washing the dishes – and I just sort of started a conversation with Nick. I said: 'Hey, Nick, why don't you go take the caravan and go with my sister around Australia, you know, and just enjoy yourselves.' As I said that, my sister sort of shrugged her shoulders and said: 'That will never happen with him.' As soon as Nick heard that he said: 'I'm going to kill you one of these days' … He sounded threatening.

Joseph, however, acknowledged in cross-examination by Spina's barrister, Max Perry, that Maria could 'dish it up as much as she could take it'. He said he last spoke to his sister about 9am on Friday 19 October 2001 – the day police believed Spina killed his wife. Maria had phoned and asked Joseph to drive her to the doctor because she had just vomited. (Even though she had a driver's licence, Spina wouldn't let his wife drive either of their cars.) Joseph told his sister he had something to do and asked her to phone him again in a couple of hours if she didn't feel any better.

Mother-in-Law Nightmare

Later that day, Joseph was astonished to get a call from Nicola Spina asking him to come over the next afternoon to see whether his pizza oven was worth repairing.

> *Joseph*: I would say in probably 28 years that I have known Nick, he would have rang me twice ... That was the first time he asked me for a favour. I think he had felt too proud to ask me ... He seemed reasonably calm about it. I was quite happy to help him out because I'm always looking for an opportunity to help somebody else. He mentioned to bring my daughter Sarah because my sister asked if she could be brought out to his place because she had some old clothes for her to try on, which she said didn't need any more.

When Joseph asked to speak to Maria, Spina told him she was at a nearby church at a committee meeting for an upcoming fair. (The priest of that church, however, told police – and Spina's jury – that there had been no meeting at the church that night.)

About 5pm the next day, Joseph rang Spina from his mobile phone to say he was on his way but Spina told him: 'Oh no, not now. Come in about an hour's time.' He added: 'Don't make it too late.' When Joseph and Sarah got to the Spinas' home at exactly 6.30pm, however, no-one answered the doorbell. Joseph suspected Spina was home after hearing a loud click inside and because of the way Spina's Jack Russells – Deana and Charlie – acted when he looked into the backyard. First they barked but then the older one stopped, looked towards the back door of the house and acted as he did when Spina was around.

> *Joseph*: He started running in a circle, a happy circle. You could say there was smile on the dog's jaws.

Under cross-examination, however, he agreed that: 'Jack Russells get excited for all sorts of reasons'. (Spina told police he, his wife and mother-in-law had been out when Joseph called, and that they had missed him by about 10 minutes.)

108   REASONABLE DOUBT

Indirectly, Deana and Charlie were part of another reason police believed Maria Spina was killed on Friday 19 October 2001. Spina's workmates told detectives that on the morning of Saturday 20 October 2001 they noticed scratches on Spina's face and arms. They said Spina had told them he got these the previous day, while playing with his dogs. He said he had slipped and fallen on the grass and hit a branch of a lemon tree in his backyard. Spina did not mention this to police; instead he blamed the scratches on the attack by his wife and mother-in-law.

Faustino Persico's story

Maria's eldest brother and Joanne's father – Faustino Persico – said Nicola Spina had 'all the time, continuously' threatened Maria.

> *Faustino*: The biggest one was: 'One day I am going to break you. I am going to kill you. I will fix up the whole family.' Those type of gestures were common.

Once, when talking to his sister on the phone, Faustino heard Nick in the background.

> *Faustino*: He said: 'Who are you on the phone with? One of these days I am going to kill the whole lot of yous.'

Nick and Maria used to go over to her big brother's house three to four times a week because she was fond his children but, in the five years before Maria was killed, Nick had only visited three or four times a year. Mostly, he just dropped Maria off.

> *Faustino*: There was the one time when he said: 'I don't really want yous to come. I want to be on my own. I am a private person.'

About two weeks before she was killed, Maria told Faustino she could never leave her husband because Nick had threatened to kill her nephews and nieces if she did.

Faustino: I was given the impression he was jealous because we were a close family.

About 9am on Friday 19 October 2001, Maria called Faustino to say she wasn't feeling well, that she had a stomach-ache. Just like Joseph, however, Faustino was busy and he also suggested she call him back in an hour if she still wasn't feeling well.

Faustino: [Long pause, wipes an eye] I didn't hear back.

Faustino Persico's account of what happened between him and Spina on the afternoon of Monday 22 October 2001 – while unaware the battered bodies of his sister and mother were a few metres away in the Spina garage – was significantly different from the story Spina had told police.

About 2pm that day, Faustino was surprised to get a phone call from Spina.

Faustino: He asked me if I could do him a favour. He said he had bought himself an answering machine and it didn't work. He asked if I could go over and fix it for him, if I could go over straightaway.

Faustino – a telecommunications company technical officer – told Spina that he was helping his other sister, Nancy, with renovations and that he would come the next day.

Faustino: He said to me: 'No, I prefer you come today to get it over and done with.'

He got to the Spina's home about 3.40pm.

Faustino: I rang the intercom at the gate and waited about three or four minutes before Nick came out to open it and he asked me if there was anyone else with me and I said, 'No,' and then he said: 'Come in. Come in,' and he took me around the back of the house.

As soon as he opened the door, he asked me to go straight into the kitchen downstairs. He asked me to have a seat. He said: 'Do you want a drink?' ... He opened the fridge and he got a lemonade and I said: 'No, don't give me a lemonade, give me a Yakult. [Spina's cheerfully rotund barrister asked if this was one of those 'healthy people drinks'.]

He grabbed himself a beer too, and sat down ... Well, he started talking. He seemed normal at the time ... We started talking about how Nancy's ... doing her kitchen ... then he asked me, you know, how's the family, about interest rates, the economy, you know. Small talk. Here and there, and then all at once he said: 'Hold on a sec. I just have to get something.' He wandered towards the billiard room ... I didn't know where he went. I thought maybe he went to grab the answering machine to come and show me, but when he comes back out he's pointing a double-barrelled shotgun ...

He was pointing the gun at me and I said to him – the gun had like a plastic bottle cover over the end of the barrel wrapped with a piece of cloth, just a cloth, roughly tied up around it - and I said to him: 'What's that?' And he said it was a silencer. Then I started laughing at him. I said: 'What sort of silencer is that?' And I said: 'What is going on here? Where's my sister?' and he said: 'She's gone for a walk with your mother.' And I said: 'Is my mother here?' And he said: 'Yeah, she slept here last night.' I said, 'What's going on, Nick? Have you had an argument?' And he said to me: 'Ask your sister. She took all the money out of the account, the whole lot – $5000. Someone must have put her up to it. You must know something about it.' I go: 'The only thing I know is that my sister did mention that you withdrew $30,000 from the joint account and you haven't explained where the money has gone and she thinks that, maybe, you are going to run off with another woman and she is very upset about it.' He goes to me: 'I'm the man of the house. She should not have withdrawn the money without my permission.'

Mother-in-Law Nightmare

I had to try to keep at ease and calm, make sure he doesn't do something stupid ... I realised he was still pointing the gun at me and I said: 'What are you going to do with that?' And he goes: 'I want you to get down on the ground and lay down. When your mum and sister come in, I want to show them that I killed you' ... I said: 'No way, Nick. I'm not getting on the ground. I have a sore back. I will get a chill on the tiles.' Then I tried to think and collect my thoughts, tried to find excuses not to get on the ground because I didn't like the idea of getting on the ground with him holding the gun at me. Then he goes to me: 'Get on the couch then,' and I was still insisting: 'No, no way, Nick. I am not getting on the couch either' ...

Then he went quiet for about 10 to 15 minutes, you know, standing there. He was probably collecting his thoughts. He said: 'What do I have to do? Act like a guard all night?' I said: 'No, Nick, you don't have to act like a guard and have the gun pointed at me. Come, sit down. I am not going to bite you. Come and sit down.' So I was able to convince him to come and sit down on the opposite side of me – still with the gun pointed at me ...

I said: 'Put the gun away, Nick. Come on, what are you going to do with that?' And he said to me: 'I'm serious. I'm not kidding. I am serious. It's not a joke.' And then I said to him: 'I don't believe there are any bullets in that gun. You're bullshitting me. Stop mucking around.' And he goes: 'You don't believe me?' and I said: 'No. If it's true, show me if there is a cartridge in the gun.'

He then cracks the barrel – with the gun still pointed at me, he cracks the barrel – he sort of twists his body a little on the side and cracks the barrel down, pulls the cartridge out, closes the chamber again and shows me the cartridge. And I said: 'No, that's probably an empty cartridge. You have got to show me that it's full.' So he grabs the cartridge and knocks it on the edge of the table where he's sitting and at that stage I realised he had had a loaded gun on me ... Because there was a twin cartridge, I knew there would be another

bullet on the other side of the barrel. I was delirious in my mind. …
I started to panic, had anxiety, distressing thinking.

I stayed quiet for a few moments and then, while I sort of put my head down a little bit, he broke the chamber again, put the cartridge back in, closed the gun. And then eventually we sat down for a little while. He grabbed himself another beer and asked me if I wanted a drink and I said: 'No, I don't feel like a drink.' Then I said: 'Is there a trigger on the gun?' And he pulled the thing back, like a pin and I knew, you know, it could go off any second now – even by a bit of a knock. He said: 'Don't do anything stupid. The gun is ready to go now.'

I kept on talking to him: 'I can't wait here all night. They haven't come yet. They probably won't come. You know Grace. If she's scared of you, she won't come.' I then started to collect my thoughts: 'What am I going to do here? Maybe I will ring my mum's and see if they are there.'

So I stood up and started towards the phone and he said: 'What are you doing?' I said: 'I will just ring Mum up and see if they are there and I will tell them to come over. I can't stay here all night.' He said: 'All right, ring' … Then I dialled my mum's home and it rang and rang until it rang out.'

He said: 'I told you they are coming. I spoke to them this morning. They have got to cook for me.'

After I hang up, I picked up the phone again and started dialling home and after I dialled the number, I said to him: 'You don't mind if I just ring Maria [Faustino's wife] and let the kids know that I will be late?' And the next thing I know he says: 'Hang up. Hang up.' At that stage all I heard was my daughter's voice saying: 'Hello'. I said: 'Hi Joanne.' And the next thing he charged up to me and pushed the gun into my guts. Because he was shoving it into my guts, I said to him: 'I'll hang up, Nick! I'll hang up, Nick!' and just hanged up the phone.

Mother-in-Law Nightmare

He asked me to sit down. After I went to sit down, he said to me: 'You realise you are my hostage.' And I tried to keep calm and not answer back.

After a few minutes I said to him: 'Come on, Nick, relax, you are my brother-in-law. Let everything go. Don't go over the top. Don't worry about it.'

Then I waited a few minutes, collecting my thoughts: What I am going to say to him to calm him down? I told him: 'Now that you are well-off, Nick, enjoy yourself, go on a holiday. You have got no kids. Make the most of it.' I said: 'There's no marriage that is perfect. We all have our arguments and disagreements at home' ...

He grabbed himself another beer from the fridge and went and sat down ... He said he had to solve his problems. They had to be solved today and he couldn't take it any more.

Spina let Faustino ring his mother a few times but kept the gun trained on him, warning him: 'Make sure you don't ring anybody else but your mum.' He knocked back Faustino's pleas to be allowed to leave.

Faustino: I said: 'I would like to go now.' And he goes: 'You are not going anywhere. You are staying right where you are' ... I thought I would try and see how he was going to react if I stood up and grab my tools and say to him I'm about to leave. As soon as I stood up, he quickly stands up and says: 'Sit down or I'll let you have it' ... Then I said: 'No, Nick, I have had enough. I am going to go now.' So, quickly he moves towards the door ... He said: 'Don't make me do it. I'm serious. I am going to blow you away.' I said: 'Relax, Nick. Don't worry about it. I am your brother-in-law' ... He pushed the gun into my guts again and he said to me: 'Get back or I'll trigger it. Get back or I'll fire.' I said: 'Come on, Nick, what's going on.' I looked down at the barrel and said: 'What's this thing at the front of the barrel? This plastic thing. What's this stupid thing, Nick? Is this your silencer?' I tried to keep things easy ...

He put himself into a stance position, his leg leaning back and his body forward, head looking at the trigger, sort of where you can get a focus. He would not look at me in the face.

My mind was everywhere. I was petrified … thinking he could take my life away in a flash. So I didn't want to push him … So, I said: 'OK, Nick, I will go and sit down. I will do this for you until seven o'clock …

Before seven o'clock, I got a call on my mobile … my friend Bert rang me and asked me where I was and straightaway I said: 'I'm at my sister's house.' And he [Bert] said: 'What are you doing?' … and the next thing, you know, Nick stands up and starts going delirious with the gun – jumping up and down. I just put my hand over the mouthpiece so Nick would know he wasn't listening and he was pointing the gun at me, you know: 'Hang up the phone! Hang up the phone!' I said: 'Nick, relax. I have got to explain to him why I hang up the phone otherwise he might think something is going on. Then he goes: 'Hang up the phone.' I said: 'I will hang up the phone but just let me tell him politely or it won't sound right to him. So I said: 'I have got to go, Bert.'

Finally, Faustino was fed up.

Faustino: About 7.30 … I did my prayers … I said goodbye to my family and decided I had to do something.

I said to him: 'I am leaving now. I am going to pack up my tools. I am going to leave, Nick. I am just going to grab my tools and I am going now. I have had enough. I can't take it any more.' He quickly stood up out of his chair with the gun still pointed at me and forced his way again … towards the door. Even though he had the gun pointed at me, I started walking towards the door saying: 'I am going, Nick,' and he said: 'Don't make me do it … Go and sit down again' … He said: You know, when I had the gun pointed at your sister's head, she wasn't scared. She said to me: 'If you are going to

Mother-in-Law Nightmare

shoot me, shoot me' ... I didn't know if that was a recent incident or something in the past. All I did was I turned my body to the side of him ... I grabbed my phone ... I took a glance to see where the zero was and dialled it three times and placed my thumb on the send button ... I lifted my hand high in the air with the phone in my hand and shouted, 'This is 31 Police Road. I am in a hostage situation. Please help!'

Well, he shook his head, not knowing what was going on and I said to him: 'I have just rang the police to let them know where I am and that I am being kept hostage,' and he said: 'Why did you do that for?' and I said: 'Because if you are going to kill me, at least they will know where I am.' He said: 'I don't believe you.' My hand came down and my thumb was still on the send button ... and he said: 'Hang it up! Hang it up!' I said to him: 'Nick, they will be here in three minutes. You can get out of all this. Grab the gun, put it back where you got it from in the cupboard where you keep it and I will go so when they will find no-one here and they will think it was a hoax.'

He took a couple of seconds to answer. He said: 'All right, I will do what I did last time. I won't answer the door when they come. Don't say anything to anybody. I'm a bit nervous.' Then he lay the gun on the kitchen table.

I went to grab my tools and he accompanied me to the gate and I got into the car and just drove.

Faustino denied shaking Spina's hand when he left. The first thing he did after leaving was to ring his brother, Joseph. He then drove his wife and children around to see their nonna. When they found she wasn't home, he went to the police station and told of his bizarre afternoon.

Under defence cross-examinaton, Faustino Persico agreed that both Spina and his sister had become very materialistic. Neither wanted to end the marriage for fear of losing possessions to the other. His sister, he agreed, wasn't afraid to swear or have screaming matches with her

REASONABLE DOUBT

husband. Like her husband, she wouldn't take her family upstairs to the 'good' lounge.

He said that on the afternoon of Monday 22 October 2001, Spina had 'very obvious ... fixed red eyes'.

The cross-examination then took a startling 180-degree turn. It completely ditched the story Spina had told police: that he had held the gun, but that it had been an afternoon of craziness in which he had never seriously threatened killing Faustino Persico.

Mr Perry: I suggest to you, what happened is that you were sitting in the kitchen, you were talking to him for a while and he told you he was going to put some eggs on for his tea.
Mr Persico: No.
Mr Perry: I suggest that shortly after that he excused himself and went to the toilet.
Mr Persico: No.
Mr Perry: And that you went into the billiard room.
Mr Persico: No.
Mr Perry: And, I suggest that you found the gun in the billiard room.
Mr Persico: No.
Mr Perry: And, I suggest that you were the one in fact, the person holding the firearm, not Mr Spina.
Mr Persico: No.
Mr Perry: Rather than he holding the gun on you ...
Mr Persico: Not correct.
Mr Perry: ... You were holding it on him.
Mr Persico: No.
Mr Perry: You understand, I am obliged to put these matters to you?
Mr Persico: Fair enough. Fair enough.

***

In Spina's April 2003 trial in the Supreme Court of Victoria, prosecutor Sue Pullen did not try to prove beyond a reasonable doubt the police theory of Spina's bloody long weekend. She didn't believe she needed to in order to have him found guilty of a violent double murder.

> *Ms Pullen*: Even on his own version of events, the prosecution says this is not self-defence ... The prosecution says to you the deaths of these two women by strangulation and assault was the result of an intense anger on the part of the accused ... that very act of strangulation causing death speaks of an intense anger ... watching as life is taken away and breathing stops, watching as that person struggles against the inevitable ...
>
> Regarding Giovanna Persico, there is no escaping this was a brutal and sustained attack – before strangulation – of a 73-year-old lady; a person the accused said ... was 'a 75-year-old who couldn't do a heavy punch ... a slap and a scratch' ... Where's the need for self-defence? ... The accused ... described Mrs Persico as going to ground quickly, collapsing quickly. No mention of strangulation. The forensic evidence has caught him out ...
>
> I suggest it [Spina's self-defence story] is not logical, is nonsensical. The accused says it's self-defence. I say it's not in a bull's roar of self-defence.

Ms Pullen told the jury that Spina's 'preparedness to tell stories inconsistent with the truth' was shown by his absurd '180-degree turnaround' on what happened between him and Faustino Persico on Monday 22 October 2001 – from telling police he held the gun because Mr Persico was a 'big man', to claiming Mr Persico had the gun.

***

Mr Perry pointed out that Spina had been incredibly cooperative with police – answering their questions and re-enacting how he killed the women, even pointing out some of the blood spatter in his home. He said Spina's account of being woken up by the women had been consistent and the prosecution had failed to prove any other scenario beyond a reasonable doubt.

Mr Perry said Maria Spina had been a 'deeply unhappy, bad-tempered woman caught in a marriage she was not prepared to leave ... an increasingly unhappy and depressed woman who has become resentful of her husband'. He said Maria Spina's claims to her family that some weeks before her death her husband had put a noose around her neck and tightened it and that he had tried to poison her, without any evidence of these things or even complaints to police, suggested Maria Spina's increasing paranoia. He pointed out that even Maria had wondered whether she had dreamed about her husband putting the noose around her neck.

Mr Perry: What if all the resentment and the anger and the perceived humiliation over the years finally came to a head that night and she couldn't take it any more and she went into that bedroom and started on her husband? ... He was attacked and during the course of the struggle, he heard words in his native tongue: 'Let's finish him now'. He fought for his life. He was terrified ...

It's very difficult in the cold, somewhat clinical atmosphere of this court to try to re-create the terror and the fear and the shock of what was occurring ... Yes, he probably did have his hands on their throats ...

If you have ever been woken up from a deep sleep, you know it takes a couple of minutes at times to get your thoughts around what's happening. But when he [pointing to Spina in the dock] is woken, he is receiving blows and he is hearing a threat: 'Let's finish him off' ...

Maria Spina is a strong lady – no two ways about it – and she is helped by another person. He fought back. My word he did! It was his only option, other than, perhaps, pulling the covers over his head and getting under the sheets ...

This is a man frightened and aware of the fact that this is not a two-dollar domestic tiff. This is heavier and much, much more serious than anything that had ever happened before.

Mother-in-Law Nightmare

Mr Perry said that if the jurors did not believe it reasonably possible that Spina had killed his wife and mother-in-law in self-defence, they should at least accept the reasonable possibility that he had been provoked into temporarily losing his self-control and was, therefore, only guilty of manslaughter, not murder.

> *Mr Perry*: He tells police: 'I lost it.' 'I don't know what happened.' 'I was like Mad Max' ... He is admitting the very loss of control that, you might feel, is the essence of a provocation defence.

He reminded the jury that the blood-spatter expert had said the wounds on the two women could have been inflicted in a frenzied fight by being bashed into the wall and door. He said the blood-spatter evidence was inconclusive because of Spina's attempts to clean it but added that his cleaning it up did not mean he was guilty of murder.

> *Mr Perry*: The accused man in a short period of time had killed these people. Then he sat alone, in an empty house, for some time wondering what to do. He had the horror of trying to clean up ... He was ... between a rock and a hard place.

He also tackled possible scepticism over Spina's claim that Faustino had pointed the gun at him.

> *Mr Perry*: At first blush, you might say, 'Well I don't think so,' but you only have to look at Faustino's evidence. This is a man who tells you he thought it was a joke ... Ladies and gentlemen of the jury, if you are invited to someone's home and, on your own account, they excuse themselves and come back with a shotgun with a cut-down container on it that has been described to you, are you going to think it a joke? Are you going to play along with the joke and see where it goes? I don't think so! This is nonsense.

Mr Perry said Faustino Persico had only called police after calling Joseph and taking his family around to see whether his mother was home because he couldn't be certain that Spina hadn't called the police first to tell them Faustino had held him hostage.

***

On 17 April 2003, after the jury deliberated for about six hours, its foreman declared Spina guilty on all counts: two murders as well as threatening to kill and falsely imprisoning Faustino Persico. Spina stood impassively in the dock.

***

In the pre-sentence plea-hearing, the prosecution called for a rarely imposed 'life means life' sentence with no hope of parole. Mr Perry pleaded for his client to at least get a chance to apply for parole at some point. He said he had been found guilty of unplanned murders, that he was nearly 56 and he had health problems that would make prison life particularly tough. He said Spina had migrated from Italy with his family in the early '60s, in his early teens. He had been a hard worker all his adult life, accruing assets worth about $700,000, and had not been in trouble with the law before. Mr Perry said that a few years earlier Maria had been pregnant with twins but, tragically, Nick Spina had been forced to agree to an abortion to save his wife's life. Mr Perry said his client 'denied strongly' claims by the Persico family that Maria had miscarried that pregnancy after Spina punched her in the stomach.

Psychologist Ian Joblin said Spina had a 'pervasive and suspicious attitude', particularly towards his wife's mother and brothers who he suspected of trying to get his wealth. Spina believed his mother-in-law had suggested her daughter stab him while he slept and claimed he heard his wife discussing changing her will with her family. Mr Joblin wasn't convinced that Spina's paranoia was delusional but said he had 'persistent persecutory ideas'.

Forensic psychiatrist Dr Don Senadipathy said Spina told him that a major issue in his marriage had been their inability to have a child.

Mother-in-Law Nightmare

After two miscarriages, Maria had been unable to conceive and they had gone on the IVF program. She had become pregnant with twins but one had miscarried and the other had to be aborted to save Maria's life. Dr Senadipathy said that Spina felt his mother-in-law had denigrated him as not man enough to have children and considered him ignorant because of his lack of education. Spina believed that after the death of her husband, Giovanna Persico had depended on and dominated his wife. Spina told the psychiatrist that things got so bad he would have liked his wife to leave him because it would have been peaceful not to be constantly attacked by her family. Dr Senadipathy said Spina had a 'chronic paranoid disorder incorporating his wife and her family, with the mother-in-law being the key person'. He said, however, that his paranoia was a low-level psychosis. He suggested that Spina was a victim of shattered dreams despite working hard to achieve them. He said Spina's paranoia was restricted to his mother-in-law and, to a lesser extent, his wife, and there was no danger of him committing more violence.

***

On 14 August 2003, Justice Tim Smith gave his verdict. He said it was likely Maria Spina and Giovanna Persico were killed on different days but that that could not be established beyond a reasonable doubt and that he would sentence Spina on the basis that in the early hours of Sunday 22 October 2001 he 'brutally assaulted both women and strangled them'.

> *Justice Smith*: The prisoner to date has shown no sign of real remorse … He still has not told the truth about what happened. It seems something caused Nicola Spina to erupt into uncharacteristic violent aggression towards his late wife and late mother-in-law … I reject his account of being viciously attacked in his sleep. The injuries which he said that he received during this allegedly violent attack were trifling in the extreme when viewed in isolation, and nothing when compared to those suffered by the two deceased.
>
> While the murders of Maria Spina and Giovanna Persico cannot be shown to have been pre-planned, they were brutal and constitute

a grave example of the crime of murder. He physically assaulted them. They tried to defend themselves. Having gained the ascendancy, he strangled one and then the other.

The judge said he was not as 'sanguine' as Dr Senadipathy that Spina was no longer a danger, saying his antipathy had extended to the Persico family, especially to Faustino Persico.

For the murders of Maria Spina and Giovanna Persico, he sentenced Spina to two life terms. For falsely imprisoning and threatening to kill Faustino Persico he sentenced him to concurrent four-year terms. He set a minimum nonparole term of 25 years: Spina would be able to apply for parole when he was about 80.

***

Outside the court, Joseph Persico fought back his tears as he said he hoped the sentence would end a 'nightmare repeating itself'.

Joseph Persico: She loved him and yet he killed her. We cannot understand it.

He denied his mother had interfered in her daughter's marriage.

Joseph Persico: She always tried to tell my sister: 'Look, let him be.' She was always trying to be understanding towards him. He couldn't see that. He couldn't understand love.

***

About two years later, Spina's new legal team called on the Victorian Court of Appeal to overturn his convictions, claiming his trial had been unfair and his sentence was too harsh.

They said he should have had two trials – one for the two murder charges and one for allegedly falsely imprisoning and threatening to kill Faustino Persico. They said Spina's jurors could have been prejudiced in deciding whether he was guilty of the murders by hearing what he allegedly did to his brother-in-law; and they would have been more likely

Mother-in-Law Nightmare

to believe he falsely imprisoned and threatened Faustino after hearing what he had done to his wife and mother-in-law.

The defence claimed Justice Smith had not warned the jurors strongly enough not to jump to the conclusion that Spina was a murderer even if they accepted that he had been violent towards his wife in the past. They said the judge should have said more about the defence case that Maria Spina was a bad-tempered, resentful woman trapped in an unhappy marriage who would be likely to attack her husband.

Nearly four months later, the Victorian Court of Appeal roundly rejected the appeal.

Not only did it find that the four charges should have been heard in the same trial – because otherwise the alleged false imprisonment of Faustino would have been 'almost unintelligible' – it found that the defence may have been helped by the same jury hearing all the evidence. Justice David Ashley pointed out, for instance, that a jury that heard that Spina had let Faustino go unharmed – after a handshake – might be less likely to accept that he had earlier deliberately murdered Faustino's mother and sister.

Similarly, the appeal judges not only denied that Spina's trial was unfair as a result of Justice Smith not warning jurors strongly enough against jumping to conclusions of guilt if they accepted Spina had been violent towards his wife in the past, but said that the judge had done Spina a favour by not emphasising his violent marriage.

But, mostly, the judges rejected Spina's appeal against his convictions because they said the forensic evidence, especially the strangling injuries on the victims' necks, 'overwhelmingly demonstrated the applicant's guilt'. They said the evidence left open the possibility that the women had been killed at 'distinctly different times' but that even if they had been killed when Spina said they were, his self-defence excuse was still 'utterly incredible'.

The judges also denied Spina's sentence was 'manifestly excessive'.

Justice Ashley: It is true that there may be said to be worse cases of murder, but once a certain point is reached, 'worse' is a largely meaningless adjective.

REASONABLE DOUBT

Despite his resounding loss, Spina applied for special leave to appeal to the High Court. In April 2006, however, he finally – after four and a half years – gave up his legal fight, abandoning the application.

Spina had lost a tough fight to get police, a jury and four judges to believe his 'I killed my wife and mother-in-law because I was defending myself after they attacked me in bed' killer excuse but, until at least October 2026, he's got an even tougher battle. It's not going to be easy to stop other prisoners laughing when he tells them he shouldn't be in jail because he fought for his life against a ferocious onslaught ... by his 'old lady' and his frail old mother-in-law.

BEING AL PACINO

'I know what you're thinking. "Did he fire six shots or only five?" Well, to tell you the truth, in all this excitement I kind of lost track myself. But, being as this is a .44 Magnum, the most powerful handgun in the world, and would blow your head clean off, you've got to ask yourself a question: "Do I feel lucky? … Well, do ya punk?" ' Dirty Harry calmly aims his massive gun at the punk's head.

Action Man coolly swaggers into the room where his nemesis is hiding; his laser gun is set on maximum stun.

Around the corner comes Robert De Niro – the super-crim in the psychological cops 'n' robbers thriller *Heat*. Slide and click – his sawn-off shotgun is ready for action: 'I am double the worst trouble you ever thought of.'

Gun in the firing position, Al Pacino expertly manoeuvres into the room: 'Freeze dirtbag!' 'Freeze, motherfucker!' He is a super-confident super-cop. He is De Niro's nemesis-but-spiritual-twin in *Heat*. His eyes dart everywhere, scanning the room for his prey. The gun scopes the room covering every corner, ready to fire at the first sign of danger.

And then BOOM! The gun fires. It does. It *really* does. It's not the movies any more. Dirty Harry, Action Man, Pacino and De Niro disappear. What's left is a kind of messy modest one-bedroom bachelor pad in inner suburban Port Melbourne. The man holding the gun is no super cop/crim. He's no Dirty Harry, or Action Man. He's 24-year-old Peter Richard Barnwell and he's in a lot of *real* trouble because he has just killed his flatmate. His silly game of Hollywood cops 'n' robbers, of jumping from behind doors like Pacino et al brandishing a big gun, has ended in real tragedy. He has just fired a bullet through a couch straight into the back of 25-year-old Luke O'Keefe's head. As the bullet hit, Luke gave the briefest of groans and died.

One moment Luke O'Keefe had been snoozing on the couch in front of the TV after he and Pete had watched Pacino and De Niro strut their stuff, the next a bullet had been fired into his brain. He didn't see his flatmate imitating guntoting Hollywood tough guys. He didn't see that Pete's prop was the sawn-off French-made Gevarm repeater rifle he had found in Luke's bag. Luke knew how his gun worked. He was careful with guns; his father was a firearms safety officer. Pete had no idea.

***

Barnwell told police that he had arrived at his Clark Street flat at about 3pm on Wednesday 28 March 2001. He called out: 'What's happening?' to Luke, who was lying on the couch watching a 'Robert De Niro, Al Pacino movie'. Luke replied: 'Not much.' Barnwell made himself a cup of tea – Luke didn't want one – asked Luke what the film was called and joined him watching it. When the movie finished, Luke decided he wanted to have a kip on the couch. Barnwell turned off the television and went to his bed to also have an afternoon nap. He slept for about 20 minutes. When he woke up, he was bored. The flat wasn't as interesting as the movie.

Barnwell: I was a bit restless and couldn't sleep and, for some reason, I looked around and saw a blue backpack that I had seen Luke bring into the flat. I wasn't sure what was in it … I opened it and I looked inside and there was a gun … I was, just: 'Wow!' – Like a kid with a toy – 'Wow! A gun. Wow!' It was a bit like a handgun but a bit bigger … It was cut down good … filed as well … I thought it was something ancient … I wasn't sure it wasn't an ancient replica … I've never seen anything like it.

I started mucking around with it like they do in the movies, jumping from behind doors and stuff, just pointing it. I went in the bathroom and had a look at it … There was a thing that slides on it. I don't know what it was … I moved this thing … It just made a noise like metal clicking on metal.

Barnwell said he had checked out the gun in the bathroom 'just in case Luke woke up and caught me going through his shit'.

Barnwell: I jumped out of the bathroom into the bedroom, like swinging it around and that … I was jumping around like a copper … I came out of the bathroom into the bedroom waving the gun around like I was Dirty Harry … Playing around like I was Action Man, I suppose you could call it, or a super hero … Just mucking around …

I was just – it sounds bad – trying to create some fun. That sounds bad now I killed someone, but I was just creating some fun with it, you know what I mean?

I jumped from the bedroom into the loungeroom, which was close to where Luke was sleeping, and it went off … I had it here, held here at my waist and I just jumped out and I don't know if I said: 'Freeze, dirt bag!' or 'Freeze, motherfucker!' – that's the game I was playing … I pointed it at a coatstand pretending it was a person … Then I've let it down and it's gone off …

It was pointed at Luke but I wasn't pointing it at Luke. It was pointed at Luke when it went off … I saw a bit of smoke and the gun spark. Luke's gone: 'Aaah' … Like he didn't make a painful noise or nothing, right, but he's gone: 'Aaah' like someone set a fire cracker off next to him … He made a noise like he got a hell of a fright but he didn't jump up or nothing …

I've gone: 'Shit! Shit! Luke!' – but he didn't answer … I didn't know what to do. I didn't know what to do and I just ran out the door … I just panicked … I grabbed my shoes and just ran out the door … I wasn't sure if I hit him. I was praying. I was praying that I got the cushion of the couch.

I run up the street a bit and thought: 'I've gotta get him an ambulance in case I have hit him,' but I was too scared to go back. I went to my pocket to get my mobile phone but it wasn't there so I started running back towards the flat and then I decided to go to the phone booth at the milk bar. So I done a U-turn and run towards the milk bar. As I was running, I realised I still had the gun in my hand.

REASONABLE DOUBT

Barnwell said he dropped the gun the moment he realised he still had it, but picked it up because he remembered there was a kindergarten nearby.

> *Barnwell*: I ducked down a lane and placed it [the gun] in a box that was sitting in the lane; a box full of soil. I ran out the other end of the lane and went to the milk bar but the phone wasn't there no more. So I started running to Bay Street, got to the corner of Graham Street and I ran into the pub …
>
> I run into the pub, dialled Triple 0 and the lady said: 'Police, fire brigade or ambulance,' and I said: 'Ambulance and the police.'
>
> I was connected to the police and told the lady what had just happened and she didn't take me too seriously … She told me to wait at the Rex [the pub Barnwell was phoning from] for the police.
>
> After that I went into a panic … I had an anxiety attack, so I bought a beer … which I pretty much skolled. I bought another, and sipped on that.

He needed a cigarette as well, but needed to get some change from the TAB to put in the cigarette machine. Sometimes when you're having a really bad day, nothing goes right. Once he got the change, the frantic Barnwell couldn't find the cigarette machine and asked the barman.

> *Barnwell*: He said: 'You must have walked past it 10 times' … I had been pacing up and down that much. I was unwrapping the cigarettes when I have heard a car screeching.

Outside the pub was like a scene out of *Heat*.

> *Barnwell*: Police were on the wrong side of the road with bulletproof vests on and sirens going. I have gone out and said, you know: 'I'm the one who called you.' They were about to draw, to draw their guns and I said: 'I haven't got anything on me' … They said:

Being Al Pacino

'What's happened?' I said: 'I think that I have shot someone. I was mucking around with a gun and it's gone off.'

It was 4.20pm.

***

Sadly and ironically, Barnwell's nightmare began just hours after he got over one of many hurdles life had placed in his way.

Born in Durban, South Africa on 16 March 1977, Barnwell was two when his family migrated with him to Australia to escape racism. As people of mixed race, in apartheid South Africa they could not vote and were barred from 'whites only' jobs. They had to live in mostly impoverished 'coloured' areas; travel on third-class 'non-white' public transport; go to 'coloured' schools and swim at 'non-white' beaches.

Their start in their new country wasn't much easier. After a brief stay in Geelong, the Barnwells moved to the Springvale migrant hostel. Finally, they got a nearby housing commission house. At first, Peter was doing OK at school, particularly at sports, but things started to unravel when he was about 12. The racism his family had fled reared up again. Goaded by racist taunts, Barnwell got into a fight with a classmate. Unfortunately he fought the wrong kid. Shortly afterwards a police officer visited his family and issued him with an official warning. That police officer, the Supreme Court later heard, was the father of the boy Barnwell had fought.

In South Africa, the Barnwells had been used to policemen supporting racists, but they hadn't expected to find the same thing in Australia. That fight – that police visit – so unsettled the Barnwells that when their son begged to go to a particular school, they refused because the policeman's son would be at that school. For young Peter it was a cruel blow. His mother Jean Barnwell later told the Supreme Court: 'From that time his schooling fell down … He could not go to the school of his dreams.' Barnwell lost interest in school, fell in with the wrong crowd and by the age of 13 was taking drugs and sniffing glue. He left school at the age of 15 in 1992. His parents separated a year later. He stayed with his father, and his mum and sister moved out. At the age of 16, he was diagnosed

130   REASONABLE DOUBT

with depression and schizophrenia. In one of his stays in a psychiatric hospital, he burnt himself by setting his bed alight. For a while, things looked promising after he got a job as a kitchenhand in a large pub. He started to believe he could make a go of a career in the hospitality industry, but then his employer learnt of his police record and he was sacked.

All up – from the age of 15 in March 1992 to April 2000 – Barnwell appeared in courts 21 times on 116 charges. Mostly they were for fairly minor property destruction. One appearance, for instance, was for smashing a CD rack in a CD shop. In February 1997, things spiralled even more out of control when Barnwell punched his father three or four times in the face. In April 1999, he was jailed for six months for breaching a community-based order.

After almost a decade of drugs and violence and courts and detention centres and jail and psychiatric hospitals, in 2000 Barnwell started to tackle his problems. He volunteered for treatment and requested stays in a psychiatric hospital.

But he was still having problems with drugs.

On 11 March 2001 – three weeks before he shot Luke dead – Barnwell went to the 'Two Tribes' rave party at the Tennis Centre. Two things happened at that rave that were to have ongoing repercussions for him.

The first was that he had some ecstasy. Known as a party drug, it had the opposite effect on Barnwell. It made him feel very sad, even suicidal. The next day he tried to cure his blues by smoking marijuana. It didn't help and he took himself to The Alfred hospital psychiatric unit, saying he was hearing voices and seeing strange things and felt very down. He was treated for a couple of days and released for continuing treatment in the community on the 16th – his 24th birthday. Barnwell later said that he had felt let down that he had to leave the hospital on his birthday. He said the nurses told him others needed his bed and that 'you present as being well'. His barrister, Michael Simon, told his pre-sentence plea-hearing that Barnwell made another 'cry for help' on the 22nd, telling a counsellor that he was 'fucked in the head and depressed'. The next day, Barnwell complained of disrupted sleep and mood swings. On the 26th and 27th, he told Luke O'Keefe's girlfriend that he wanted to be readmitted to a psychiatric hospital for more treatment. On the 27th – the day before he shot Luke – Barnwell missed an appointment at a clinic to get his medication and treatment.

The second significant thing to happen to Barnwell at the Two Tribes rave was that he met Luke O'Keefe. They had been friends for a short time a couple of years earlier but had lost contact. At the rave, Luke said he needed a place to crash for a couple of days and Barnwell offered his flat.

Three weeks later – by 28 March – the friendship between the two had become a little strained. It was only a one-bedroom flat and had got a little crowded with Luke's girlfriend often around. Barnwell was also fed up with Luke's rowdy partying and messy ways.

Barnwell: We had a pretty good relationship, except he had outstayed his welcome a bit. I said he could stay a couple of days 'cause he needed somewhere to stay …

When I asked him to leave and that, he just kept going: 'Settle down.' I've gone: 'I am sick, sick in the mind. I need a place where I can settle. I can't have all this partying and that.'

Luke and Peter had lived very different lives. Luke had grown up in Port Melbourne. He had excelled at sports, particularly Australian Rules football. He played for the Victorian Junior Football Squad and had been selected to train with the Richmond Tigers Football Club, but a curvature of his spine cruelly cut short his footy career. He had done a horticulture course and had worked as a landscape gardener, but was unemployed when he was killed – hence the lazy, video-watching midweek afternoon. Luke also had dreams of making it as an actor. They weren't just dreams, either: he already had scored a role as boxing legend Lionel Rose's sparring partner in *The Lionel Rose Story*. He also had an eight-year-old daughter.

At 1.30pm on 28 March 2001, Barnwell went to a local clinic to get the medication he had failed to pick up the day before. He was injected with

REASONABLE DOUBT

40mg of an antischizophrenic drug and 'felt good' – no depression, no schizophrenic-like symptoms.

> *Barnwell*: My mood was down, but I cheered myself up sort of thing.

He went to the bank, withdrew money and paid the rent, bought some cigarettes and headed home.

Ironically, Barnwell killed his friend just a few couple of hours after his medication had made him feel good, *not* on the many times over the years such silly, dangerous play-acting would have been much more un-derstandable. He hadn't done it the day before when he missed his psy-chiatric medication, or when he said he felt 'fucked in the head', or when he said he was hearing voices, or when he said he was feeling deeply depressed. He had stupidly killed his mate when he felt good; when he felt sane; when he couldn't blame his mental state.

Barnwell pleaded guilty to reckless manslaughter, admitting that his play-acting with a loaded weapon had been criminally careless.

At the pre-sentence plea-hearing, psychiatrist Lester Walton said he believed Barnwell's schizophrenic-like symptoms were caused by drugs. He said Barnwell had not had a psychotic episode in jail while off illegal drugs, even though he had also not been on his psychiatric medication. He said Barnwell's play-acting just before the gun went off was very childish, but not psychotic.

> *Dr Walton*: There is a striking immaturity about his conduct. I mean, it's like kids playing Cowboys and Indians except, of course, it is a life game … [but] I cannot go past Mr Barnwell's own descrip-tion: that he engaged in recklessly irresponsible play-acting with a firearm and that that behaviour was not a very direct product of mental illness.
>
> Currently, he doesn't exhibit strikingly immature behaviour. He is coherent, rational, cooperative. He is normal …

He has been responsible for the death of a friend. I think it is fair comment that that has had a fairly major impact upon him. He seems to be applying himself to what drug rehabilitation is available in prison, apparently with good results. I mean it hardly constitutes a guarantee, but I think he is, at least at this stage, fairly genuinely motivated to remain drug-free.

On 5 July 2002, Justice Philip Cummins gave his verdict. He noted that even with a cursory glance Barnwell should have seen that the 'nasty firearm' he was playing with was loaded.

Justice Cummins: You did not realise the gun was loaded, cocked and ready for firing ... You then commenced play-acting with the weapon ... You started jumping around the bedroom pointing the gun and pretending you were someone like Al Pacino. This would have been a harmless and immature set of actions except that you had in your hand a weapon which was in fact loaded ... You jumped into the loungeroom, still play-acting and pointing the weapon. In doing so, and unexpected totally by you, the weapon discharged. Tragically, it shot the deceased once in the head and he died instantly.

The judge said neither Barnwell's psychiatric condition, nor the medication he had had just hours before, had anything to do with Luke O'Keefe's death. He said, however, that he accepted that Barnwell had 'substantial and genuine remorse' for his 'grossly negligent actions' and, despite his long criminal record, was genuinely trying to rehabilitate himself and keep off drugs.

Justice Cummins: Looking through the thicket of your prior convictions, Mr Barnwell, I still think there is substantial potential for good in you and I think, if you keep off the drugs, you could have a good life once released ...

Mr Barnwell, for the manslaughter of Luke O'Keefe, I sentence you to four years' imprisonment. I direct that you serve a minimum of two years' imprisonment before you are eligible for parole. Mr Barnwell may be removed.

Outside the court, Luke's father Leon Kalaitzis said he hoped his son's death would be a wake-up call that 'guns are not toys'.

Mr Kalaitzis: I am actually a shooter and I'm a firearms safety officer and I never blame firearms. I always blame the people behind them. Any child knows you never point a loaded gun at anyone, or play with a loaded gun. It's just commonsense.

SLEEPWALK OF DEATH

Bernie Brown's sleepwalking escapades were a bit of a joke with his family.

> *Brown*: On a couple of occasions I found myself sitting in the loungeroom with a cup of coffee in my hand … I woke up with a warm cup of coffee in my hand! On another occasion, I woke up with a smoke *and* a cup of coffee, just sitting there smoking and drinking coffee. Other times, I woke up sitting in the doorway of my son's room just staring at the wall. Another few times, I was in my daughter's room just kneeling down on the floor in the bedroom, just next to the bed and then I'd wake up and go to bed.

Brown said that he had been a sleepwalker as a child growing up in a Western Australian orphanage.

> *Brown*: I used to wake up in strange, strange places … In like the airing cupboards. They didn't have doors, just little alcoves in the hallway with sheets and pillows and stuff and I used to wake up in there on one of the shelves. I also used to wake up in bed with my younger brother, or sleeping on the floor beside my older brother's bed – and they were in different dormitories.

He said that at the orphanage he had walked in his sleep three or four times – that he knew of. After being taken into a foster home at the age of 13, he did not sleepwalk, or at least did not know whether he did or not, for nearly 25 years – until 1988. That was when he fell while painting a railway station and hit his head hard. He believed that caused ongoing headaches, memory problems and made him more easily irritated. Brown also believed hitting his head somehow renewed his childhood sleep problems.

> *Brown*: I snore very loudly and quite often stop breathing when I am sleeping. I don't know that personally, that's just been relayed to me. My wife Susan would give me an elbow to get me breathing again.

He also said he had had a few 'night terrors'.

> *Brown*: I would just wake up very cold but sweating, you know, at the same time. Just terrified, absolutely terrified.

Some nights he slept on the couch so Susan – his wife of 10 years – could get a decent sleep. For Brown, sleep was often anything but restful; he would wake up in the morning feeling 'virtually brain dead'.

> *Brown*: Just no energy, can't think straight, nothing really registers for a while.

In August 1992, Brown's sleepwalking increased. That was when for three nights in a row, he made his strange nightly visits into the bedroom of his 13-year-old stepdaughter, Kathryn. He found himself kneeling next to her bed, staring at nothing. The first time it happened Kathryn asked: 'Dad?' 'It's not Dad, it's your mum,' he oddly replied. Again she said: 'Dad?' This time he replied blankly: 'Oh, you're awake,' and walked out.

Brown's increased sleep disturbance might have been triggered by his rising anxiety about losing his job as a house painter. Although considered a good worker, there was very little work in or around the tiny town of Harrisville (population about 500), about 100km southwest of Brisbane, just south of Ipswich.

> *Brown*: Work was getting scarce. There was talk of laying people off … I was very upset.

Sleepwalk of Death

The 41-year-old was so worried, he organised a day off on 26 August 1992 so he could talk to another contractor just in case he lost his job.

He never made it to that interview.

In the early hours of 26 August 1992, according to Brown, his sleepwalking stopped being a joke, stopped being a weird eccentricity, and caused a tragedy.

***

On 25 August 1992, Brown had come home at his normal time of about 4.30pm. Susan and Kathryn were arguing so he got a beer – a light one – and went to tinker in his workroom. After a while, his wife joined him. They discussed whether Kathryn should move to another school. Kathryn overheard some of it.

> *Kathryn*: Mum wanted me to go to another school and Dad's sticking up for me ... I heard him say: 'Why are you always picking on Kathryn?'

Brown had a shower and then another light beer before the family sat down to dinner at about 6pm. After dinner Ben and Kathryn went to their rooms – Ben, 15, to do some homework, Kathryn to listen to her music. The family then watched a science-fiction video. It was so bad Susan and Bernie went to bed about five minutes before it finished – about 10.30pm.

In bed, Brown said later, he and Susan continued discussing whether to move Kathryn to another school.

> *Brown*: We were just throwing the fors and againsts around and I suggested she had been picking on her a bit much.

During the evening Brown had a couple of Panadol, some Sudafed and a couple of other drugs to try to get rid of a headache. He said that at about midnight he got out of bed to take a couple of Mogadon.

REASONABLE DOUBT

Brown: I hopped back into bed and we spoke for a while longer. I don't know exactly how long – about half an hour to an hour – and then I kissed her goodnight and we rolled over and went to sleep.

He said the next thing he remembered was waking up about 5am.

Brown: I had to have a leak … I sort of sat up and looked across at the time on the digital readout. I saw '5' – that's all I saw. I put the touch lamp beside my bed on and I got up and walked down my side of the bed and across the foot of the bed and I just looked across to my left and it was just a bloody mess …

I just stood there for a second, then I sort of moved forward. I didn't really run because it's not that many steps to take, and I sort of shook my wife and I felt for a pulse in the neck …

Pausing and shaking his head, Brown tearfully said: 'There was no pulse. I felt nothing.'

Brown: I tried talking to her but there was no response … I said words to the effect: 'Come on, it's time to get up' …

I went to make two cups of coffee. I don't know how far I got with making it. I went back to the bedroom and I said: 'Your coffee has been made. Come and have a coffee.' She didn't answer …

I was a mess. I was crying. Then I tried to sit her up and put her legs over the edge of the bed … and I said: 'Come on, stop fucking around. It's not funny.' And I was shaking her …

I was getting, I think, a bit angry because she wouldn't answer and she slid off the bed onto the floor and I thought she was just, just foolin' around, you know. So, I put her back on the bed. I lifted her under the arms onto the bed and that was when I realised I had blood on me.

And all I can remember saying virtually from the start of the whole incident until just before I realised there was blood on me, I just kept saying: 'Oh no! Oh, Jesus, no!' and just virtually talking to

Sleepwalk of Death

nothing. I mean obviously God wasn't, wasn't there but that's who I was talking to and it didn't make any sense later on.

Brown said he then started taking off the blood-soaked sheets.

Brown: My wife hates a mess … And for some reason I thought: 'I have got clean up this mess because if she sees a mess she is going to kill me.' That's what I was thinking.

I just started grabbing everything off the bed … I took it down to the car. I had no shoes on at the time, I don't think. I just kept going back and forth to the car, I think with sheets – whatever it was – I was just grabbing everything.

I wanted to hide it, which now seems stupid because she wouldn't have found it.

When I got rid of all the sheets and stuff, I grabbed something off the floor, I don't know what it was, a rag, and I started wiping the [blood off] the wall … I didn't want her to see the mess.

My wife felt very cold easily, so I covered her with the … doona. It was some time then that I realised she was dead …

The next thing I remember was having a shower … I was some time under the shower and it was then that I stopped crying … I didn't feel any better but I stopped crying …

I was walking around for a while thinking: 'Jesus, I can't let the kids see that mess.' So woke I them up for school and told them their mum was sick and that she was sleeping and virtually just let them get their own breakfast and whatever.

Ben and Kathryn both said they had found it strange to be woken up by their stepfather instead of their mother at 6am. They also found it odd that their lunches hadn't been prepared.

Ben: He came in and woke us up and then I dozed back off to sleep and then he came back in and gave us $5 and said like: 'Here's $5 for lunch because your mother is sick,' or something. 'She's in bed, so you buy your lunch today and I'm going to stay home.' He said that she had had to go in to the doctor and they got some sedatives and something and she was asleep and that she wasn't to be disturbed ...

He seemed a bit nervous. He was sort of pacing around a bit.

He just sort of mentioned that about two o'clock he went and took her to the doctor and they spoke to the doctor and he said that my mother was under a lot of stress and that she would have to go to have a lot of rest and then she would have to seek counselling or something ...

He said there might have been a bit of a row and he was surprised that I didn't get woken up by it ...

Ben said his stepfather seemed very tense that morning, that he was constantly pacing around the lounge and up the hallway. Kathryn agreed their stepfather seemed a bit upset that day.

Kathryn: He said that mother was sick and he took her to the doctors and that I didn't have to eat my breakfast, which I normally did. He said: 'Don't go and see her because she needs her rest and when she wakes up she will just have to have a meal and go straight back to sleep.'

Brown's increasingly convoluted lie even extended to him putting some of the blame on Kathryn.

Kathryn: He said that she was tired and I said, 'Is it because of me?' and he said, 'Yes.' He said that they got up at two o'clock in the morning and took her to the doctor and he asked me if I heard the car and I said, 'No.'

Kathryn was so upset that her behaviour at school might have triggered her mother's breakdown, she wrote a note to her and put it in a glass

Sleepwalk of Death

cabinet. Poignantly, Kathryn did not know that her mother had been shot twice in the back of the head *and* hit with a claw hammer in her bed some hours before.

Kathryn: He said: 'I'll give it to her when she wakes up' … He said he's got to stay home and look after Mum.

Despite being told not to disturb her mother, Kathryn could not resist a quick peek.

Kathryn: He was in the loungeroom, I think. I quickly walked past and I think I saw her laying in the bed with the covers on her.

It was only later that she found out that she had caught a glimpse of her mother's bloody corpse.

Nothing had woken the teens that night – not their parents arguing in their nearby room, not gunshots and not their mother's screams. It seemed Ben and Kathryn's sleep was also extraordinary, but not in the way their stepfather's was.

After the children left for school, Brown said that he kept up his logic-defying refusal to accept his wife was dead.

Brown: I kept walking around the house, just pacing up and down and I kept asking my wife to 'Come on, stop fooling around.'

Finally about 9.30am – four and a half hours after he said he had found his wife's dead body lying in their bed – Brown phoned a friend. Weeping and stuttering badly he said, 'I've done something really bad and I think I am going to jail.' He went to see a lawyer and then the police were notified.

Senior Constable Paul Foley got the call to check the Brown home in Hall Street, Harrisville just before 10am. When he got to the home – an old hospital divided into units – he had to climb a chicken-wire fence and negotiate his way past a German shepherd pup and a 'little black dog which was quite savage'. He found the home very neat and tidy and all the doors closed. In the master bedroom he saw a waterbed 'roughly covered' with a white doona.

> *Sen Constable Foley*: I felt this blanket and felt two legs. I then went to the foot of the bed and pulled back the blanket and found the deceased person.
>
> She was lying face up with her left arm across her stomach and the right arm wedged between the side of the waterbed and the waterbed's bladder. There seemed to be a large quantity of blood around her skull, her face and left shoulder … and blood spatter on the wall behind the bed, on the bed and on the bedhead. She was only wearing a T-shirt and necklace.

The policeman discovered a bloody claw hammer under the waterbed. Police also found – inside a silver case in a locked gun cabinet in Ben Brown's room – the .22 Springfield rifle used in the killing. In the boot of Brown's car they found blood-stained sheets, a pillow and a pillow slip, each with a bullet hole, and a pair of Brown's grey tracksuit pants with two discharged .22 calibre cartridge cases in the pocket.

An autopsy found that Susan Brown had been shot once in the lower back of her head and once in the upper back of her head. She also had cuts on the right side of her head, which could have been caused by a claw hammer.

When police asked Brown how his wife died, he told them: 'I don't know. I think I shot her. I don't know. I have no idea.'

***

So in June 1993, 10 months after 36-year-old Susan Brown's gruesome death, a Queensland Supreme Court jury had to decide whether her husband was guilty of her murder. His barrister, Debbie Richards, said her client could not remember anything of the death of his wife but that the most likely explanation was that he had killed her in his sleep and, therefore, was not guilty of her murder.

Ms Richards: Brown was acting while not conscious of his actions, while not in control.

Prosecutor Kevan Townsley said that Brown had cold-bloodedly murdered his wife and that his claim to have been sleepwalking at the time was a 'furphy'.

In his cross-examination of Brown the prosecutor tried to cast doubt on his claim that he had increasing bouts of sleepwalking in the weeks before he killed his wife, asking him why he didn't tell a doctor about them, especially as that would bolster his worker's compensation claim over the fall at the railway station.

Brown: Because I had enough problems at the time with my headaches, memory and the dizziness … I didn't want to keep running to the doctor with all sorts of complaints.

He said he had not realised his sleepwalking would be important to his compensation claim. He agreed that he and his wife were shooters and would go out hunting animals, but he denied this meant he should have more quickly realised that his wife had been shot dead. Mr Townsley also quizzed Brown about his reaction to finding his wife's bloody body.

Mr Townsley: Did you scream for help or anything like that?
Brown: No … I was just shocked. I didn't do anything for a short time …
Mr Townsley: But you did yell and scream?
Brown: Not that I know of.
Mr Townsley: This was someone you loved?
Brown: That's correct.
Mr Townsley: Did you rush out to see if your children had been murdered?
Brown: No.
Mr Townsley: Didn't cross your mind?

144   REASONABLE DOUBT

Brown: No, nothing entered my head except what I saw.

Mr Townsley: You were … with her body from 5 o'clock to 9.30 – four and a half hours … So, if you were so inclined, you could have rung for an ambulance and the police, couldn't you?

Brown: If I had thought of it, yes.

Mr Townsley: Why didn't you do that?

Brown: Because I assumed I had done it.

Mr Townsley: You assumed you had done it?

Brown: That's correct.

Mr Townsley: How quickly did you realise that?

Brown: I don't know when I first realised it, but it was some time after I started taking the bed clothes off and having a shower …

Mr Townsley: You have got no memory of all of this?

Brown: No.

Mr Townsley: You didn't do it?

Brown: Not as far as I am concerned.

Although the defence's main argument was that the jury could not dismiss the reasonable possibility that Brown had been sleepwalking – an unthinking automaton – when he killed his wife, it said someone else could also have killed Susan Brown when her husband was either sleeping next to her, or had gone to the toilet. To back this admittedly less-likely possibility, Ms Richards pointed out that police had found fingerprints in the bedroom they could not identify.

Mr Townsley: You weren't woken up by the report of two shots of a .22 rifle?

Brown: No …

Mr Townsley: Why did you want to get rid of the blood-soaked bed clothes?

Brown: Because, the way I was thinking at the time, I knew my wife hated a mess of any sort and I was determined to get rid of that mess before she saw it because at the time I thought: 'If she sees all of this shit, she will kill me.'

Sleepwalk of Death

Mr Townsley: You would, however, have felt for the pulse and found none before you removed the sheets?

Brown: That's correct.

Mr Townsley: How could she kill you?

Brown: It doesn't make any sense to me.

Mr Townsley: It's nonsense you have made up, isn't it?

Brown: No.

Brown denied the prosecutor's claim that he (Brown) had early on suggested a psychiatric defence to his lawyer, saying he had not known his lawyer would go with the sleepwalking 'automatism' defence until a few days before the trial. He said he could not remember suggesting soon after his arrest that he should have a psychiatric examination because he was a Vietnam vet.

The prosecutor also asked Brown why he told his children such an elaborate false story – about taking his wife to the doctor in the early hours of the morning.

Brown: I did not want to let them go in and see the horror that was in the bedroom ...

Mr Townsley: There was something she said in that discussion with you in bed that triggered the shooting ...

Brown: No.

Mr Townsley: ... that you are not telling us?

Brown: No, there was nothing said.

A sleep disorder expert, Dr Phillip Lethbridge, told the jury that it would have been possible for a sleepwalking person to have gone to the Browns' gun cabinet, unlocked it, taken out a gun, walked back to bed, shot Mrs Brown twice, hit her with the claw hammer, put the fired cartridges into his pocket, returned the gun to the cabinet, locked it away and then returned to sleep beside the bloody corpse. He said that, if true, Brown making himself a cup of coffee and lighting a cigarette while sleepwalking showed he was capable of complex actions while sleepwalking.

146   REASONABLE DOUBT

Dr Lethbridge said people had committed quite complex crimes while sleepwalking. He said the most famous recent example was a Canadian man who drove more than 20km to his in-laws' home, where he beat and stabbed his mother-in-law to death with a tyre lever and a kitchen knife. In the bizarre 1987 attack Kenneth James Parks, 23, of Ontario, also badly injured his father-in-law. On the evening of 23 May, shortly after falling asleep on the living-room couch, Mr Parks got up, put on his shoes and jacket – but no socks or underwear – and left the house, leaving the front door open. He drove 23km to his wife's parents' townhouse. He took a tyre iron from the boot of his car and opened the townhouse's door with a key. He later remembered, according to a report in *The Journal of American Academy of Psychiatry and the Law*, seeing his mother-in-law's face and hearing the children yelling from upstairs and running up the stairs calling out to them. The children later said they only heard Mr Parks grunting. Luckily, the robot-monster uncle did not go into the children's bedrooms. Instead, he drove to a nearby police station and babbled out a confession.

> *Mr Parks*: I just killed someone with my bare hands. Oh my God, I just killed someone; I just killed two people. My God, I've just killed two people with my hands. My God, I've just killed two people. My hands; I just killed two people. I killed them; I just killed two people; I've just killed my mother- and father-in-law. I stabbed and beat them to death. It's all my fault.

At his trial Mr Parks claimed he had been asleep the whole time – on the drive to his parents-in-law's, while attacking them, and on the drive to the police station. The jury heard that he and his family had a history of sleepwalking and sleeptalking. It also heard that the year before the killing he had been very stressed: he had worked 10-hour days as a project coordinator for an electric company; lost money on betting at the horse races; stolen $30,000 money from his employer to cover these debts; been sacked after this theft was discovered; and had been charged with theft.

His problems had put a strain on his marriage but – as Canada's highest court, the Supreme Court, noted in 1992 – Mr Parks' wife's parents always supported him. He got on really well with his in-laws, particularly with his mother-in-law, who called him a 'gentle giant'. Mr Parks' jury found him not guilty of murder, accepting the defence's sleepwalking claim. The judge rejected a prosecution call for Mr Parks to be kept in a mental institution, ruling that sleepwalking was not a disease of the mind. Both Ontario's appeal court and Canada Supreme Court upheld this decision, throwing out prosecution appeals.

What the jury in Brown's trial did not hear was that sleepwalking has been a nightmare for legal systems around the world since at least 1846. That was when a celebrated Boston lawyer, Rufus Choate, managed to persuade a jury that his client was sleepwalking when he slit the throat of a famously beautiful high-class prostitute so badly her head was nearly severed. Albert Tirrell's highly publicised trial heard that he had become so besotted with Maria Ann Bickford that he left his family to live near her. It heard he wanted her to give up prostitution but she refused – the money was too good. After brutally slaying Maria, Albert started three fires in the brothel, which the prosecution said he did to hide the evidence – not the sort of thing a sleepwalker would do. The jury, however, disagreed and took less than two hours to find Tirrell not guilty. He was set free and lived the rest of his life a free man.

Dr Lethbridge told Brown's trial that while a third of children have walked in their sleep, only three per cent were regular sleepwalkers and only one per cent of adults were sleepwalkers. He said adult sleepwalkers had usually been sleepwalkers as children. The neurologist said Mogadon was one of the drugs believed to trigger sleepwalking and that sleepwalkers tended to walk more in their sleep when they were stressed. He said it was possible for a sleepwalker to continue sleeping through gunshots, particularly if a pillow had been used to stifle the gun's noise. He agreed, however, that it was unusual for sleepwalkers to try to conceal what they had done.

On July 1 1993, Brown's jury took less than two hours to find him guilty of murder. As the verdict was announced, Brown sighed and told

REASONABLE DOUBT

Justice Brian Ambrose he had 'absolutely nothing to say'. Shortly afterwards, declaring it a 'horrible crime', the judge sentenced Brown to life in prison – the only sentence available in Queensland for those convicted of murder.

Outside the court, Susan Brown's mother, Moureen Deakes said she was 'more than happy' with the verdict and sentence.

> *Ms Deakes*: No-one else will suffer the way we did now that he's been put away. Knowing what he did, the terrible fear was that he would be released and hurt someone else.

But it wasn't over.

In December 1993, Queensland's Court of Appeal overturned Brown's conviction and ordered a new trial. The appeal judges ruled that Justice Ambrose had unfairly undercut Brown's chances of being believed by telling the jurors that when they came to consider what he said in the dock they should treat him as any other witness but 'keep in mind' his interest in the case; that they should look 'carefully' at his evidence. They said even though the prosecution case had been strong, Brown could have been acquitted if the jury had believed him. The judges said Brown 'was undoubtedly entitled to have the jury consider the possibility of somnambulism … properly'.

Despite this win – about a year later and before his new trial started – Brown surprisingly ended his legal tussle. On 4 January 1995 he pleaded guilty to murdering Susan. He told Justice Des Derrington: 'A lot of people have been hurt by this whole bloody nightmare. I can't help them any more, but I'd like to say sorry for everything that happened.'

Once again he was imprisoned for life.

A SPIRITUAL DEATH

Breatharians are fed by the Light of God. Breatharians *breathe* God ...

The term Breatharian applies to someone who chooses neither to eat nor drink. These people obtain their nourishment from the universal life force directly ...

In order to understand how a Being can be sustained by only Light, we need to understand that which is sustaining them i.e. prana – also known as the Universal life force of 'liquid light'.

Prana is a subtle element which pervades each cell of every living tissue and fluid in an organism like electricity through atoms in a battery ...

An organism can be sustained by etheric realms and by prana alone – some individuals have achieved this through manipulating their consciousness to higher vibrational frequencies that in turn change the molecular structure of their physical, emotional and mental bodies ... These beings are called breatharians ...

In June 1993, at the guidance of my Inner Teacher, I underwent a magical 21-day process. I say magical as it truly brought more magic into my life. For eons of time beings have existed purely on Light, yet in modern society this natural state of Being is often disbelieved ...

The 21-day process is not a process of denial or of 'fasting' one's way to ascension. It is a process of mastery – a sacred, spiritual journey that is being pioneered to present to humanity (and the Western

150   REASONABLE DOUBT

world) simply another option. One can be vegetarian, vegan, fruitarian, liquidarian or breatharian. It is not a miracle, or something to be feared, but a reclamation of our natural state of being …

Being nourished by prana is like riding in a Porsche. Getting energy via food and digestion is like riding in an old jalopy. One ride is just so much smoother than the other …

When one has ceased to require physical nourishment from food, all the energy used in the digestive process can be, and is, redirected elsewhere. The individual benefits of the redirection of this energy, and of no longer requiring food, are too numerous to mention here. Also as each individual is unique so will each experience be unique.

On a global level, imagine a world without hunger?

These are some of the things Jasmuheen, the Australian 'guru' of breatharianism, wrote in her book *Living on Light* and in her New Age rainbow-hued, swirly, starry, moon-festooned Cosmic Internet Academy (CIA) website. They were the sorts of ideas that persuaded Lani Morris, a 53-year-old mother of nine children aged from about eight to 32 – to fly from her Melbourne home to Brisbane to become a breatharian. She wanted to live on 'prana', on air and light – to 'breathe God'. She had even named one of her children Jasmuheen. Shortly before deciding to try breatharianism, Ms Morris separated from her husband of 30 years and also had to try to come to terms with the death of her 23-year-old son. Ms Morris's ex-husband tried to talk her out of becoming a breatharian, but Lani wouldn't be dissuaded.

What Ms Morris probably did not know was that in 1983 (according to the online encyclopedia 'Wikipedia') the founder of the Breatharian Institute of America, 47-year-old Wiley Brooks, was caught coming out of a 7-Eleven with a Slurpee, a hot dog and Twinkies. He later stopped preaching Breatharianism to 'devote 100 per cent of his time on solving why he needed some type of food to keep his physical body alive'.

Ms Morris also may or may not have known that those who had interviewed Jasmuheen (born in 1957 as Ellen Greve) had been surprised

A Spiritual Death

to find the fridge in her luxury Brisbane home – with its gold-coloured statue of the Virgin Mary in the front yard – full of food. (Jasmuheen said it was for her vegan second husband, Jess Ferguson.) Before handing over $700 for the 21-day breatharian introduction, Ms Morris may also not have realised that Jasmuheen said she channelled Count St Germain, who she claimed (according to *The Skeptic* magazine) had been alive for hundreds of years in incarnations including William Shakespeare, Merlin, Christopher Columbus, Joseph the (foster) father of Jesus, and the prophet Samuel. According to 'Wikipedia', Jasmuheen had also claimed that her DNA has expanded from two to 12 strands to 'absorb more hydrogen', but had refused to have a blood test to prove this, saying she did not understand the relevance.

About 15 months before Ms Morris went to Brisbane to become a breatharian, a 31-year-old kindergarten teacher called Timo Degan had died in Munich shortly after trying to do the same thing. According to an article in the *Sunday Times* in Britain, Mr Degan fell into a coma on the 12th day of his bid to live on prana. A hospital spokesman said he had 'an almost total circulatory system collapse' and looked as though he had been in a 'concentration camp'. After four weeks on an intravenous drip, Mr Degan recovered but soon afterwards fell over, fatally injuring his head.

Presumably unaware of the darker side to this 'live on light and air' philosophy, in June 1998 Ms Morris met Jim and Eugenia Pesnak. She believed they would lead her to a magical way of living by guiding her through the 21-day 'process' to breatharianism.

The Pesnaks had been breatharians for less than three years and they weren't the sort of people normally expected to belong to New Age cults. Jim Pesnak was a 60-year-old retired engineer; his 61-year-old wife was a retired tax agent. They had been married for 33 years and had four adult children, none of whom shared their parents' belief in breatharianism.

Jim Pesnak was born in 1938 in Estonia, then part of the USSR; Eugenia was born in Poland in 1936 but, because of the Nazis, they suffered similar childhoods. Both families were taken in cattle trucks to Germany and

152 REASONABLE DOUBT

forced into slave labour as 'Eastern workers'. After the war both families also spent three years in different German refugee camps before migrating to Australia and settling in Brisbane. In 1964, after university and two years of national service, Jim Pesnak became an electronic engineer at the Queensland Electricity Commission. He stayed there until he was made redundant 23 years later. Eugenia worked as a clerk in the tax department for 10 years until 1965, when she married Jim and started having children. From 1975 – a few years after their fourth child was born – Ms Pesnak worked as a tax agent until she retired in 1983 to help Jim care for his father.

The Pesnaks belonged to the Russian Orthodox Church but, in the 1980s, they became interested in other spiritual philosophies. In August 1995 Jim Pesnak became a breatharian. His wife soon followed. They said they were both put through the 21-day process by a breatharian called Dr William Moulton. After that, the Pesnaks said they put about 30 people through the same 'process' – seven days without food or drink followed by 14 days with some orange juice and other liquids – without any problems.

Sadly, that was not the case with Ms Morris – not by a long, long way.

***

The Pesnaks met Ms Morris at Brisbane airport on Saturday 13 June 1998 and drove her to their home in the bayside suburb of Ormiston, where they set her up in a caravan out the back. Then, adhering to Jasmuheen's 21-day process precepts, they left her alone.

Ms Morris kept a diary of her attempt to be a breatharian. On the first day the excited believer wrote that she felt a tingly sensation as she entered the caravan. She was told that that indicated the cleansing had started – that the spirit guides were there.

Quite quickly, however, there were signs this 'cleansing' wasn't going to be easy.

June 13: I started to read but couldn't concentrate ... head feels heavy mind sluggish ... Eyes feel odd.

A Spiritual Death

June 14: On entering the caravan after my shower, my ring finger and little finger became tingly and numb again ... Spent Sunday sleepy, itchy. Head groggy. Legs a bit shaky. Dream of interplanetary craft. *June 15*: Sitting around listening to tape. Read little. Tired, very tired. Smell like ice-cream.

On the fourth day of her fast, Ms Morris wrote of pain in her lower back, hips, ankles and knees. Lying down or sitting didn't help. She was forgetful and her mouth was dry. She would scold her stomach for feeling nauseous.

June 16: Went to shower. Came back feeling exhausted. Exhaustion comes from stomach region. Had a few words with it [her stomach]. Tasting bile in my mouth. Feeling nauseous. Had lot of words to say to stomach, pancreas etc ... Can't wait for end of these operations and mouthful of orange juice ... Is this a rebellion of the mind? ... Africa has been on my mind a lot ... Imagine what could be done without the necessity of food ... No more famine ... Beautiful sunshine today ... Would love a drink. Anything would do. Skin itchy and shrivelling ... Breasts smaller. Wish it was my stomach.

After this, it was not clear when Ms Morris made her diary entries. What is clear is that her neat handwriting turned into childish scrawls with lots of loops. It is also increasingly clear that it's the diary of a dying woman.

Ms Morris's diary: Feel like death. Mind gone. I have stayed fairly well so far because my mind has been in control. Don't know how I am going to last out if it goes ...

Dreamt of fruit juice last night. I was walking through jungle collecting exotic fruits ... walking through markets with arms full of fruit ... In my kitchen with this gigantic juicer, boxes waist-high all over the kitchen full of fruit and great jugs of fruit juice enough for whole family to bathe in and drinking all these exotic blends of fruit ...

> Every morning I think of cups of Earl Grey tea. Yesterday I caught myself reminiscing over tomato and coriander soup … today it's Black Forest and pancakes with maple syrup and ice cream and hot chocolate with marshmallow.

Her last legible words were: 'My first drink will be tomorrow night. Hope I can last that long.'

Her final diary entry was just a spiral.

On the sixth day of the fast – Friday 19 June – Ms Morris was so forgetful she got into the shower fully dressed. About 4pm, the Pesnaks heard a thud coming from the caravan. They rushed in to find their guest on the floor. She told them: 'Stupid me,' and they lifted her up and put her back in bed. Jim Pesnak later told police that they did not ask Ms Morris then how she felt or whether there was anything wrong.

Jim Pesnak: No … She looked all right.

He said, however, that it was unusual behaviour for breatharian inductees.

Jim Pesnak: People normally don't go as far as falling over. People say that, you know: 'I'm woozy,' and they'll sit down, or: 'I'm woozy. Please Jim, give me a hand to go to the toilet.' People don't normally fall over.

Ms Morris spent most of the next day – Saturday 20 June – sleeping and could only mumble when awake. The Pesnaks looked in on her 'just to make sure that she didn't fall or something'.

Jim Pesnak: If she can't get up, I don't want her on the floor for hours and hours.

He said that that evening Ms Morris drank two litres of the orange juice she had so avidly anticipated. She struggled, however, to lift her right arm and was a 'little bit sort of fazed out', but Mr Pesnak said this was 'nothing unusual'.

A Spiritual Death

Mr Pesnak said that the next morning, he found that his fasting guest had vomited and urinated in her bed, 'wasn't very talkative', and had started hicupping. He said none of this was 'normal behaviour' for breatharian wannabes.

Still, the Pesnaks did not call in an ambulance.

They were concerned enough, however, to phone the man who had introduced them into breatharianism – Dr William Moulton. Dr Moulton understood he was being called as a breatharian, not as a doctor. He and Jim Pesnak agreed that Ms Morris's disturbing symptoms were a sign of her spiritual struggle getting rid of the body's poisons. He was not asked to come over and see Ms Morris for himself. (Dr Moulton has since rejected breatharianism.)

Jim Pesnak told police that he did not believe Ms Morris was in any physical danger and thought she was fighting an 'ego battle'; that she had a spiritual blockage caused by her 'childish' refusal to let go of her 'emotional burdens'.

Mr Pesnak: This is a spiritual battle, not a medical procedure ... When the question comes up, 'Should I call a doctor?', the answer is, 'No, trust in God' ... If I had called in an ambulance, they would have stopped the cleansing.

Eugenia Pesnak told police: 'As far as the process is concerned, sometimes a doctor's intervention can be fatal.'

On Monday 22 June, Ms Morris could not speak and was using sign language to try to communicate with the Pesnaks. She was also still hiccupping. The next day her right leg was weak and she couldn't control her bladder. She could not write with her right hand and could only scribble with her left. Most disturbingly of all, she began spitting out black flakes. Mr Pesnak said he gave Ms Pesnak some milk diluted with warm water.

Still, they didn't call an ambulance.

On the next day, Wednesday 24 June – the 11th day of Ms Morris's introduction into breatharianism – things deteriorated alarmingly quickly. At 7am, the black spittle was much more obvious.

156 REASONABLE DOUBT

Mr Pesnak: The black stuff was gushing out of her mouth …

By about 11am, she was breathing hard and hyperventilating. He said that despite her desperate state, Ms Morris refused to drink. By midday Ms Morris was struggling to breathe.

Mr Pesnak: She was having problems, real problems … Her throat was constricted. She stopped breathing for a while. I was pressing down on her chest, and she started breathing again and now she's lying on her side, sort of just breathing but very laboured now. You can see her, sort of, chest and her stomach really trying hard to get the air in.

Mr Pesnak put his fingers into Ms Morris's mouth and found it 'full of black stuff'. He had his fingers in her mouth for about 10 minutes. Desperate to get air into her, Mr Pesnak put a crudely made tube down her throat. Still, he did not call an ambulance. Instead – at 2.16pm – Mr Pesnak once again phoned Dr Moulton. He was not home. On Dr Moulton's answering machine he left this message: 'Can you help me? Well, what can I do or, or would it be possible for you to come over after work and have a look at her, or, I don't know, for some advice, or should I call an ambulance and what do I tell them?'

Finally – shortly after leaving this message – Mr Pesnak called an ambulance. Unconscious and severely dehydrated, Ms Morris was put on a respirator and a life-support machine. One lung had collapsed and the other was severely damaged.

The process that was supposed to enable her to live just by breathing had destroyed her lungs.

Ms Morris died about a week after being taken to hospital. An autopsy revealed that she had died of pneumonia; that she had had a stroke and acute kidney failure. A neuropathologist who examined Ms Morris's brain found that she would have had a reasonable chance of surviving if an ambulance had got to her before Tuesday 23 June. After that, medical treatment would not have been able to save her life.

A Spiritual Death

In his interview with police, Jim Pesnak denied there was anything uncaring about the way he and his wife had run the 21-day breatharian process with Ms Morris.

Mr Pesnak: I know there is a duty, and you treat them humanely and you get an ambulance when something goes wrong … When I realised something was going wrong, I called the ambulance straightaway.

***

Almost a year and a half later – in November 1999 – the Pesnaks were tried in the Brisbane Supreme Court, accused of criminal negligence manslaughter.

Prosecutor Charlie Clark said the Pesnaks' failure to call an ambulance was a gross breach of their duty towards a fellow human being.

Mr Clark: The fact that we might be a follower of the breatharian cause does not give an excuse to ignore that duty. There is not a defence of breatharianism in the criminal code …

Members of the jury, you don't have prejudice against them because they are breatharians, but can it be fairly said that breatharian philosophy, as it applied to Lani Morris's declining state of health, was a reasonable belief?

It might be honestly held, but can it be said to be a reasonable belief?

Any ordinary and reasonable person was going to look at Lani Morris and be dialling Triple 0 … in that six-day period [the six days before Ms Morris died].

Mr Clark said that the Pesnaks' criminal disregard for Ms Morris was especially shown by the message Mr Pesnak left on Dr Moulton's phone, even as his guest was battling to breathe and vomiting up 'black stuff', even as she was dying.

Mr Clark: Can I close with these final, very telling words of the accused: 'Or should I call an ambulance and what do I tell them?'

Why in heaven's name does he need Moulton's advice as to what he should tell the ambulance officer, if and when the ambulance officer arrives?

If he has got a genuine concern for her health, it is quite easy: he tells the ambulance officer what has occurred.

The Pesnaks' barrister, Neil Macgroarty, acknowledged that a doctor had found that Ms Morris became too sick to stop her fast, but he said his clients were not guilty of manslaughter because at the time they honestly and reasonably believed she could have ended her fast if she had wanted to. He also said the Pesnaks three calls on three consecutive days to Dr Moulton to ask his advice showed that they were not uncaring. He said Dr Moulton had told them not to worry about the black flakes in Ms Morris's spittle, telling them that that had happened to him when he did the 21-day process. Dr Moulton also told the Pesnaks that the fact that Ms Morris could draw a spiral seemed to indicate that she had not had a stroke.

Mr Macgroarty: If you look at the spiral ... there is a definite pattern repeated over and over again ... that is indicative of a person whose mind is conscious ...

If you like, members of the jury, as it turns out his [Jim Pesnak's] crime, I suppose, was to rely on Dr Moulton ...

He [Mr Pesnak] has not conducted himself with such disregard of the life and safety of Lani Morris as to amount to a crime against the state and to be conduct deserving of punishment.

Mr Macgroarty said Jim and Eugenia Pesnak believed in breatharianism.

Mr Macgroarty: It's not as if my clients are some sort of fraudsters going around to get money out of people ... They are people who genuinely ... believe in this process.

He told the jurors, however, that they did not have to believe in breatharianism to find the Pesnaks not guilty.

A Spiritual Death

Mr Macgroarty: There is one fact in this case that I say, and that is this: any person alive needs food and drink to survive. There is no two ways about that, members of the jury. You and I, I suggest, would not agree with the beliefs of Lani Morris or Jim Pesnak or Eugenia Pesnak. It is fundamental: you have got to eat and drink to survive.

They are not on trial for their beliefs ...

What they believe you might classify as 'silly', but you don't jump to the conclusion that because they are silly and have silly beliefs, therefore they are guilty of this serious criminal offence.

The jury took just three hours to find Jim and Eugenia Pesnak guilty of manslaughter.

In sentencing the couple about a week later, Justice Margaret Wilson said she accepted that they had been 'fine, upstanding members of the community' who had brought up their children in a loving environment, and that they had cared for Jim Pesnak's elderly father. She also accepted that they had not meant to harm Ms Morris.

Justice Wilson: You are entitled to your spiritual beliefs. The sincerity of your beliefs has not been questioned. You have not attempted to proselytise others but simply to provide spiritual support to like-minded persons. The death of Ms Morris has demonstrated just how dangerous was the 21-day process and how misguided your belief in its essentially spiritual character.

Justice Wilson told Jim Pesnak that his failure to take 'appropriate action in the face of Ms Morris's deteriorating condition' was 'quite frightening'.

Justice Wilson: Mr Pesnak, your recklessness was of a high order. Mrs Pesnak, not only did you make no endeavour to dissuade your husband from his course of conduct, you actively assisted and encouraged him.

REASONABLE DOUBT

In trying to come up with just sentences, the judge compared their case with that of 'Vollmer and others', which involved a woman dying while three people (including the woman's husband) pinned her down and pushed on her stomach and throat, believing they were exorcising demons from her. (The story of this bizarre and fatal 'exorcism' appears as 'Fighting demons with Gladwrap' in *Killer Excuses*, Wayne Howell, The Five Mile Press, 2005.) Justice Wilson noted that the longest sentence handed out to these 'exorcists' was two years' jail with all but four months suspended. The judge, however, refused to impose a similar sentence. She said the fatal 'exorcism' had taken a few hours and the victim's death was 'totally unforeseen', whereas the Pesnaks had neglected Ms Morris in the face of a 'demonstrable decline' in her health over six days.

> *Justice Wilson*: It is important that other members of the community be deterred from engaging in such dangerous, cruel and inhumane conduct, albeit in the pursuit of spiritual beliefs … Jim Vadim Pesnak, I sentence you to a term of imprisonment of six years … Eugenia Pesnak, I sentence you to a term of imprisonment of three years.

Six months later the Queensland Court of Appeal also said it was important 'to impose a substantial term of imprisonment in the hope of deterring others from engaging in such objectively dangerous and unacceptable conduct whilst pursuing personal religious or spiritual beliefs'. Nevertheless, the judges agreed to substantially cut the Pesnaks' jail terms. Jim Pesnak was sentenced to four years, and Eugenia Pesnak was sentenced to two years' jail. But the good news for the Pesnaks didn't end there. The judges also agreed to set minimum terms after which the Pesnaks could apply for bail – 18 months for Jim Pesnak and nine months for Eugenia Pesnak. They said the Vollmer case was a major reason they had decided the sentences were too high.

***

And what of the woman who inspired this fatal fast?

A Spiritual Death

In her book *Dancing with my DOW (Divine One Within)*, Jasmuheen wrote:

Interviews with Mr Pesnak and his wife share how Lani refused all of his help and attention for a number of days and he was loathe to interfere with her free will and decision to continue. Her choice to go through the 21-day process is not the issue for the courts, the concern is that the caregiver did not act soon enough to seek medical care for her. I have been working with the prosecution as an independent expert witness. I had never met nor been involved in any way with either the Pesnaks or Lani Morris. Immediately after this occurred, the Self Empowerment Academy issued very strong guidelines imploring people to act responsibly at all times.

According to Britain's *Sunday Times*, Jasmuheen said that perhaps Lani Morris was not coming from the right place of integrity and did not have the right motivation.

In October 1999, Jasmuheen took up a challenge by Channel 9's *60 Minutes* for her to prove she could live without eating or drinking and agreed to be monitored 24 hours a day in a hotel for seven days. After four days, however, the show abandoned the experiment upon the advice of the head of the Queensland branch of the Australian Medical Association, Dr Beres Wenck. Jasmuheen had lost about six kilograms, was dehydrated, her pupils were dilated and her pulse rate had doubled. Dr Wenck said he feared her kidneys would fail if the experiment continued.

Jasmuheen did not let this nationally televised apparent exposé of her as a sham stop her. She blamed her problems on the show, on pollution from a nearby freeway and a lack of sleep, not on the lack of food. She said she only got about three or four hours sleep a night because a guard kept checking that she wasn't secretly eating or drinking. She also pointed out that 68 per cent of 1596 callers to the show answered 'yes' to the question: 'Do you believe a person could live for six months on nothing but air and light?'

REASONABLE DOUBT

In her letter written on 31 December 1999 for her *The Elraanis Voice*, 'international community newsletter' of 'Inspiration, Information and Illumination', Jasmuheen welcomed readers to the new millennium and told them her five-week world tour to seven countries and 12 cities talking about 'dancing with the divine' went as 'graciously and successfully as ever', despite the media.

> Thankfully, even though there has been so much media misconception evident about my work, few that come to my lectures bother to read the newspapers or watch the news, finding it all too depressing and preferring to create realities of singing hearts and honor among all. I have come to realize … my real message as a scribe for Spirit is just too boring and so the media prefer to sensationalize my private lifestyle choice of being fed by prana instead. Weird but true.

It's clear when she discusses the Pesnak case that she is far from contrite. She certainly does not accept that Lani Morris's death revealed the 21-day breatharian initiation to be dangerous nonsense. She even implies that Ms Morris died because she failed to push herself through her 'self-imposed limitations'.

> My mind goes to the 21-day initiation process that has caused so much controversy in the media this last year or two. I think about Jim and Eugenia Pesnak now serving jail time for providing a physical place for Lani Morris to undergo the process. Unable to attend the court proceedings, as I was in Europe on tour, I have no in-depth knowledge of what occurred, yet the jury found them negligent and that they could have acted sooner to save Lani's life.
>
> I remember discussing this with a friend in Germany who has literally overseen hundreds go through this 21-day initiation, and I asked at what point he would have interfered. *'I don't know when I would have,'* he replied, saying how it is so hard to tell what is a barrier that needs jumping over like a mental block that is expressing itself physically. My translator, a deeply spiritual woman, agreed. *'Sometimes*

A Spiritual Death

we just have to push ourselves to break through, that's what initiations are about – going beyond self-imposed limitations!' I know what they mean.

Yet how can initiates of ancient rites of passage share this with a modern-day world that has forgotten the importance and significance of such things as breaking barriers, and taking leaps of faith? ...

As I have always stated, the 21-day process is an initiation for a spiritual warrior, it was never intended to be offered as armchair entertainment, or as a circus for the media (which some may say my naivety with *60 Minutes* allowed it to be) ...

Yet the 21-day process is not about fasting per se. It is about stopping internal and external energy flow so that in the stillness the DOW can be experienced in all its glory. It is also about trust and surrendering and taking a leap of faith, and yes it is about symbolically dying and being reborn.

She told Brisbane's *Sunday Mail* in April 2000: 'Some people find that after the first 21-day they never need to return to food again, preferring to be pranically nourished; others don't connect deeply enough with the divine to sustain being nourished with prana without negative side-effects.'

Also in 2000 Jasmuheen 'won' two prizes she didn't want. The Australian Skeptics awarded her its Bent Spoon as the 'perpetrator of the most preposterous piece of paranormal or pseudoscientific piffle'. She also scored an international Ig Nobel for 'her book *Living on Light* which explains that although some people do eat food, they don't ever really need to'.

In 1999, *The Skeptic,* 'A Journal of Fact and Opinion', hoped that the Pesnak trial would ensure breatharianism – the 'myth of living on light' – would 'disappear without a trace'. In his article 'Breatharians Found Guilty', Barry Williams noted that the Pesnaks had claimed they had honestly and reasonably believed in breatharianism but said – as the court found – sincerely believing something is not good enough if that belief puts somebody else's life in peril. But Williams doubted the beliefs *could* have been genuinely held.

164 **REASONABLE DOUBT**

Williams: We can only question how sincerely anyone can hold a belief that they are living on cosmic energy when they must actually be eating and drinking. How can anyone be so self-deluded as to deny the evidence of their own actions?

In the same issue in an article called 'Breatharianism – just a lot of hot air?', Rosemary Sceats concluded: 'Personally, coming from a family of unreconstructed foodies, I find this idea of living without food a bit hard to swallow.'

HYPNOTISE ME

What do you do when seven people see you shoot a woman dead in her car on a sleepy suburban street? Startled by a screech of tyres on gutter, they look up from their Sunday morning gardening, dishwashing or TV viewing to see you fling open your car door and storm over to a little red sports car you have just forced to stop. They jump and blink as you fire, 'Bang! Bang! Bang! Bang!' into that car. They gape as the attacked car ramps the gutter and careers across a vacant lot with your car in hot pursuit. Some look for a film crew – 'This sort of thing doesn't happen in our neighbourhood', 'It's a movie, right?', 'It can't be for real, can it?'

What do you do when – after seven people have seen you shoot a woman in a car – you race to the home of a friend, tell them you have shot your ex–de facto, beg them to hide you and they refuse? What do you do if you then shoot yourself in the chin but survive and find yourself charged with murder? Do you plead guilty and hope for a couple of years off for not wasting the court's time? Not if you're David 'Benny' Ibrahim, you don't.

***

On 27 September 1998, 28-year-old Sue Chircop made the fatal decision to borrow the snappy red Probe sports car usually driven by her 31-year-old sister Carol. Sue didn't have a licence, but her driving ability was not going to be the problem that day. It wasn't going to kill her. What *was* going to kill her was driving towards her in a ute armed with two loaded .25 pistols. She was going to be killed by her sister's former de facto, David Ibrahim, who was furious that Carol had failed to pick up their five-year-old son, Jake, from an access visit.

Ibrahim was also bent on revenge against Carol and her father, Frank. He believed that six months earlier Frank had shot at him as he ran for his

166   REASONABLE DOUBT

life through a paddock and that his daughter had helped her father. Carol told Ibrahim's trial that Ibrahim owned guns and once even put his toddler son's hands around a gun and helped him fire shots into the air. She also said that he beat her.

Just days before the shooting, Ibrahim had left a mental institution. Staff noted he had told them he wanted to kill his ex–de facto before she took their son to Queensland. The day before the shooting a psychiatrist at Royal Melbourne Hospital diagnosed Ibrahim as angry, not depressed. On that day too, according to Carol Chircop, Ibrahim told her: 'Tell your dad his number is up. I'm coming after him and I have covered my arse by putting myself in a psychiatric hospital.'

About midday on 27 September 1998, in Copernicus Way, Keilor Downs, on Melbourne's western fringe – near where he used to live with Carol – Ibrahim saw Carol's little red car. He had driven his red Ford ute all the way from his mother's home in Newport on Melbourne's bay. He mowed down the red Probe and forced it to stop in the gutter by blocking its path. He flung open his ute's door and angrily strode over to the red car, .25 Browning pistol at the ready. Bang! Bang! Bang! Bang! He pumped four bullets through the front and side windows. Two hit Sue Chircop in the back, one scraped her boyfriend's arm. Mortally wounded, just minutes from death, Sue Chircop floored the accelerator, ramped the gutter and drove across the vacant lot. Having escaped her killer, Ms Chircop collapsed at the steering wheel and died. Her terrified boyfriend, Tom Falzon, fled the car, jumped the fence of a nearby property and begged its residents to take him in. They refused and he hid in the garden.

After losing track of his dying victim, Ibrahim drove to the nearby home of long-term friends, the Prevolseks. Shaking, he disturbed Margaret Prevolsek as she did her gardening. His fury had so blinded him that *he still thought he had shot his ex–de facto, not her sister.*

Ibrahim: Margie! Margie! You've got to do me a favour. I've just shot Carol. I just need you to hide me for an hour so yous can calm me down. I need time to think. Can I put my car in the garage?

As Mrs Prevolsek ran inside to get her husband, Tom, Ibrahim added: 'Wait a minute, I'm just going to get my guns.' Inside, Mrs Prevolsek interrupted Tom's television watching by announcing: 'Benny's here. He's just shot Carol.' Both of them thought Ibrahim was 'very angry, very mad'. To Mr Prevolsek, he 'seemed to be boiling' – his eyes were rolling.

Ibrahim: Tom, I need a favour. I have just shot Carol. Can I put my car in your garage?
Mr Prevolsek: I have got kids here. I have got a family. Don't get me involved.
Ibrahim: What should I do?
Mr Prevolsek: Go in the paddock. Leave your car in the paddock.

Mr Prevolsek later recalled: 'That's when he just turned around and put the gun under his chin and shot himself.'

Mrs Prevolsek: He put the gun under his chin. I think he used two hands. Then I heard a bang when he pulled the trigger and he dropped to the floor. Then there was blood coming from his neck and on to the floor. His body was moving. He blocked the whole hallway. I didn't know what to do. I panicked and thought about what he might do to the kids. I ran up and down the loungeroom in panic.

As the wounded Ibrahim lay in the hallway, Mr Prevolsek squatted next to his friend.

Mr Prevolsek: Benny, you fuckin' idiot. How could you do this in front of my kids?

Mr Prevolsek grabbed Ibrahim's two pistols and threw them in his garage. Then he phoned for the police and an ambulance.

Later that day, doctors removed the bullet from next to Ibrahim's nose. It had passed through his neck and mouth but, amazingly, had not made it to his brain. After the operation, police charged him with Sue Chircop's murder.

168   REASONABLE DOUBT

In hospital, Ibrahim said he had no memory of shooting Sue Chircop. He asked the police officer guarding him: 'Am I in trouble? Have I done something really bad?' Two days later when a police officer showed him a newspaper report of the shooting, Ibrahim asked: 'Was that me?' Later that day, Ibrahim asked his police guard: 'Would you shoot me and put me out of this misery?'

***

That was the prosecution's story. The story Ibrahim told a Supreme Court jury two years and nine months after the shooting was slightly, but significantly, different.

Ibrahim denied that on the day he killed Sue Chircop he was angry with Carol for not picking up their child. Disappointed, maybe, but not angry. He also denied seeking revenge against her and her father. He said he was petrified of Frank Chircop, who he said had shot at him twice. Ibrahim said the first shooting was in 1990 when he drove around to see Carol at her family home during one of their many split-ups.

> *Ibrahim*: I drove in the court. I was stopping the car. Frank Chircop was standing on the balcony with a gun, right. He shot at the car …
> He got the car on the left-hand side. I didn't know what was going on. I just took off. The next day, I spoke to Carol. She just laughed and said, 'If you want to know why he did that, go and ask him.'
> I was scared of the bloke. I didn't know what he was going to do next.

Ibrahim said his next major confrontation with Frank Chircop was in March 1998 – about six months before the shooting.

> *Ibrahim*: I was walking home back through the paddock. I saw the red Probe Carol was driving. She drove on the wrong side of the road and her car like drove up a bit on the gutter … Carol winds down her window. I don't really remember if she yelled out 'You're fucked. You're fucked,' before or after I was shot. The passenger-

side door opened. When the passenger-side door opened the interior light went on. I seen Frank hop out of the car. Frank Chircop – this bloke here [pointing to Mr Chircop in the court]. He went around to the front of the car … He had something in his hands. It was a long-barrelled gun. It was a shotgun … The gun went off. When I heard the gun go off there was a flame that came out of the gun. I turned around. I ran in the paddock. Frank chased after me. A second shot went off. That's when he got me in the back of the head … What struck me in the back of the head felt like pellets that hit me, pushed me to the floor, so I fell face down on the dirt … I didn't see Frank get back in the car but as I got back up and I started to run again, I turned my head and the car was driving off.

Ibrahim agreed that he had not told police until some weeks later that Frank had shot him. Frank Chircop was never charged over the incident. Carol Chircop agreed that she had stopped her car to berate Ibrahim on that day but said that her sister, Sue – not her father – was with her at the time. She denied her father owned a gun or that Ibrahim had been shot, although she said she had heard 'a sound like a car backfiring or a gunshot'.

Ibrahim denied beating Carol – except for one slap a few years earlier – and said the main problem in the relationship was her frequent gambling on poker machines and demands for money. Carol Chircop acknowledged playing pokies about three times a week.

In his trial, Ibrahim said it was just coincidence that he came upon Carol Chircop's red Probe about 11.45am on 27 September 1998 near her home. He denied stalking his ex–de facto or her father with murderous intent, saying he had been delivering a gun back to a friend as a final act before committing suicide when he saw the red Probe.

Ibrahim: I was sad. I wasn't eating much. There was just nothing to look forward to. There were threats against my life. I didn't know what to do … My head was just all over the place …

That day, to me, right, in my own mind I didn't have anything to look forward to so I had the full intention of taking my own life …

I remember seeing the car as I was driving to my friend's house. I seen the car. I wanted to ask Carol why she never picked up Jake. I pulled the car over.

Defence barrister: How did you do that?

Ibrahim: That I don't recall, actually how I blocked it off … I jumped out of the car. The driver raised her hand … There was a gun in her hand. I didn't know what to do. I shit myself. I pulled out a gun and I fired.

Barrister: How were you feeling at that time?

Ibrahim: I was shitting myself.

Barrister: When you fired the gun what were you trying to do?

Ibrahim: I was trying to stop her shooting me.

Barrister: Can you remember, now you look back on the event, who it was who was pointing the gun at you?

Ibrahim: At the time I thought it was Carol, but I know now it was Sue.

Barrister: Now everyone knows, of course, it was Sue that was in the motor car but when you look back on the event, when you think about the event and go through it in your mind, what is your recollection?

Ibrahim: My recollection, right, it is still Carol …

Barrister: When you saw the gun pointing at you what did you think was going to happen?

Ibrahim: I thought she was going to shoot to kill me. She pulled a gun at me. I seen the gun.

I fired the gun … I thought I just fired twice. After that I don't remember much at all … The next recollection was, I remember waking up, right, at the hospital. I don't remember any more than that …

Barrister: Did you have any intent to shoot Carol prior to or on that day?

Ibrahim: I had no intention of harming anybody but myself. I just wouldn't do that.

Hypnotise Me

Under cross-examination by prosecutor Geoff Horgan SC, Ibrahim stressed the fear he felt when he shot Sue Chircop.

Ibrahim: My life was in danger. I had no choice. There wasn't time to think of anything else. I did not set out to harm anybody but myself, Mr Horgan.

I was scared. What was I supposed to do? Let her shoot me?

Ibrahim's excuse of self-defence had some big hurdles to overcome. These included that no gun was found in the sports car, that Sue Chircop had been shot in the back and that while Carol might have had some motive to point a gun at her bitterly estranged ex–de facto, Sue Chircop appeared to have no reason to shoot Ibrahim. Another problem for the defence was that Ibrahim refused to name the friend to whom he claimed to be returning the gun when he happened to see the red Probe. Saying he did not want to get the 'friend' into trouble and also that he feared for his safety, Ibrahim refused to name the gun owner, even when he was threatened with contempt of court. The prosecution pointed out that this meant his claim could not be checked with the friend. If Ibrahim had shot in self-defence he also had to explain why he hadn't told the Prevolseks this. Finally, the defence team also had to explain why Ibrahim had taken two years – and two hypnosis sessions – before remembering seeing a gun and firing in self-defence.

Defence barrister Roy Punshon SC tackled the 'no-gun-found-in-the-Probe' problem by telling the jurors it was reasonably possible Tom Falzon had taken the gun when he fled the car. The prosecution hit back, saying it was 'absolute nonsense' that Mr Falzon would hide the gun rather than defend himself with it.

The defence said it was also possible that Sue Chircop, being part of the Chircop family, which hated and had terrified Ibrahim, could have felt she had a reason to point a gun at Ibrahim.

The prosecution said a person who had just defended himself would not chase after the person he had just defended himself against.

Mr Horgan: That's not a person who is fleeing, who is afraid for his life. That's a person who is seeking revenge to finish off the job. He goes to the Prevolseks straight afterwards and he doesn't say to the Prevolseks, 'Listen, I've just had the most shocking experience. I've had to defend myself, I am scared for my life' … It was, 'I shot Carol. I need a place to hide.' That's not self-defence, members of the jury.

The prosecutor said Ibrahim's attempted suicide was the 'final act of a desperate, violent, impetuous man, a man who had done what he wanted to do, namely kill. The Prevolseks would not hide him and give him time to think, so this desperate, violent, impetuous man tried to kill himself.'

Mr Horgan: His actions after the event … are all indicative of somebody having committed a murder and being conscious of the fact.

The defence rejected this.

Mr Punshon: He's panicked. It's the behaviour of a man whose mind is everywhere and his behaviour becomes explicable in terms of panic and confusion. Realises he's shot his wife. You will remember exactly how the Prevolseks described how he looked. He was not normal.

The defence argued that Ibrahim's failure to tell the Prevolseks that he had acted in self-defence was 'understandable given the traumatic experience he had just been through and a memory fragmented by illness and disability'.

That left the problem of why it had taken Ibrahim about two years to say he had seen a gun and fired in self-defence. Why had he only remembered the gun – or indeed anything about the shooting – after two sessions of hypnosis?

A memory expert – neuropsychologist David Stokes – told the court that Ibrahim suffered a 'high anxiety' disorder, which made it difficult for him to register stressful incidents in a way that could be remembered later.

Had hypnosis successfully retrieved a genuine memory from Ibrahim of seeing a gun being pointed at him – even though that memory falsely put that gun in Carol Chircop's hand? Had Ibrahim duped his hypnotist into helping him 'trick up' an excuse of self-defence? Had hypnosis allowed Ibrahim to really think he remembered seeing a gun pointed at him, when in reality he hadn't? For just the seventh or eighth time an Australian jury got to watch an accused person being hypnotised. Hypnosis was on trial.

Hypnosis was defended by a former president and the then-treasurer of the International Society of Hypnosis, a man with 35 years' experience in psychiatry, Professor Graham Burrows. Professor Burrows told the court he was convinced that in two hypnosis sessions he had managed to get Ibrahim to genuinely remember the shooting of Sue Chircop. He said that initial testing had found that Ibrahim was hypnotisable. His hypnotisibility score was 3.5 out of 5. Professor Burrows said he managed to get Ibrahim to recall, even relive, the shooting by getting him to see it as if he was watching it on television.

Prof Burrows: He developed what we call eye catalepsy, his lids flickered like mad and there was a lot of eyeball roll, which is … something you can't simulate …

He was really quite distressed … I thought it was genuine …

I believe he thought he saw Carol … He was very hot, sweating, anxious … I think it was a panic attack. He was reliving the experience.

The jury saw a video of Ibrahim being hypnotised by Professor Burrows. Unfortunately, for about half of it they could not see his face because the camera got stuck panning down but when they did see him, they saw a sweating, heavy-breathing man apparently in a trance. They heard him apparently remembering the day he killed. Breathing quickly, he talked about seeing Carol 'pulling something out'. Breathing faster, he told Professor Burrows it was a 'gun' and added: 'I shot … the person holding the gun.' Asked why, he replied, 'I was scared.'

174 REASONABLE DOUBT

Under cross-examination, Professor Burrows agreed that many eminent psychiatrists did not believe that hypnosis could retrieve genuine memories or, at least, that hypnotised subjects could not distinguish between genuine and false memories. Professor Burrows, who said he was also an advisor to Australia's False Memory Association, agreed there was a 'healthy debate' in psychiatric circles about the possible effectiveness of hypnosis in recovering memories. He even agreed that subjects who felt great pressure to produce memories could 'recall events that never occurred'.

Mr Horgan: People can believe they saw things that never happened, or they can believe they saw things differently from the way they actually occurred?

Prof Burrows: Yes.

Mr Horgan: Hypnosis can add to this process. Agreed?

Prof Burrows: It can. Badly used … That's why it's [hypnosis to recover memory] been used in this court and this land only, as far as I know, only about six or seven times in 35 years.

The prosecutor then went in for the kill.

Mr Horgan: Doctor, let me suggest to you that in that [hypnosis] session you put into his head the idea of self-defence. You created, in that session, the idea of self-defence …

Prof Burrows: I don't think I did …

Mr Horgan: [You asked Ibrahim] 'Yeah well, I was just interested in whether you felt that she did actually pull a gun out and that you acted in self-defence?' He has not suggested anything to you at that stage about acting in self-defence. Never once.

Prof Burrows: OK, that is true.

Mr Horgan: You introduce the idea, don't you?

Prof Burrows: I suppose I must have, yes, unintentionally.

Mr Horgan: Whether it's unintentional or not … it invalidates the whole process.

Prof Burrows: Does it?

Hypnotise Me

Mr Horgan: What do you think?

Prof Burrows: I don't know.

Mr Horgan: You introduce self-defence …

Prof Burrows: Wrong word usage. I accept that.

The professor stressed, however, that he found 'offensive' the prosecutor's suggestion that he had tried to school Ibrahim in an excuse of self-defence.

Nearly two years and eight months after Sue Chircop was shot dead, Ibrahim's jury deliberated for just two hours before declaring him guilty of murder. When the verdict was announced, Ibrahim rolled his eyes briefly and shrugged his shoulders almost imperceptibly.

Outside the court Frank Chircop said he was 'very, very, happy; more than happy' with the verdict. He also took the chance to slam hypnotism.

Mr Chircop: It's bullshit, I tell you. You get that professor fellow to hypnotise me without drugs and I will tell him any sort of bullshit I like.

About a month later, Justice John Coldrey said that at the time Ibrahim fired the fatal shot, he believed he was shooting Carol Chircop.

Justice Coldrey: In fact, you had not. Cruelly and tragically, you had shot her sister Sue … Your failure to accurately identify your victim may well be attributable to your state of anger at the time of the shooting. The anger was a manifestation of the ongoing animosity you felt towards your former de facto wife. I have no doubt the jury would have been satisfied that when you fired the fatal shots, you intended to kill the person you believed to be Carol Chircop.

The jury might not have accepted that hypnosis had produced a genuine memory of a gun being pointed at Ibrahim, but Justice Coldrey was willing to accept that Ibrahim had not just used hypnosis to try to get off murder.

Justice Coldrey: There is a considerable body of expert opinion that hypnosis produces illusory memories … I am prepared to find that your evidence of shooting in self-defence was the result of what may be described as confabulation or false memory rather than any wilfully false account by you.

The judge said he accepted that Ibrahim had been in a state of emotional turmoil – including feelings of depression, hopelessness, anger and resentment – when he murdered Sue Chircop.

> *Justice Coldrey*: Nonetheless, this was a grave offence. It was premeditated … You set out armed and with the intention of confronting Carol Chircop, and shooting her.

The judge noted that in the run-up to the shooting, as well as getting psychiatric help, Ibrahim had also been self-medicating on marijuana and, perhaps, cocaine.

The judge said he had taken into account Ibrahim's deprived childhood. The seventh of eight children, Ibrahim regularly ran away from his drunken, violent father. From the age of nine he lived in foster care or boys' homes until his older brother Nick took him in when he was about 13. With a low-normal IQ of 80, Ibrahim struggled at school, leaving in the first term of Form 3. After that, Ibrahim was mostly unemployed except for a little work in the building industry and at an abattoir.

Justice Coldrey sentenced 30-year-old Ibrahim to a maximum 19 years' jail and set a minimum nonparole sentence of 14 years.

After the sentencing, Professor Burrows said he still thought that Ibrahim had been properly hypnotised.

> *Prof Burrows*: I thought that on the basis of the balance of probabilities that what he actually thought he saw [the gun being pointed at him], he probably did.

But Professor Burrows acknowledged that hypnotists could never be certain their subjects were not pretending or that recovered memories accorded with what really happened.

He said, however, that that did not mean serious hypnotism could not play its part in the justice system, but that it was probably more helpful in police investigations, rather than as evidence in court. Professor Burrows said, for instance, that hypnotism could help witnesses remember licence plates on cars.

Two years after Ibrahim was sentenced, his lawyers tried to persuade the Victorian Court of Appeal that his trial was unfair because his judge had not warned the jury strongly enough against assuming he was guilty because of what he did *after* the shooting. They argued his case was similar to that of Gabriel Omar Chang, who won a new trial for this reason.

Chang denied murdering a woman friend who died in his flat even though he admitted hitting her head with a meat tenderiser and was caught near her half-dug bush grave wearing a blond wig. He admitted trying to bury her – and trying to disguise himself with the wig – but said he had only done so out of panic. He said she had died after he pushed her away and she accidently fell and hit her head on the arm of a chair. He said he only tapped her with the meat tenderiser to see if she was really dead. (See the full story in 'Blond wig and meat tenderiser', *Killer Excuses*, Wayne Howell, The Five Mile Press, 2005, page 100.)

The judges, however, rejected the defence claim that – like in the Chang case – Ibrahim may have been convicted just on what he did after the killing.

Appeal Justice Geoffrey Eames: The Crown case was a particularly powerful one, with seven eyewitnesses … none of whom saw a gun in the hands of the victim … The whole case turned on the question of whether the victim had produced a gun, thus causing … [Ibrahim] to shoot in self-defence. If the jury concluded beyond a reasonable doubt that the victim did *not* have a gun at the time, then the accused must have been convicted of murder …

This was an exceptionally strong case. Indeed, there was force in the submission … [by the prosecutor] that not only was it an overwhelming Crown case, but the defence case bordered on the incredible.

WARNING SHOT

Massacre
Terror Hits Abortion Industry

A FANATICAL anti-abortionist yesterday became Australia's worst mass murderer, killing dozens of people inside the country's most famous abortion clinic.

Up to 41 people are believed to have burnt to death, trapped inside an inferno at the Fertility Control Clinic in East Melbourne.

Several fire trucks raced to the blaze at the historic building just after 11am yesterday, but by the time they had doused the flames, the building was completely destroyed.

Then firefighters made a gruesome discovery – piles of incinerated bodies.

The victims had no hope of escaping excruciating deaths – they had been tied up and gagged and the clinic's doors had been jammed shut with specially adapted metal tubes.

It's believed several had also been shot.

The massacre comes five years after the killing of 35 people at Port Arthur – the world's worst single-episode murder-by-shooting spree in peacetime.

Not far from the smouldering clinic in Wellington Parade, police yesterday found a chilling message made out of letters circled in a newspaper article. It was:

Anyone who protects sewerage is sewage and will get treated like sewage and the same goes for anyone who works on or with patronised sewerage. By the time I get through, there will not be an abortionist in Melbourne left deathless. We will now see if the Vic Police are in the same class as the Nazi Gestapo and try to protect these slaughters.

In scratchy handwriting, firefighters found another spine-chilling note taped to the clinic's front door:

We regret to advise that as a result of a fatal accident involving some members of staff, we have been forced at short notice to cancel all appointments today.

Among the clinic's ruins the semi-charred remnants of another note in the same handwriting was found:

Please wait in the waiting room (an arrow pointing the way). *There could be a 10-to 15-minute delay today.*

Investigators say kerosene was sprinkled through the building and set alight with blazing sticks.

Set up in the face of mass anti-abortion demonstrations in 1972 by pioneering abortion rights campaigner Bertram Wainer, the clinic was the first in Australia to openly provide abortions. Since it started, anti-abortion campaigners have kept up an almost daily protest outside its front gate.

All over Australia, abortion doctors fear their clinics could be the next victim.

Police have no clues as to who committed this massacre.

Warning Shot

***

If things had gone the way Peter James Knight had fantasised – and planned – for months, this is the kind of newspaper article he would have been reading on Tuesday 17 July 2001. While the rest of Australia would have been reeling from the news, Knight would have been gleefully reading an article like this while sitting hidden in his camp in dense bush in Candlebark Park, not far from the 'Mcmansions' of Templestowe in Melbourne's east. The 47-year-old would have been congratulating himself on single-handedly dealing a killer blow to Australia's abortion industry.

***

Knight had started thinking of taking on the abortion industry many months earlier while sitting in the ramshackle tin-and-logs humpy he called home deep in the Killabutta State Forest, Gumble, in central New South Wales – about 800km north of Melbourne. The nearest town – Molong – was about 15km away. Molong was about 35km north of Orange and about 90km north of Bathurst – where Knight was born on New Year's Day 1954.

The youngest of six children, Knight was four when his farming family moved to Molong. About seven years later they moved to Orange. It was then, at the age of 11, that Knight lost interest in studying at his Catholic school. As he put it later, he became a 'TV addict'. He did not have any friends at school and left at the age of 16, after finishing Year 10. Knight and his four older sisters and older brother were closer to their devoutly Catholic mother than their father. He later said his childhood was 'not one of the greatest, but not bad either'. He had got on well with his mother and siblings but not so well with his father, believing he drank too much alcohol. He later said that while his father had been domineering, he had not been violent. By his early 20s, Knight had developed extreme views. One sister remembered him calling his father a 'murderer' because he wasn't opposed to the sale of cigarettes.

When he was 22, Knight went travelling. For two years he moved around, occasionally getting jobs picking fruit. Then, for about 15 years, he lived in Brisbane working as a factory hand. He became more and more reclusive. One of his sisters remembered his flat was infested with cockroaches. Finally, he left Brisbane because it got 'too big' and had become 'a different place to what it used to be'. He returned to central New South Wales and set up a camp in the Killabutta State Forest because it 'was as good a place as any'.

Because he believed the Bible forbade the taking of oaths, Knight decided not to work, pay taxes or collect the dole. Around his humpy, he planted fruit trees, grapevines and vegetables and dug a metre-deep dam, but the trees bore little fruit and he mainly lived off flour discarded from a nearby flour mill. At first he trapped rabbits, but stopped because he found it a 'disturbing and vicious practice'.

Locals dubbed him 'the Yowie', but considered him a harmless eccentric – intelligent and polite but painfully shy and odd. Occasionally the heavily bearded Knight would cycle into Molong but he would mostly walk with his head down and seldom spoke to anybody. He didn't completely cut ties with society, however, regularly cycling 50km to Orange to see his elderly father and sister.

'Several kids used to go out there and eat his fruit; he'd never take money or anything,' John Farr, a former Molong mayor, told the *Age*. 'I understand he used to get very mad about people who sold cigarettes to children.' Neighbour Bill Evans said: 'He seemed like a bit of a sad sort of bloke, but I thought he was just harmless.' Shirley McLaughlin remembered her son, Adam, getting on well with Knight, even helping him trap rabbits. 'He seemed harmless. We never had any trouble with him. He kept to himself. A lot of young fellas used to go out there and throw rotten eggs in his water and harass him but he never retaliated in any way,' Ms McLaughlin told the *Herald Sun*.

One anecdote elderly neighbour Bob Evans (Bill Evans's father) told the *Herald Sun* seemed to shed some light on Knight's odd character. In 1997 Knight's sister asked police to look for him. She was worried because he had not visited their elderly father for his birthday. Before a search party could even be gathered, however, Knight resurfaced. For Mr

Evans that was strange enough, but what happened next was just bizarre: 'He knocked on the front door, poked a $20 note at me and said he was sorry to have caused so much trouble – this from a bloke who'd hardly spoken to me in 10 years.'

By late 2000, Knight was no longer satisfied with being a hermit; with not causing anyone any trouble. He had had lots of time to think of what was wrong with the world. Now it was time to act.

His first plan to make a difference was triggered, on a visit to Melbourne, when he looked through the *Yellow Pages* for a printer. A couple of pages before 'printers' he found ads for 'pregnancy termination services'. That revelation of the availability of abortion helped him choose his crusade: he would force the telecommunications giant Telstra to remove all ads for abortion clinics from the *Yellow Pages*. Without any *Yellow Pages* ads, Knight thought, thousands of unborn babies' lives would be saved. Knight decided to enlist the help of anti-abortion groups to start a boycott of Telstra.

Fired with a zealot's enthusiasm, Knight took his plan to Right to Life. Unused to society's niceties, he turned up unannounced at its Melbourne headquarters during the Christmas holidays in January 2001. Luckily for him, the organisation's president, Margaret Tighe, was catching up with some paperwork. Ms Tighe thought he was 'a bit scruffy looking, but there was an attempt to be neat'. She said he was 'very intense and un-smiling' while asking her to help him boycott Telstra because it allowed telephone directory ads for abortion clinics. Knight wasn't put off when Ms Tighe told him Right to Life wasn't big enough to organise such a boycott and, anyway, it also advertised in the *Yellow Pages*. He wouldn't stop talking, so Ms Tighe fobbed him off by asking him to write his plan down for consideration by a committee.

Ms Tighe said Knight returned soon afterwards with his 'well-written' proposal, 'closely written on a scrappy-looking piece of paper', but she said it was signed 'Peter Sweeney'. He returned a couple of times but even Ms Tighe, who is known for her forceful opposition to abortion, found Knight too intense. Once, she asked her assistant: 'Go and get rid of him please.'

Knight also had little support for his idea from the regular protesters outside the Wellington Parade clinic. Richard Grant of The Helpers of God's Precious Infants told Knight he didn't think Telstra was responsible for what went into the *Yellow Pages*. Like Ms Tighe, Mr Grant also found Knight 'very intense', remembering that he 'spoke only a few inches from your face every time'.

Disappointed at his failure, Knight travelled to a 12 March anti-abortion protest outside Sydney's 2UE and then retreated to his forest humpy. His failed mission had confirmed his misanthropy: people were stupid and cowardly. He decided to go it alone.

He started gathering twine and metal brackets and other bits and pieces to use in a lone assault on the abortion industry. Like an Australian version of the Unabomber, this recluse was determined to make his mark on the world.

A couple of months later, Knight snared the most important things he needed – a Winchester rifle and some ammunition. To get these, he rode about 60km west to Parkes and broke into a sports shooting store. Presumably, to placate a God unhappy with those breaking his Commandments, Knight left the shop owner a letter:

> Sorry mate but I had to do it. Keep the bill for the items and remember the price of the rifles. It may take a year or a bit more, but I'll pay you back when I can with interest.

Knight then made his way back to Melbourne. By June 2001 he had set himself up in a well-hidden camp in Candlebark Park – a perfect base from which to launch his assault.

On 4 June 2001, Knight broke into his enemy's camp. He didn't take or destroy anything in the Wellington Parade clinic; he just checked the lay of the land. He also mingled with protesters, paying particular attention to the security guard, noting that they – first a woman and then a man – left just after 10am.

In the days before Monday 16 July 2001, in his little hideaway, Knight meticulously prepared. On a newspaper, he painstakingly circled individual letters to make his 'no abortionist in Melbourne left deathless' threat. He bought two four-litre and four two-litre plastic containers and filled these with kerosene. For each of these he got a second lid in which he punctured holes – so he could sprinkle kerosene all over the clinic. He also filed and drilled blue metal tubes so they could jam doors – to stop abortionists trying to flee the inferno. To start that inferno, Knight wrapped foam over the tops of some sticks and bought three cigarette lighters – not for lighting cigarettes.

He wanted to turn that clinic into the hell he believed abortionists deserved to be in.

Knight figured with the security guard gone and his Winchester, he should be able to persuade those in the clinic to bind and gag themselves. People were, after all, stupid and cowardly. He sewed pieces of cloth as gags and made sure he had plenty of twine.

Also to give himself time, Knight wrote a couple of polite and official-sounding notes to stop anyone stumbling inopportunely into his scheme.

The most careful preparation went into the Winchester. He adapted it so that he could fire it from inside a hessian bag.

On the morning of Monday 16 July 2001, Knight – wearing a rolled-up balaclava, shabby desert boots, jeans, a flannelette shirt and dirty white gloves and sporting a longish greying goatee beard – rode his bicycle laden with paraphernalia for a massacre to the East Melbourne clinic. He hid the bike nearby in a rubbish bin enclave and waited till 10.20am – until the protesters and, he thought, the security guard, had left. With his high-power rifle hidden in the hessian bag and carrying a large plastic bag, Knight walked through the clinic's front door. Already inside were 41 people, including about 26 members of the public. Some were there for abortions, but many just wanted fertility control advice or various other female health services.

Moments after quietly walking in, Knight's plans for a horrific crusade began to fall apart.

His first problem was that the unarmed security guard – 44-year-old Steven Rogers – had *not* yet left for the day. He had been having a smoke outside with a partner of one of the clinic's patients – carpenter Tim

184   REASONABLE DOUBT

Anderson. On his way home, Mr Rogers made the fatal mistake of asking an odd-looking man what he had in his big bags.

A four-months-pregnant law student, Lillian Kitanov, was just a couple of metres away from Knight ('a male with scraggy clothes') and Mr Rogers when they met. She was at the reception counter organising an appointment with a doctor (it wasn't for an abortion) and remembered it was a 'calm' conversation, but then …

> *Ms Kitanov*: I remember the male actually showed him [the security guard] what he had in his Hessian bag … and I had seen the gun … The security guard was taken aback but not really stressing out or worrying … [The gunman said] 'I've got a gun here … It's for real,' and the security guard goes: 'Are you serious?' and the gunman said: 'Yeah man, I'm serious.' I realised the situation I was in and the security guard has taken a step back.

The law student said that just at that dangerously awkward moment, her construction-worker boyfriend, Sandro De Maria, who had gone to get her Medicare card from the car, tried to get into the clinic. Knight was blocking the door but moved aside, telling Mr De Maria: 'You're right, mate. Come in.'

> *Ms Kitanov*: The gunman had the gun pointed at the security guard … Nothing was said at all. The whole room was calm. We were just watching. I was just watching because I couldn't believe it … Then the gun goes off … and the gunman actually shot the security guard and I saw him shoot. It went to his left shoulder and then he just went up against the cabinets, the filing cabinets and then I saw the gunman had turned the gun towards me. I just saw him look around. The only people that were in the room at that stage were myself and Sandro. I don't know where the receptionist went after the security guard had got shot …
>
> After he shot the security guard, I just saw the gun within seconds come to be pointed at my stomach. I was about 30cm away …

I was basically just waiting to get shot; the way he had shot the security guard – just so cool and calm. I could just see that he was looking for somebody else and when he came to point the gun at me, I was so scared.

I was looking at the barrel of the gun, where the bullet comes out. I was waiting for the bullet to come. I was clenching my hands ... I was just waiting for the impact.

Then all of a sudden, I just remember seeing two hands grab the barrel of the gun and push it away from me and up into the ceiling and I saw Sandro. It was Sandro that actually grabbed the gun off the gunman ... Sandro had the gun pointed at the ceiling and the gun was going all over the place ... They were coming back over to me ... I was screaming and hysterical and Sandro was just wrestling with him.

... As Sandro was scuffling with him and Sandro had him round the chest, I heard Sandro say something like: 'Help me,' or 'Get him,' and there was another guy [Tim Anderson] had actually come and grabbed the man with the gun from behind his neck and shoulders.

Sandro was trying to keep it in the air in a stable position and the gunman was trying to get Sandro's hands off the gun. I saw Sandro try to get the gun off the gunman. He actually punched him in the face to try to get him to let go of the gun ... Three times I saw him [Sandro] punch him ...

I thought of going around to the reception desk and ringing the police but I was too nervous and scared so I ran out of the entrance of the clinic and started yelling out if anybody had a mobile phone to ring the police ...

I ended up running back into the clinic to see if I could do anything ... Sandro was scuffling with the gunman ... close to the door ... I couldn't get to walk in because they were right in front of me.

Mr De Maria said that he first realised something was up when in the periphery of his vision he saw 'something going up'.

Mr De Maria: When I turned I saw what looked like a hessian bag and a split second later I heard a shot being fired ... I saw the gunman recoil ... I was just standing there in shock. I didn't actually see the security guard being shot ... I just had my eye on him [Knight] ... He was holding [the gun] to his shoulder and his left arm would be holding it under the stock as in the firing position ...

After that, he lowered the rifle down to about waist level. He kind of looked a little bit to his right and then to his left around the room ... Then he saw Lillian standing to the left near the door and he pointed the gun around her stomach area ... I was looking at him in the face, at his eyes and the way he looked around the room ... I could just see he was looking for his next person to shoot and when he'd seen Lillian and pointed the gun, he had locked on. I believe he was ready to shoot by the look in his eyes ...

At that point when he was pointing the gun at Lillian, I kind of lunged at him – at the gun.

I grabbed the barrel and lifted it up, so it pointed up. He had kind of moved back and with that another shot had gone off, which must have hit the ceiling because the rifle was pointed up. I have pushed him back against the wall, still holding the rifle up and holding him ... I actually kicked him in the groin ... I don't know if I connected or not in the struggle of it all.

He was trying to pull the gun away from me and I still had a hold of it.

I knew not to let go of this gun.

A big guy [Tim Anderson] grabbed him from around the shoulders. I then got the opportunity when I could just hold it [the gun] with my left hand and I remember hitting him in the face a couple of times. At that point, he had kind of released the firearm and someone from behind me – I didn't know who – had grabbed the firearm out of my hand.

He was crouching low ... because Tim was holding him from behind and I punched him again and he fell to the ground. After he had fallen to the ground, the guy that was helping me had grabbed him by the back of the hair and he was trying to pull him to the ground ...

I then grabbed his arm and I pinned his elbow to the ground and bent his wrist backwards so he didn't move ... He just said: 'You're hurting my wrist. Let me go.' Which, obviously, I refused to do and a couple of times he was just moaning because it was hurting, or whatever.

During the struggle at one point, when we were near the back waiting room, I saw the security guard. He was leaning up against the cabinet and he had blood coming out of his mouth. His eyes had rolled back. [Mr De Maria wipes away a tear.] ... I then saw him again later on – a few minutes – and he was on the ground ... I saw blood, a pool of blood everywhere ...

When the police came ... I remember telling them: 'It's all right, the guy, he's unarmed.'

I saw someone had ripped open his [Mr Rogers'] shirt and I saw where the actual shot hit his chest. [Mr De Maria breaks down in tears] I saw the bullet wound. His chest was all black from the shot. I saw the blood.

Tim Anderson remembered Steve Rogers borrowing a cigarette from him and the two of them having a smoke and a 'bit of a chat' before Mr Rogers went back inside to pick up his keys and head home.

Mr Anderson: Maybe five, 10 minutes later, I was reading a book and I heard ... a loud bang ... It startled me. I looked up from my book. From where I was sitting, I could just see into the reception area. I could see some smoke and fibre floating in the air ... I suppose from curiosity, I leant forward on my chair and noticed two people wrestling ... I got off my chair and went into the waiting room ... Just to stop them wrestling and making a noise ... to get them out of the reception area ...

As I came in, where they were sort of moving around and as they spun around, an object came in front of me. It was in a plastic bag ...

inside the bag I could see a long metal tube … things just clicked together and then I realised it was a gun. I grabbed, I suppose, both men … with the intention of making that gun mine …

We sort of wrestled in a group back towards the reception area … The gun was in front of me … I grabbed the gun and moved it away from the other two people and as I did that someone else [Brett Cassar] came from behind me … the momentum took it towards him and I asked him to grab it and take it out of the room.

Mr Anderson said it took him a while to work out which of the wrestlers was the gunman.

Mr Anderson: I stood back and from, I suppose, reactions and the way people look it became apparent to me who had previously had control of the gun.

He didn't let up after Mr Cassar took the gun out of the clinic.

Mr Anderson: I suppose I panicked a bit. I didn't know if he had anything else … so I punched him in the back of the head … but the punches weren't seeming to do anything. The person [Mr De Maria] from the other side was also punching him and he didn't seem to falter … I lifted my knee into his thigh a couple of times and then dragged him to the ground … We had him pinned down. He expressed a bit of discomfort … He was asking if he could be turned over because his back was hurting … I just said, you know: 'Stay there. Don't fight us and you won't actually get hurt.' I remember asking him: 'What have you done?' but there was not really a response.

Mr Anderson said that when he and Mr De Maria finally had Knight subdued, he heard a woman saying she had called the police.

Mr Anderson: As I turned to look where the voice was coming from … I noticed a man slumped against the cabinet. [Mr Anderson pauses, choking back tears.] I recognised it was Steve, the security guard. I said to the people who told me they had called the police: 'Get an ambulance! Get an ambulance! He's been shot!' ... Then I thought: 'We're in a clinic.' So I yelled: 'Get a doctor! Can someone get a doctor!' Then I looked at Steve. I told him to 'Hang on'.

Brett Cassar said that after hearing a bang, he looked in the waiting room and saw three men struggling. When he moved towards them to try to break it up, one yelled out: 'Grab the gun.' He did that, ran out of the clinic, down the road, dumped the rifle at a nearby florist and returned.

After hearing a bang, seeing two men struggling *and* the stricken Mr Rogers, one of the clinic's nurses ran upstairs to find a doctor. When she couldn't find one, she joined many other terrified nurses who had locked themselves in the changeroom. They only ventured out when everything was quiet.

One of the clinic's doctors, Kathy Lewis, heard two gunshots about 10.30am. Thinking they had come from outside, she went to the window to see what was happening but when she heard 'a lot of confusion and screaming' she realised the shot had come from inside the clinic.

Dr Lewis: I went down the main staircase towards the gunshots to see what was going on ... I saw a person on the ground being held down by two other men and he was struggling quite a lot and I said to them: 'Where's the gun?' They said: 'No, it's gone.' I said: 'Do you need a hand?' They said: 'No, help that guy.' They meant Steve. It was only then that I realised Steve was slumped in the corner against the filing cabinet ... He was unconscious ... I went across to see what I could do for him ... I can't actually remember whether he was still breathing at that time or not. I think Jamie, the clinic manager, was in the area ... and I said: 'Go get Greg Levin or one of the other doctors. Get him to bring a resuscitating machine from the theatre' ...

REASONABLE DOUBT

I pulled Steve down so he was lying flat on the ground, so I could start trying to resuscitate him. I tore the clothes off the front of his chest – I could see he was bleeding from there. When I looked, there was a large gunshot wound to the right-hand side of his upper chest …

Choking back tears, Dr Lewis remembered her futile attempts to revive Mr Rogers.

Dr Lewis: I tried to do CPR with Steve and I remember the whole time saying: 'Don't do this to me, Steve. Don't die.' I tried to resuscitate him. By that time Greg had come round with the resuscitating machine, but it was too late …

The police arrived soon afterwards. They were approaching really cautiously. They didn't know if the person had been disarmed yet. I went outside and said: 'Get in here. Give us a hand. Get him, he's unarmed. Handcuff him.'

Soon after that the ambulance guys arrived and confirmed that Steve had indeed passed away.

Knight's grandly horrific plan had been ruined. He had been caught redhanded with a high-powered rifle, moments after shooting a man. He had fired two bullets, had another five loaded and another seven in his pocket. He also had obvious paraphernalia to create an inferno. But all that did not mean Knight was going to make it easy for police.

Far from it.

Soon after arresting Knight, police realised that they had a real oddball on their hands. He didn't say much, but what he did say was very strange. For instance, he told one constable: 'You are in a bad position there. I can turn and grab your gun and that will be the end of it.'

Knight wasn't just odd. He was obstructive. He refused to give his name. When a magistrate pointed out that this was slowing his case, Knight replied: 'That's OK by me.'

For three weeks, he was known as Mr X. Police made a public appeal for anyone who knew him to identify him. Mr Rogers' grieving mother, Shirley Rogers, joined in the national plea. Tearfully, she said her son had been a real family man – a father of five and a stepdad to two.

> *Ms Rogers*: We need to know who did this and why.
>
> Steve had everything to look forward to in life. He had just been told he was a grandfather for the first time and he was so happy, and then it was all taken away from him.
>
> We have lost everything. I've lost my son, his wife has lost her husband and my grandchildren have lost their father.
>
> He was shot in cold blood. He was killed for no reason. It doesn't make any sense at all. It's a nightmare.
>
> Steve hated violence. He took the job at the clinic because he thought he would be safe.

At first, even Ms Tighe did not realise Knight was the 'Peter Sweeney' she had found so disturbingly intense six months earlier. On the day of the shooting, she had been preparing to go on holiday, when a reporter phoned and told her of the clinic shooting.

> *Ms Tighe*: I said: 'Oh that's terrible.' And then I said: 'But nobody has been killed, have they,' and he said: 'Yes, he's dead,' and I said: 'Oh dear God, that's terrible.'
>
> It was all over the newspapers and on the TV and one of my colleagues Father Eugene Ahern said: 'Thank God we don't know the man,' because we didn't recognise him. I didn't recognise him at the time.

She said it was only weeks later, when she saw a big photo of 'Mr X' in a newspaper, that she recognised him and called police.

> *Ms Tighe*: I told my secretary at the time: 'Oh my God, Joanne, that's the guy that came to the office.'

Finally, the mystery was solved when Molong residents identified 'Mr X' as their 'Yowie'.

Knight's identity might no longer have been a mystery, but he still would not cooperate. At his trial in Victoria's Supreme Court in April 2002, he refused to follow normal court protocols and stand up when asked to do so or to bow when the judge entered the court. He also would not get a lawyer, cross-examine witnesses, call any witnesses in his defence, or give evidence himself. He did, however, plead not guilty to a charge of murder.

While he was waiting for his trial, Knight wrote to Ms Tighe from his jail cell arguing that young Australians had to be protected from 'callous butchers'. He claimed that if his jurors were opposed to abortion, he would be found not guilty. Then he threatened. Knight wrote:

> If that happens, since abortionists and pro-abortionists alike are a gutless lot only capable of attacking the defenceless … once I am released then there will not be an abortionist about the place prepared to remain in operation – guaranteed.

Even after prosecutor Bill Morgan-Payler QC opened his case by telling the jury: 'But for the bravery of these men [Mr De Maria, Mr Anderson and Mr Cassar] who intervened, there would have been a tragedy of dreadful proportions', Knight was still confident. His opening address was extraordinarily brief.

> *Knight*: In response to the prosecutor's opening, I will make my response both brief and to the point. Accusations are accusations. Evidence is evidence. The prosecution has many of the first, and little of the second.
>
> Having seen the evidence they will produce through him in this trial, it is obvious to me it does not support their accusations and I am confident that when the final word is said in this trial you will be of the same opinion. I will let the evidence speak for itself.

Warning Shot

In closing his case for the prosecution, Mr Morgan-Payler told the jury the evidence that Knight had deliberately and without lawful excuse killed Mr Rogers was 'simply overwhelming'.

After four days of saying almost nothing – of not giving evidence, not cross-examining, not objecting – Knight chose Mr Morgan-Payler's final address (when barristers are not normally allowed to object) to make his only objection in front of the jury.

Mr Morgan-Payler: Remember: 'Yeah mate, it's for real.' He said that just before he fired the shot. 'Yeah mate, it's for real.' Lillian Kitanov heard that …

Knight: I would like to interject here. The correct term was, it was insinuated, was: 'Yeah man, it's for real,' not: 'Yeah mate, it's for real.'

What could it possibly matter if the evidence was that he had said: 'Yeah man, it's for real' instead of: 'Yeah mate, it's for real'? Was it just an obsessive man's pointless pedantry?

To Mr Morgan-Payler it didn't matter whether it was 'mate' or 'man', his point was that seconds before firing the shots, Knight had been 'cool and calm'.

Mr Morgan-Payler: And the rifle? What position was it in when that shot was fired? … It was raised to his shoulder. Where was it pointed, this rifle all ready to go with the hammer cocked? Was it pointed up to the ceiling? Was it pointed down to the floor? To one side or the other? No. It was pointed straight at Steven Rogers, straight at his upper body …

Not only does the firing of … a 30/30 calibre rifle at close range into the chest of a person speak loudly of an intent to kill, but look at the planning, look at that note: 'a fatal accident involving some members of staff'.

He went there with murder on his mind. Steve Rogers may not have been his primary target … But it does seem likely that Steven Rogers got in the way.

REASONABLE DOUBT

Mr Morgan-Payler said that Knight could not claim that he had killed to protect the lives of unborn babies.

> *Mr Morgan-Payler*: Whether his sentiment be right or wrong, an unborn foetus as far as the law is concerned is not a person, is not a separate life and so as far as the law is concerned, one cannot act to defend that life because it is not a life.

The prosecutor told the jury not to find Knight guilty of a massacre he never carried out.

> *Mr Morgan-Payler*: But for the intervention of Steven Rogers there might have been an appalling catastrophe, but that has nothing to do with this trial at all. The only relevance of that is that it indicated he had killing on his mind when he went into that clinic.
>
> We invite you to convict him properly on the evidence, not out of horror at the potential disclosed by the evidence ...
>
> Protecting the lives of young Australians and discouraging people from involving themselves in abortions are lofty sentiments, but they are not, we submit to you, in any way a defence to the terrible murder that was committed in this case.

In his closing address, Knight finally revealed what his defence was: it had been an accident.

> *Knight*: The major issue you need to resolve in this trial is whether the security guard was shot by the first bullet, which was deliberately fired, or whether he was shot by the second bullet, which was accidentally and unintentionally discharged during the course of a struggle.

It was a truly bizarre final address to a jury. Knight's demeanour ranged from calm and methodical to shrieking and ranting.

Warning Shot

Like all those giving final addresses, Knight was not allowed to introduce new evidence. He was only allowed to summarise the sworn evidence given in court. He couldn't, for instance, just tell the jury that he fired the first shot in the air because that would have been giving evidence. He could only point to evidence given in the trial.

His two-hour speech included a maths lesson, a personal attack on the prosecutor and a fiery sermon against the swearing of oaths in law courts. What Knight's extraordinary diatribe/lecture/closing address/sermon did not do, however, was explain the evidence of the planned massacre. He also did not apologise for killing Mr Rogers or even offer any sympathy to the dead man's family. He started by venting his frustration.

Knight: At last, at long last, there is some light at the end of the tunnel. For the past four days, I have been dragged to this courtroom and been forced to listen – to endure – some of the most useless, some of the most irrelevant and some of the most stupid evidence and testimony any prosecuting barrister must ever have had the effrontery to present. But if you are amongst those who, like myself, have been forced to suffer these past four days, then forsake not all hope: I bring good news. During this address, I will not attempt to emulate the prosecution strategy of raising all the irrelevant issues they could lay their hands on. I will, instead, confine myself to those issues which are relevant and informative and which are not totally and absolutely bloody useless …

When this had been done … and you have had time enough to fully consider the implications, then – unless you are already aware of just how inept the Office of Public Prosecutions is – I think you will be quite satisfied that they should never have put me on trial, on this evidence, to answer a charge of murder.

Knight told the jury that evidence from Mr De Maria and Ms Kitanov showed there was 'little doubt that when the first shot was fired, the gun was held at my shoulder'.

REASONABLE DOUBT

He then tried to prove mathematically – geometrically – that this first shot could not have been the one that hit Mr Rogers. He pointed out that the autopsy found that the 'projectile' that hit Mr Rogers near his right shoulder had entered with an 'approximately 20 degrees upward and backward angulation'. He pointed out that Ms Kitanov had said he had been about a metre and a half from Mr Rogers when the gun was fired. Then Knight became a maths teacher.

Knight: Now if you take that angle of 20 degrees, what does that say about what level this shot was fired? Well, a metre and a half: that's three units of half a metre, which means by the time that the bullet struck the security guard, it would have travelled slightly more than the one unit of half a metre.

So, it is clear where that bullet came from: half a metre lower down, which would make it around my waist area.

But, as the witness says, the first shot was fired from the shoulder. Now the obvious question which arises from this is: Where was the rifle positioned when the second shot was fired? If this bullet was fired from about waist level and struck the security guard, would that not explain the entry of his wound?

To back up his claim that the first shot had been a deliberate above-the-head warning shot, Knight also pointed out that a bullet hole was found in the ceiling approximately above where Mr Rogers had stood – about where someone would direct a warning shot 'to coerce people to move'.

Knight also pointed out that Mr De Maria had said that just before the first shot from the shoulder he had seen an 'upward motion' of the gun.

Knight: So you can assume the rifle was raised up a split second before that first was fired. Now why was that done? If you deliberately intended to shoot that security guard and you had a rifle at your shoulder aimed at that person there [he aims an imaginary gun from his shoulder], would you not take careful aim and pull the trigger [mimics pulling the trigger]? No movement up at all.

Warning Shot

But De Maria, of course, says there is an upwards movement, there just before that gunshot and that is what you do if you aimed to fire a warning shot over that person's head. If they have been told to move over there and they take no notice, a warning shot would be one thing you could do.

He was so convinced of the force of his logic, Knight did not appear to appreciate how disconcerting it might be for a jury to have a gunman – even one who claimed to have shot accidentally – to aim and fire an imaginary gun at them.

Knight also explained his seemingly strange objection to the prosecutor's final address – insisting the evidence had been that he had said: 'Yeah man, it's for real', not: 'Yeah mate, it's for real'. The reason turned out to be that he believed it was less likely the jury would accept that he had said it at all.

Knight: I think I might say that if either of the two women on the far side were to take the witness box, they would tell you that is not my manner of speech: 'Yeah man, it's for real.'

As to whether he intended killing, Knight disposed of the chilling 'there will not be an abortionist in Melbourne left deathless' letter from words circled in a newspaper in one sentence.

Knight: The question of intention being such an important issue, it still remains to show whether or not I planned to harm the security guard. First … the newspaper with the circled letters – you can make of that what you will.

Then, once again, he had those in the court squirming with some extraordinary argument. To prove he had not intended to harm the security guard, Knight detailed the terrifying lengths he had taken to prepare for his attack on the clinic.

REASONABLE DOUBT

Knight: Now if I had planned to harm this security guard or intended to harm this security guard, would I arrive at the time indicated
by the witnesses there … 20 or 25 past 10 when, as other witnesses
say, the security guard usually left at about 10 o'clock?

The next question follows: Was I aware of the security guard's
schedule?

Is it likely that I would have went into the premises without first
having obtained a fair idea of what went on in there?

In fact, I can tell you that the person who held the position of
security guard prior to the deceased was a woman who was slightly
short, was very stockily built, had short dark hair, drove a maroon-
coloured Mitsubishi which was commonly parked opposite – or
approximately opposite – the premises and she had always left the
premises and driven off by 10 past 10.

Knight's logic to the jury seemed to be: you should clear me of the guard's
murder because I intended to kill a whole lot of others, but not him.

Knight finished his final address with an often screeched harangue
against legal 'mumbo jumbo'. For him, taking an oath to God to 'tell
the truth, the whole truth and nothing but the truth' was an insult to God
because God's commandment that people should tell the truth should be
enough. He didn't mention anything about 'Thou shalt not kill'.

Knight: I would like to explain the reasons why I did not call any
witnesses for my defence and this will also explain the reasons why
I did not cross-examine any prosecution witnesses … That has to
do with the matter of oaths and, of course, their twin brothers are
affirmations and declarations.

My response to this nonsense – as it has been in many years past –
is when will people ever start to grow up? Just what purpose does
this ridiculous mumbo jumbo serve?

He said most people 'true to the nature of fools' took oaths because they needed something more than God's commandment to force them to tell the truth.

> *Knight*: They say to themselves: 'I reckon if it will get me to do what God's advice could not get me to do and tell the truth, then that's got to be a good thing. God's advice, all things considered, is just not much chop but me own word, me own guarantee; now that's BIG time and if anything at all is said about it when I am kicked upstairs I will say: "Sorry old fellow, but I needed something that had a bit more go and a bit more officiality than your word to get me to tell the truth in court." '
>
> If they do not think it will get you to tell them the truth in court, then give me one sensible, practical, nonchildish and nonridiculous reason why they persist and insist on it …
>
> Anyone who thinks this enforced regulation, this done-on-cue mumbo jumbo is the way to tell God anything, has a very feeble relationship with Him. Why don't they simply grow up and charge anyone who has given false testimony in court, but then that would be just too simple and sensible for peacocks like these …
>
> Under no circumstances would I participate in this nonsense myself and under no circumstances would I place pressure on anyone else to do so.
>
> For anyone to say that taking an oath makes it more important for them to tell the truth, only goes to show what little regard they have for telling the truth in the first place and what little regard they have for God's advice.

Knight's other explanation for not having a lawyer and not playing a more active role in the trial was his intellectual cockiness and his certainty of his innocence.

> *Knight*: There are only two things I had need of for this trial. The first of these was a list of depositions and evidence confirming just

how poor and how ridiculous the prosecution case would be. This was obligingly supplied by the Office of Public Prosecution.

The other thing I had need of was a prosecuting barrister with no brains at all, and here too – once again – the Office of Public Prosecutions has come to the fore and generously supplied the solution.

What the hell would I need a barrister for, when it was plain and obvious the prosecuting one has gotten all the evidence I needed anyway.

To close, I make a final word on the matter of oaths. It may not have cost me very much in this trial, but it is only a matter of time before this ridiculous nonsense costs some people their chance at justice.

After deliberating for almost four hours, the jury of eight men and four women declared Knight guilty of murder. As had been the case throughout the trial, Knight refused to stand up when the jury or judge entered and after the verdict he also refused to give his details. He was 'Mr X' again. Then, suddenly, he leapt to his feet and shouted out to the jury: 'You'll be made to pay the penalty.' Later, he said he had meant that they would pay their penalty in the afterlife.

Outside the court, Shirley Rogers told *Herald Sun* reporter Norrie Ross: 'I think Knight was going to go in and kill all the doctors and burn the place down but Steven foiled his plan … I think they should lock him up and throw away the key because, the way he was talking, I think he would be a dangerous person to be on the street. He more or less threatened to do it again … Tonight, I am going to say a prayer to him [Steven] and I'm going to say: "You've finally got your justice." '

At his pre-sentence plea-hearing, Knight continued to refuse to have a barrister act for him. Justice Teague, however, asked barristers Roy Punshon SC and Reg Marron to be 'friends of the court'. While not acting for Knight, they were there to try to look after his interests although this was difficult without his cooperation.

Warning Shot

The big issue was whether Knight was mentally ill or just odd. If he was found to be mentally ill, his whole trial would have been declared a nullity – as if it had never happened. Two psychiatrists came up with very different conclusions.

After regularly interviewing Knight over eight months, Dr Don Senadipathy found that Knight had 'chronic paranoid schizophrenia' and had 'committed the crime driven by his delusional interpretation of the Bible'. Dr Senadipathy said Knight was still psychotic and that he was a 'highly dangerous man who would remain unpredictable' and a 'high risk' even in jail. He said he was not optimistic that Knight could be cured and recommended he be held and treated in a 'secure hospital setting'.

> *Dr Senadipathy*: His delusions control his life. He has no insight to accept that he set out to commit a horrendous crime. He does not have the ability to show emotions and there is no remorse. This is in a man who believes in God and acts according to what he believes is stated in the Bible. Abnormal thoughts and beliefs drive him … He lacks motivation and drive to lead a normal life.

He noted that Knight was so obsessively opposed to smoking that in hospital he refused to speak in front of any nurses he believed were smokers. Dr Senadipathy also noted that even though he had almost nothing, Knight gave what he could to charity. He warned, however, against allowing him back into the community: 'I agree with the comment of his sister that he is capable of an even more sinister crime.' That sister was worried her little brother might do something serious – 'like Martin Bryant'.

Another psychiatrist – after interviewing Knight for nearly two hours – found 'little objective evidence of mental illness, including schizophrenia'. Dr Justin Barry-Walsh agreed that Knight was paranoid and had strongly held odd views (Knight told him he considered himself 49 years old, not 48, because he dated himself from the time of his conception, not birth) but he did not believe he was delusional.

Dr Barry-Walsh: He spoke generally freely and at length and would have been happy to continue with the interview past the point at which I terminated it ... He spoke spontaneously ... He showed flashes of humour and made several jokes ... Generally, he seemed to be someone who was mistrustful of others, particularly those with authority ...

He did not characterise himself as being a recluse. He felt a recluse was someone who doesn't want company. He suggested he could, in fact, be happy to have company but was fussy about company. He indicated he had always been a hard judge of other people. He said that he only demanded the standards in other people that he would demand in himself. He wouldn't tolerate people that used drugs, that wouldn't give to charity, that were too greedy or smoked cigarettes.

In relation to the court process, he accepted that he had been found guilty. He felt that perhaps he could have put his case to the court somewhat better than he did.

He expanded more generally on his views about law and order ... He felt the death penalty should be mandatory for 'serious crimes' such as armed robbery and child molestation but optional for murder.

He indicated to me that there were times when people had to take the law into their own hands. He said this did not make him an anarchist and he appreciated that one had to have government but, by way of analogy, he suggested that if he was living in the time of Adolf Hitler, it would have been appropriate to have to take the right action ...

He believed he had the right to take the law into his own hands at the time of which the offence was committed ... He was unwilling to talk about the harm he might have perpetrated as a result of the offending and, in particular, was resistant to the notion of relating his Christian views to the offence and its aftermath ...

He likes to invent things and solve problems ... [but] he was reluctant to talk to me in detail, suggesting that if he did, I might think he is a 'nutcase'. He tells me he succeeded in designing a perpetual

Warning Shot

motion machine, but if he broadcasts this, this might have him 'off to a mental hospital'. He also tells me he has designed a better mousetrap ...

He views the government as responsible for his predicament because of their condoning the abortion law.

Dr Barry-Walsh said it was not surprising that he and Dr Senadipathy disagreed because Knight was 'in the grey area between a person who is odd and unusual and socially deviant and a person who is clearly and frankly mentally ill'.

To try to break the psychiatric opinion deadlock, Justice Teague called for a third psychiatrist. The tie-breaker, Professor Paul Mullen, noted: 'There is a pathway from obsessive concern through fanaticism to delusion' and it's 'no easy matter in men like Mr Knight to know when they have moved from the enthusiasms of extremism to the madness of delusion'.

Prof Mullen: On occasion, when I have seen Mr Knight he has been able to discuss his views with a degree of openness and even to be able to contemplate the possibility of error. On other occasions, there has been a rigidity and grandiose claim to absolute knowledge ... suggestive of delusion ...

He is undoubtedly a very unusual individual who has developed a number of convictions which he holds to be absolutely true and self-evident and which he is arrogant enough to believe he has the right to impose on others. At times, given his personality and the lack of any of the usual checks and balances on extremism and hubris, Mr Knight's fanaticism may well merge into delusion. In my opinion, however, he does not have an established and ongoing delusional disorder ...

Mr Knight still believes that he was in the right on that day when he shot and killed Mr Rogers. One can only hope that eventually the awfulness of what he did to Mr Rogers, and the pain that he inflicted on the family and friends of Mr Rogers, will lead Mr Knight to some awareness of the need to moderate all views with an element of humanity and respect for others.

Mr Knight may well require psychiatric care in the future ... [but] he would not, in my opinion, currently be a candidate for a hospital order.

So, it was 2–1 in favour of Knight being sane.

Then Knight had his go. In his scratchy scrawl, he attacked Dr Senadipathy's schizophrenia diagnosis, saying it broke the law.

Knight: Section 8 (2) of the Mental Health Act states, (2) 'A person is not to be considered to be mentally ill by reason only of any one or more the following – (b) that the person expresses or refuses or fails to express a political opinion or belief.'

My attitude, as it had been termed, in regard to oaths has as its source a religious foundation from Biblical scripture. Firstly James, chapter 5, verse 12 says: 'My friends, above all else, don't take an oath. You must not swear by heaven or by earth or by anything else. Yes or No is all you need to say. If you do anything more you will be condemned.' Secondly, Matthew chapter 5 verse 33 says: 'You know that those of old times were told, "Perform your oaths unto the Lord." But I say unto you, swear not at all, neither by heaven, for it is God's throne, nor by the earth, for it is his footstool. Neither shalt thou swear by your right arm or by your left or by any other oath. But let your communication be Yay or Nay, for whatsoever is more than this comes of evil.'

The 2nd of these extracts is part of what is commonly referred to as the sermon on the mount – one of the foundation stories of the Christian religion. Hardly what could be criticised as being extreme or obscure religious literature. It seems to me somebody's adherence to Christian doctrine is hardly reason to consider them to be schizophrenic. It shouldn't be, but if it is, that raises all sorts of new possibilities. Let me further say that I have no desire at all to see the validity of that trial brought into question ...

> Given that Mr Senadipathy's diagnosis is based on invalid criteria, and given that any report forthcoming from him would be of doubtful legality, I consider that the court has before it everything it requires for a decision to be made ... The trial has taken place; the witnesses have given their evidence (confused though much of it was), the jury has made their decision (and what a decision). It is now up to the judge to make his. Based not on one misguided and legally doubtful psychiatric report, but ... on whatever degree of culpability, and whatever degree of responsibility he thinks I have for the charges presented to him.
>
> I am not someone of weak faith. I know that nobody can do anything to me which has not been permitted by God, for my own eventual good.
>
> Sincerely
>
> P Knight

Despite Knight's plea and the opinions of Professor Mullen and Dr Barry-Walsh, Mr Punshon and Mr Marron told Justice Teague he would be entitled to find that Knight had been delusionally schizophrenic when he killed Mr Rogers. They pointed out Dr Senadipathy had made his diagnosis after talking to Knight over eight months.

The prosecution urged Justice Teague to take the rare step of jailing Knight for the rest of his life without any hope of parole. Up until that time (August 2002) – since 1986 when Victorian judges were given the power to set minimum terms for those convicted of murder – only five murderers had been sentenced, and were serving, 'life means life' sentences. They were: Stanley Brian Taylor, who bombed the Russell Street police complex, killing a policewoman in a declaration of war on society; triple murderer Ashley Mervyn Coulston; the abductor and killer of six-year-old Sheree Beasley, Robert Arthur Selby Lowe; Leslie Alfred Camilleri, who abducted, raped and murdered two teenage girls near Bega in New South Wales; and Peter Dupas, who killed and sexually mutilated the body of his psychotherapist.

Mr Morgan-Payler: A murder committed with an intention to kill in the course of a campaign to effect social change must rank as one of the gravest examples of the crime of murder.

He said Knight had shown no remorse for what he had done, was not psychiatrically ill and had threatened the 'gravest crimes if, and when, released'.

Mr Punshon and Mr Marron, however, called for Knight to be given a hope of eventual freedom. They denied that what he did amounted to a declaration of war against society and said he should only be punished for murdering Mr Rogers, not for what he might have done.

Knight was still hanging on to an impossible hope that Justice Teague would exonerate him – despite the jury's verdict. In another letter, Knight told the judge there were 'many factors which the sentencing act states should be considered by a judge when determining a sentence'.

Knight: But as far as I am awhere [sic] nowhere in that act, or anywhere else, does it specify how much <u>importance</u> should be placed on each, or any of those factors … Each case has its own unique characteristics … But in <u>all</u> cases, there is one factor which must always be given a lot of importance. In some cases it may be the only factor which has <u>any</u> importance. That factor is, the actual degree of responsibility or culpability the judge considers the defendant has, for the charge he has been convicted of.

It is obviously the first factor which should be considered, and whenever the answer is zero, as it is in this case, then it should be the only factor given any importance. No other factor has any importance here.

Knight told Justice Teague to reject as 'inaccuracies, falsehoods and unsubstantiated opinions' anything the three psychiatrists told him about why he shot Mr Roger.

Knight: I have refused to speak on the subject, despite their numerous attempts to elicit dialogue on the subject.

Warning Shot

Their comments on my motives, my plans, and my intentions and on what they consider my future actions might be, are nothing better than guesswork.

Dr Senadipathy proposes that it was my intention 'to kill the doctor or doctors working at the clinic, and perhaps set fire to the building'. Others have made a variety of suggestions (guesses), some very much different. The only thing that such a diversity of opinion shows is that none of them can confidently say what my intentions were. I am the only one who knows.

Some rather foolish people have suggested to me that I should have given my own account of things at that trial. I had, and have, no intention of doing so of course for the reason … that it usually does little good to tell people something they do not want to believe …

The other reason I have not spoken is that it could well make it more possible that I might be convicted. Not of the charge which was levelled against me here, but of other lesser charges which I have heard suggested could possibly eventuate. I considered, and still do, that if I remained silent on this matter that no OBJECTIVE jury or judge would have, or will, convict me of any charges in relation to the events of 16th of July apart possibly from one or two very minor charges. But I have not been charged here with any of those. They are irrelevant here. The only charge under consideration here is murder.

In November 2002 – almost a year and a half after Knight walked into Australia's most famous abortion clinic with a rifle, fourteen bullets, metal doorstoppers, foam-tipped sticks, kerosene, twine, gags and cigarette lighters – he was sentenced for murdering the security guard who asked if he was serious.

Justice Teague: The murder of Steven Rogers was a very serious crime. It is to be treated more seriously because … you were a loner on a personal crusade … to effect social change. Steven Rogers was just doing his duty. He got in the way of your crusade. He was one of those who was characterised by you as being in 'the abortion racket' ...

You went to the clinic with a plan to massacre. You made Steven Rogers pay the supreme sacrifice because he got in the way ...

I am not disposed to accept the diagnosis of schizophrenia. You are clearly a person who [however] ... rigidly and unshakingly, adheres to certain beliefs. You are a man who is intolerant to an extreme ... You exhibit a fanaticism which at times may well merge into delusion ...

You have murdered one man in the context of having planned a massacre of many ... You represent, now, a considerable danger to the community. In July 2001, you were able to put together a collection of items that had the potential to result in the deaths of dozens of people who were going about their normal lives in the East Melbourne clinic ...

You have not shown any remorse ... The closest you have come to that has been to argue that his death was just bad luck. In all the circumstances, I am satisfied that life imprisonment is called for.

The judge told Knight that with 'significant reservations' he had decided to fix a nonparole term, to give him a chance of eventually being released from jail. He said he had done so because this was his first criminal conviction and because his mental state 'does border on a delusional disorder'.

Justice Teague: Mr Knight, I sentence you to imprisonment for life. I set a nonparole period of 23 years. Remove the prisoner.

***

Almost another year and a half later (March 2004), Knight fought another lone legal battle. This one in the Victorian Court of Appeal started with an extra bizarre twist – Knight was wheeled into court strapped upright Hannibal Lecter–style to a metal stretcher. Unlike the *Silence of*

Gatto vs Veniamin: Defence Underworld-style Dominic 'Mick' Gatto (above) and Andrew 'Benji' Veniamin (below) were odd friends in Melbourne's underworld. At the back of his favourite restaurant, Mr Gatto fatally shot Veniamin. He said it was self-defence; the police said it was revenge for the murder of another underworld figure, the man Gatto called 'Pa' – Graham 'The Munster' Kinniburgh. *Newspix / David Crosling (Gatto) / Jessica Lee (Veniamin)*

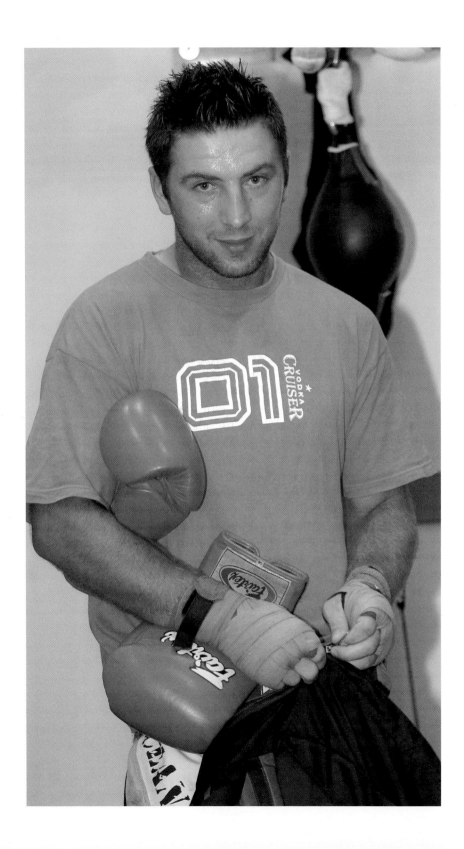

David Hookes: A Cricket Hero Dies At the SCG in 2004, Australian cricketers and fans remember David Hookes, Australia's Centenary Test larrikin hero. It was Australia's first international cricket match since one punch by bouncer Zdravko Micevic (opposite) killed 'Hookesy' outside a Melbourne pub. Mr Micevic said he threw the fatal punch in self-defence; some witnesses said he did so in anger. *Newspix / Cameron Tandy (Micevic) / Glenn Campbell (Hookes)*

A Spiritual Death Jim and Eugenia Pesnak (above) walk into the Brisbane Supreme Court to fight charges they committed manslaughter by failing to call an ambulance in time to save a starving woman's life. Lani Morris died while the Pesnaks were inducting her into Breatharianism, which claims people can live on just air and light. *Newspix / Steve Pohlner*

Already Dead For nearly 40 years after a car crashed into her twin brother's pram, Judith Anne Cengiz had been a dedicated sister. She regularly visited Lindsay Jellett at his home for the intellectually disabled. In the end, however, police said she twice ran her car over her brother so she could inherit his compensation payout. *Newspix*

Sniper Wife Mother of five Claire Margaret MacDonald donned a camouflage jacket, grabbed a bolt-action long-distance rifle, hid in a sniper's nest, lured her husband of 17 years into range, and fired six shots at him from 48 metres away. She denied murdering him, however, saying he didn't deserve to live and that she had to kill him to protect herself and their children.
Newspix / Richard Cisar-Wright

Being Al Pacino The tragic cost of a silly game: a young man is killed and a family grieves. Luke O'Keefe (pictured) was shot in the head while his flatmate was pretending to be an Al Pacino–style cop. Luke's grandmother Lesvia Kalaitis holds his portrait. His father Leon Kalaitis and his seven-year-old sister Sadie are in the foreground; his uncle John is behind them.
Newspix / Jay Town

Insanely Homesick When he was promoted and transferred to Australia, Canadian businessman Gerry Skura had no idea the homesickness of his wife Marie would make it a nightmare odyssey he would be lucky to survive. *Newspix /Jessica Lee (Gerry Skura) / Joe Benke (Marie Skura)*

Just Anger John Edward Whiteside (below left) and Kristian Peter Dieber (below right) said they fatally bashed Keith Hibbins (above) in a park because they thought he had just raped a woman. He hadn't. He had bolted from them because he was gay and thought Whiteside and Dieber were gay bashers. *Newspix / Jay Town (above) / Shaney Balcombe (below)*

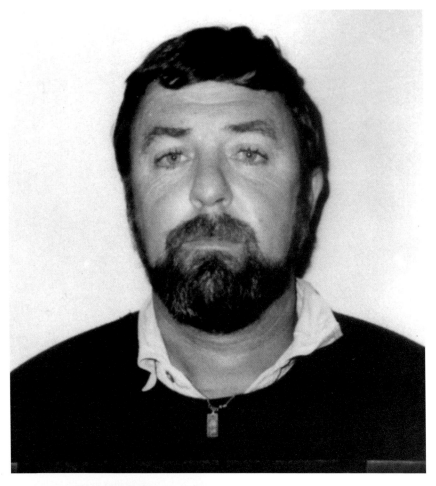
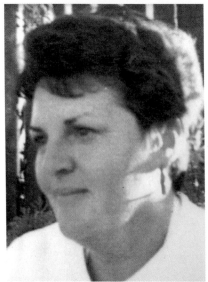

Sleepwalk of Death Bernard Charles Brown said that if he did kill Susan Brown – his wife of 10 years – by shooting and hitting her with a hammer in their bed, he must have done so when he was sleepwalking. *Newspix*

the Lambs villain, however, Knight was not wearing an ice hockey mask or a straitjacket. He also was not on the stretcher because of security fears, but because he was refusing to come to the appeal hearing.

His reluctance to appear was especially odd because he was asking the court to accept his appeal even though he had missed the deadline by five months. In his appeal, Knight told the three judges he should get a new trial because Justice Teague had been 'obviously not nearly learned enough' and 'dimwitted'.

He also argued that he had been deprived of an impartial jury because jurors who had held strong views – for or against – abortion had been excused from sitting on the jury. Knight argued that the only people who could have given him a fair hearing would have been people opposed to abortion. He said only those opposed to abortion 'were even-handed towards the unborn as well as the born'. Knight denied that he had agreed to excluding jurors with strong views on abortion. He said when Justice Teague asked him whether he was 'content for me to adopt that course' he had only said 'Yes' because he was 'content to see this judge be foolish enough to give grossly improper directions to the jury pool. And, not being a complete fool myself, and being mindful that what had been promised or proposed by the judge, would constitute sure-fire grounds to get an appeal upheld, then, quite naturally, I was content to see this judge make a blunder of such magnitude.'

Once again Knight's too-clever-by-half cockiness failed him completely. The appeal judges rejected as 'specious' his claim that only those opposed to abortion could have impartially judged his case. They then noted that even if they had accepted the point, Knight would not have been able to argue it because he had not tried to dissuade the judge from doing it. Barristers and accused people are not allowed to 'store up' appeal points without alerting the trial judge. The judges refused to grant Knight an extension of time to make a full appeal, saying he had 'failed to show any reasonably arguable ground of appeal, let alone one that would probably succeed'. Appeal court losses don't come any more resounding than that.

After his big loss, Knight was once again obstructive: he was a dead weight as security guards carried him out of the court.

210 REASONABLE DOUBT

While the justice system was struggling to deal with Knight, the bravery of the three men who stopped him committing a massacre was recognised. Mr De Maria was awarded Victoria's second-highest bravery honour – the Star of Courage – for those who act with conspicuous courage in circumstances of great peril. Mr Anderson received a Bravery Medal; so too did the man who could not collect his – Steven Rogers. Mr De Maria said the shooting had taught him to value life more, had made him realise anything can happen: 'I saw that with the security guard, he was just within a couple of minutes of going home and he never made it.' When trying to explain why he did what he did, Mr De Maria looked teary-eyed at his baby daughter who had not yet been born when a fanatically anti-abortionist gunman pointed a loaded gun at her pregnant mother's stomach.

'I couldn't stand there and do nothing. I look at her and I would never forgive myself for it. So, I had to do something.'

JUST ANGER

After a day of watching footy and drinking beer, two young men bash a couple of older gay men in a city park. They chase them through the park and pounce when one of the gay men falls. They punch or kick his head, side and hips. When the man's partner shouts: 'Leave him alone,' the attack stops long enough for the man to scramble to his feet and flee to safety. His partner is not so lucky. Pins in his arms and legs – a legacy of falling off a roof eight years earlier – means that he runs like the tin man from *The Wizard of Oz* and the two fit, sports-loving younger men easily catch him. Then, according to a woman who happens to be watching from the seventh-floor hospital room where her cancer-stricken husband lies dying, the younger men punch 'the crap' out of the older man. He slumps unconscious on the road, and dies 11 days later without regaining consciousness.

The fatal bashing of 45-year-old Keith Hibbins just after 7pm on 25 April 1999 seemed to be a particularly gruesome and tragic case of a gay-bashing – but it wasn't. The excuse 27-year-old John Edward Whiteside and 23-year-old Kristian Peter Dieber offered made it a far more bizarre and much trickier proposition for the justice system.

Whiteside and Dieber admitted bashing Keith Hibbins and his partner of 15 years, David Campbell, but insisted they had *not* done so because they were gay but because they thought they had just raped a woman. They said they had not meant to kill or even seriously injure Mr Hibbins. They had only hit him because he was trying to escape their citizen's arrest, because they wear justifiably angry.

***

Like tens of thousands of footy fans on 25 April 1999, Whiteside and Dieber went to the big Anzac Day clash between the Essendon Bombers and the Collingwood Magpies at the MCG. Friends of friends, they met at the game by chance. A friend drove Whiteside to the game. Whiteside had woken up late after spending much of the night watching World Cup cricket on the television. Dieber and a group of friends took a train to the game.

Afterwards, Whiteside's friend offers to drive him home but he decides to have a few more drinks at the nearby MCG Hotel and take the train with Dieber and co. About 7pm, they start walking along Wellington Parade towards the city to have a few more drinks at the famous Young and Jackson's pub before catching a train to their outer-suburban homes – Whiteside to Stoda Street, Heathmont, and Dieber to Appleby Place, North Ringwood. They walk past the Fitzroy Gardens – home to Captain Cook's Cottage, a model Tudor village, a conservatory, picturesque ponds, a 'Fairy Tree', a couple of fountains, Victorian-style rotundas and lots of brushtail possums. They cross Lansdowne Street and walk on the border of Treasury Gardens, home to a pond memorial to the assassinated US president John F Kennedy. A little way up the street is the Peter MacCullum Cancer Institute. As Whiteside and Dieber and their friends walk beside the Treasury Gardens their discussion of the footy (the Bombers beat the 'Pies 108 to 100) stops suddenly. In front of them is a hysterical, weeping 23-year-old woman – Euginea 'Jenny' Tsionis.

Tsionis is wearing tight black trousers and a flimsy white top. She has no shoes and only one sock. As Dieber and Whiteside's group approach, she yells: 'Are you going to rape me too?' She throws her wallet at them, saying: 'Just take it, and leave me alone.' One of Dieber and Whiteside's friends lends the distressed woman his Essendon footy team jacket. Whiteside puts his black-and-white Collingwood footy scarf around her neck. Then, with a jogger who comes to help, they discuss what to do. Inside Tsionis's wallet they find $550 and hail a taxi but Tsionis tells them she wants the police. When the police are on the line, Tsionis is asked whether she has been raped. She doesn't give a definite answer but when asked if she has been sexually assaulted, she says: 'Yes.' The jogger tells Dieber and Whiteside that not long before he had seen two men arguing with the woman. Amid all the hullabaloo, a senior park ranger talks to Tsionis.

Ranger: I asked her if she had been raped, to which she looked at me then she put her head down and gave what I thought was a false-sounding cry. I again asked her if she had been raped, to which the reply was again a false-sounding cry … I felt that she hadn't been raped; however, I was very cautious in case I was mistaken.

The ambulance medic finds Tsionis curled up in a foetal position, weeping and crying out: 'Why me?' When the police turn up, she tells them she has been sexually assaulted. About two hours later, she tells a doctor that she was raped. In a police statement, she writes that a 28- to 30-year-old man 'with a deep voice, dark short hair, one length straight-style' grabbed her in the gardens, spun her around, forced her pants down – without undoing her zip – and that then she 'could feel his semi-erected [sic] penis in between my legs near my upper thighs. He didn't penetrate my vagina with his penis … All I could think of was: "Why me?" '

It was traumatic stuff, but it was all nonsense. Tsionis made the whole thing up. She hadn't been raped; she hadn't been molested in any way. The former tabletop dancer wasn't a victim. What she was, was angry and stoned – and staggering, zigzagging drunk. She was in the Treasury Gardens that cool evening not because she had been raped, but because she had argued with her boyfriend, Tony Beck. She started that day with a bong of marijuana for breakfast. Then she and Mr Beck had gone roller-blading along the St Kilda foreshore. She had then had two bourbon and cokes and two 'cowboys' – Bailey's and butterscotch schnapps – at the Esplanade Hotel before they walked along the St Kilda pier. After that, Tsionis and Mr Beck tried to get some lunch at a popular nearby restaurant but it was booked out so they sat at the bar drinking alcohol. They sat there drinking alcohol all afternoon. When she left in the early evening, Tsionis 'felt quite drunk'; her head was spinning. As they were driving through the CBD past Flinders Street Station, Tsionis and Mr Beck argued. Mr Beck later said Tsionis had wanted to continue drinking at another pub and he thought she had had enough alcohol. Tsionis told police she couldn't remember what they had been arguing about. She did remember being so furious that she threw her shoes at her boyfriend and stormed out of the car at Treasury Gardens. Mr Beck drove his car on to the gardens' grassy verge, got out and tried to coax her back but Tsionis refused, and he drove off.

Nearly a month after her hysterical 'cry wolf', Tsionis formally admitted she had made it all up. On 15 October 1999, she was sentenced to a two-month intensive corrections order after pleading guilty to making a false report to police, possessing amphetamines and breaching a community-based order. The magistrate heard that in the past she had been a victim of domestic violence, and that she cared for both her mentally ill five-year-old son and for her schizophrenic mother at her Ringwood home. A month later in a fiery cross-examination at Dieber and Whiteside's murder committal hearing, when asked why she had lied to police about being raped, Tsionis replied: 'I cannot answer that question.' When quizzed about lying to Dieber and Whiteside's group, Tsionis said: 'I have been punished already for that.' Upon being reminded that two men were facing murder charges as a result of her lie, Tsionis retorted: 'I didn't go and tell them to do that … It didn't give them the right to do what they did.'

***

Back in Treasury Gardens on 25 April, Dieber and Whiteside know none of this. They only know that the sobbing woman in front of them is saying that two men have just raped her. Nothing in their lives has prepared them to suspect that she may be lying.

Whiteside grew up in Ferntree Gully, then a semi-rural suburb. Brussels sprouts and beans grew across the road from his home. The Whitesides were a big, close, hard-working, sports-loving family. Whiteside was the youngest of five children. His boner/butcher father played district cricket and football; he had been the captain/coach of the Canterbury football club. His mother also played cricket. Later she played lawn bowls for Victoria. When he was 14, Whiteside's father died. He then helped his mother make ends meet by mowing lawns. She died in 1998 – a year

Just Anger

before Mr Hibbins did. At school, Whiteside struggled academically but thrived at sport, especially cricket. He left Knox Technical School after Year 10 and took up an apprenticeship with an airconditioning firm. He eventually got a full-time job there and developed a reputation for his skill and know-how in the area. Psychologist Elizabeth Warren found Whiteside's propensity for rage was low compared to other men of his age. She found him a 'warm, friendly sort of chap'.

Like Whiteside, Dieber loved sport, especially cricket, and had a supportive family. While Whiteside had struggled academically at school, however, Dieber had excelled. For four years in a row, he came in the top five per cent in a national mathematics competition. By Grade 3, he was the school chess champion – even beating the principal. In Year 11, he was on his school's student representative council and learnt to play the piano. His final-year school mark put him in the top 10 per cent in Victoria. Dieber also represented his school in football, athletics, table tennis and cricket. He captained the North Ringwood cricket club's 3rd eleven and coached their under-14 side. He was known as a quiet student of the game, enjoying the tactical finesse of spin bowling. At Monash University, Dieber got distinctions or credits in his Bachelor of Economics but knocked back an offer to go on to Honours. He wanted to start earning money to help support his family. He got a job working on the accounts of a security guard company and by 1999 he was a trusted and respected employee responsible for several workers. Dieber's father was a retired butcher. He had migrated to Australia from Austria in 1969, at the age of 26. In 1999, 23-year-old Dieber was living with his parents, his 27-year-old sister Jodi and her five-year-old son. For the young boy, Dieber was not just an uncle – he was a father figure.

Dieber and Whiteside's lives had not prepared them to treat a distressed woman's rape claim suspiciously, or even cautiously. The alcohol they had drunk that day may also have had something to do with it. Before the footy, Whiteside had drunk two cans of full-strength beer and Dieber had downed four or five pots. During the game, they had both drunk beer. Afterwards, in the hour or so they were at the MCG Hotel, Whiteside had five or six full-strength beers and Dieber had five drinks – beer and spirits.

Whatever the reasons, upon hearing Tsionis's rape claim, Whiteside and Dieber have none of the park ranger's doubts and race off into the park, determined to catch the rapists and hand them over to police. They are so fired up with their 'citizen's arrest' mission, they do not even find out what the 'rapists' look like.

In their semi-drunken search, Whiteside and Dieber advise a family to leave the park as there has been a rape. The family thank them and do just that. Dieber and Whiteside ask some others whether they have seen 'two guys' recently. Then they come upon two guys – Mr Campbell and Mr Hibbins.

Up until that moment – like Whiteside and Dieber before they met Tsionis – Mr Campbell, 47, and Mr Hibbins had been having an enjoyable day. Life partners for 15 years – they called each other Davo and Keitho – they had spent the day up country in Marysville visiting a waterfall and had bought a nice red at a winery. On their way back to the inner-suburban Collingwood home which Mr Hibbins had architecturally designed and Mr Campbell had landscaped, Davo decided he needed some olive oil to cook the dinner to go with that red. To get the money, they went to the ATM at the Peter MacCullum Cancer Institute but, because of the big footy game, they had to park quite a distance away. As Mr Campbell told Steve Dow for his book *Gay*, on the way back to the car, he said to Keitho: 'Oh, let's go and look at the possums.' Mr Hibbins and Mr Campbell liked walking through the park and watching the wide-eyed brushtail possums. But that night Mr Hibbins and Mr Campbell never see the possums. Instead, they meet two aggressive-looking younger blokes reeking of alcohol who tell them a woman has just been raped.

Mr Campbell: They both came towards us and said in an aggressive voice that a woman had been raped in the gardens. At that point, I felt that there was going to be trouble judging by the aggression in

Just Anger

the males' voices. Keith and I said in unison: 'We'll call the police.' They replied that they had already called the police. I said: 'What does the guy look like?' The first male [Whiteside] said: 'We don't know.'

That's when Mr Hibbins makes his fatal mistake. As well as being known for its possums, a part of the gardens is known as a gay hangout. Knowing this and noting Dieber and Whiteside's aggression, Mr Hibbins and Mr Campbell jump to a tragically wrong conclusion.

> *Mr Campbell*: I thought they might have been gay bashers. I look gay and so does Keith ... I don't know the exact words Keith said, but he was asking why they were so aggressive with the two of us. Keith then said we were going off to get the police.
>
> Keith then said to me, 'We've got to get out of here. Run!' ...
>
> It was obvious just before Keith said 'Run!' that both males were getting more aggressive and that Keith and I were the subject of that rage. When Keith said, 'Run!' we ran. When we started to run, I knew that the two men were chasing us ...
>
> I can recall tripping on something. As I was getting up off the ground, something hit me on the mouth and nose; I am unsure whether it was a fist or foot. I was then pushed back down on to the ground, front first. Whilst I was on the ground, I was being struck a number of times to the legs and face ... I heard a voice say, 'I'm gonna fucken kill you' ...
>
> I recall Keith saying, 'Leave him alone.' I knew Keith had come back to help me ... I was able to get off the ground and started to run again.

Mr Campbell makes it to Lansdowne Street and hails a car. He begs the couple inside it: 'Somebody help us please. I've been bashed.' When the car stops, Dieber abandons his chase and goes back to help Whiteside deal with Mr Hibbins.

REASONABLE DOUBT

From the quiet of her dying husband's room on the seventh floor of the Peter MacCullum, Beverley Skinner sees the bashing of Mr Hibbins against a parked car. She thinks he's hit about 20 times.

> *Ms Skinner*: He [Whiteside] just started beating into him … He was just punching the crap out of him. He was using fists and elbows … but I did not see any … kicking. He was not stopping. He wouldn't stop for no-one. It was an outrage. He was a bloody animal – savage.

A witness on the ground – Ross Junor – calls for an ambulance as he watches the assault and hears Mr Hibbins screaming for help. As he speaks to the ambulance service operator, Mr Junor's voice rises as he realises how serious the assault is: 'They're getting stuck into someone up here. Make it quick!'

With Mr Hibbins unconscious, Dieber and Whiteside look for Mr Campbell. The man and woman he flagged down a few moments earlier – Paul and Michelle Rogers – are consoling him at the hospital's entrance. When Dieber and Whiteside rush at him, Mr Campbell flees inside the hospital and Mr and Mrs Rogers block the bashers' path. The taller, more aggressive one (Whiteside) tries to push past them to get to Mr Campbell. Both men loudly tell the Rogers that a girl has just been raped in the park. Whiteside asks: 'What would you do if you approached two guys, you told them that and they ran off?' Ms Rogers tries to tell the angry, slurring, alcohol-reeking young men how wrong they are. When they tell her the man she's protecting in the hospital is a rapist, she replies: 'Don't be silly, he's gay.' Whiteside sneers: 'Well, he would say that, wouldn't he.' Dieber snorts: 'That's a likely story.'

Dieber and Whiteside stay near Mr Hibbins's unconscious body until police arrive. Still certain he's in the right, Whiteside tells police he punched Mr Hibbins four or five times. When asked why, he tells the police officer: 'You know, they know.'

Lying unconscious on the street, Mr Hibbins has two black eyes, a badly bruised left ear, extensive bruising down the left side of his neck up to his jaw and a badly bruised chest. Worst of all, there is bleeding into his brain.

Just Anger   219

***

In interviews with police into the early hours of the next morning, Whiteside and Dieber gave very different versions of what led to the fatal bashing of Mr Hibbins. Dieber said he and one of his friends were 'pretty stunned' when a distraught woman screamed at them, 'Do you want to rape me too?' and then 'just collapsed and just dropped to the ground'.

> *Dieber*: Johnny has said to me: 'She said she got raped by two men' … So basically me and Johnny just walked through the park trying to find, you know, two guys and we spoke to people and just asked them: 'Have you seen two guys running through here?' … We were as calm and rational as you can get … I mean it's not like we were a head full of steam and, you know, 'someone had to pay': that wasn't what it was about.

Dieber said after a few people calmly denied seeing two guys running by, they saw two guys 'just hanging around' in there.

> *Dieber*: Johnny might've said: 'Hey, you blokes, have you seen any two blokes running through here or hiding in here?' And they said something along the lines of: 'Why?', or something, and Johnny said: 'Because a girl's been raped,' and I think they said: 'Why don't you call the police?' and Johnny said: 'Well, the police have been called,' and that's when they sort of just started heading off … Johnny said: 'What are you going for?' and that's when they started running and that's why I guess me and Johnny were pretty convinced that they knew something about it [the 'rape'] … They just absolutely sprinted away … Johnny said to me: 'Catch him. Catch him' … and he chased the other guy.

His version of the first time they caught up with Mr Campbell and Mr Hibbins did not include Mr Campbell tripping over; Mr Campbell getting kicked or punched; and certainly nothing about anyone yelling 'I'm gonna fucken kill you', or Mr Hibbins telling them to 'Leave him alone'.

220 REASONABLE DOUBT

Dieber: We just grabbed 'em like 10 metres away and just said: 'What are you doing?', you know, 'What are you running for?' ... I just grabbed the guy and said: 'Look, wait here, we'll let the police ask the questions, all right,' and then he just pushed us and sprinted away.

According to Dieber, what happened the second time they caught Mr Hibbins – on Lansdowne Street – was nothing like the 'savage' beating Ms Skinner said she saw.

Dieber: I chased the shorter one [Mr Campbell] but I couldn't catch him and then I looked up the street and Johnny had caught the other one and I went up there ...

I thought I'd help Johnny because I was dead set convinced that they knew something about this girl getting raped. Johnny ... was just trying to hold him ... So I came up and just said: 'Listen, mate just fucken ... stay there and wait for police' ...

Johnny was just, you know, arguing with him: 'Just wait here, wait for the police to get here. They've been called. Let them ask the questions.'

And the guy, you know, is obviously yelling at us, you know, the usual: 'I'm gonna kill you, you dobber,' and whatever ...

The guy was saying some violent things – I can't repeat what he was saying without swearing – he was saying basically 'Get lost'.

When the police tell him to 'feel free' to say what was said – not to worry about saying swear words – Dieber says: 'I don't know exactly what he said.'

Dieber: We wanted to keep him there, and he was resisting. Like, Johnny probably hit him a couple of times. He was still struggling and I threw a couple of punches. I am not sure if any landed ...

Later in the early-morning interview with police, Dieber says he hit Mr Hibbins 'three or four times' and that probably two of the blows hit Mr

Just Anger

Hibbins around his nose. But he also said: 'I've never hit anybody so … I am not a particularly good puncher or anything.'

Dieber: He, me and Johnny were just grappling with each other and we obviously wanted to keep him in that place, like for the police … I hit him then and, yeah, basically he wanted to get away at all costs …

I thought if he's raped someone, you know, who knows, he might have a knife – anything. So I have thrown a few punches …

Anyway, he ended up falling over and we went to find the other guy and we just went round the corner. There was this couple there and they said: 'The police are on their way that guy is over there.'

We said, you know, 'Excellent,' and just sat down on the ledge. Me and Johnny just voluntarily sat down and waited for the police.

Dieber tried to make the police understand why he and Whiteside were so convinced Mr Campbell and Mr Hibbins were rapists.

Dieber: If I told you a girl's been raped, what are you gonna do? You're gonna go: 'Really! No I haven't seen anyone … I'll keep an eye out' … and when I say: 'The police have been called,' you're not gonna just sprint off, are you?

It was pretty weird. I mean, we weren't aggressive to 'em. It's not like they sprinted because we were assaulting 'em. That's not the case at all …

She got raped by two males and they were two males in the park who happened to absolutely sprint when we asked them about it.

He denied that either he or Whiteside held Mr Hibbins while the other punched him, or that they hit Mr Hibbins 20 times, although he admitted they could have hit his head 'something like' 10 times.

Dieber: It's pretty hard to hold someone if they don't want to be held … Johnny hit him a few times, not overly hard, just sort of trying to, you know, make him realise that he's not getting away. He just kept on fighting and stuff and trying to get away ...

I am a security guard, so I know you can use like reasonable force to make a lawful arrest ... I thought it was pretty much reasonable force. I think the real injury must have been done when he hit the ground.

My objective wasn't to hurt him ... But what else can you do? Like, I didn't have handcuffs, or anything like that. I thought, you know, you could use a bit of force to make a citizen's arrest ...

It all happened so quickly, but he either got punched or pushed to the ground and obviously must have hit his head to have ... the injuries that he's got which I am obviously sorry – sorry – about, but that wasn't our intention, just to bash someone. I mean, I have never done anything like that in my life.

Whiteside told police that when they came upon Tsionis she threw her purse at them and screamed: 'Take whatever's in it.'

Whiteside: She was just *that* frightened, it wasn't funny ... It was pretty scary ... You could see something had happened to her majorly and she just said she had been sexually assaulted ... Like, we heard plain as day she just said: 'Two blokes sexually assaulted me ... I have been raped.'

I have said: 'OK,' like sort of shocked because ... like that's not every day you would walk down the street and a woman has just been raped ...

I should have probably stayed put and stayed with my friends and probably stopped being a bit of a hero and left the police to catch the blokes who did it ... but at the time, I just thought it might be the safest thing to do to just have a gander around, have a look around, so that's what I did.

He said that after talking to two or three groups of people, he and Kristian Dieber came upon 'these two gentlemen'.

Just Anger

Whiteside: They got very nervous and started walking the other way saying they'll ring the police themselves when we said the police were already at hand, but then they started to run – which was pretty suspicious – and we ran after them to find out, you know, why they were running.

The two gentlemen just acted very, very strange and when they started to run off that just wasn't a good look. It looked like they did it …

As we were chasing them, I remember shouting out to them, you know: 'Why are you running?' It was pretty strange: two blokes just start running as soon as you mention police and they just couldn't wait to get out of the park as quickly as they could hightail it … They just done a bolt on us.

Contradicting his mate's story, Whiteside said that Dieber [not he] caught Mr Hibbins on Lansdowne Street. Dieber, he said, dive-tackled Mr Hibbins on the street and that he only arrived as Dieber was struggling to his feet.

Whiteside: I grabbed him [Mr Hibbins] … The guy's actually taken a swing and I have gone bang, bang and hit him a couple of times in the jaw … He chucked a swing at me and I hit him a couple of times … It wouldn't have been more than four times. He wasn't knocked out with any of the punches. It was just basically a clout …

I happened to hit him four times. It was just short sharp hits. It wasn't like I stood there and king-hit him four times. It was fast. It was just: whack, whack, whack, whack. You know what I mean? … I was chucking the swings basically in self-defence to some sort of degree …

I was shaking him at the time saying: 'What's going on?' Basically: 'How come you're running away? You obviously know something that's going on' … We got into a wrestle … I got my shirt ripped and stuff like that … I don't know where the other half of my

224   **REASONABLE DOUBT**

shirt is … He nearly got on top of me and that's when Kristian hit him because I was in trouble … I called out to Kris 'I need help' … Kris hit him and that's when basically he was unconscious, I daresay … He hit the deck.

Like Dieber, Whiteside did not mention anything about Mr Campbell tripping, or being kicked, or having his life threatened. He also strongly denied that Mr Hibbins's head was punched anything like 20 times.

Whiteside: No, that's not true. If he took 20 blows to the head, he must have one hell of a jaw. I don't know too many people who could take 20 blows to the jaw.

I'm guilty for hitting him – if that's what you're saying – but, I mean, he chucked the first one …

I'm the last person that normally goes out looking for a fight and stuff like that and trying to knock blokes' heads off and stuff like that … Listen, I don't get into fights. I am not a fighter. The last time I had a fight it was with my brother and he kicked the snot out of me …

I don't have a criminal record at all so, you know, what's happened I am not happy about it but if this guy's got hurt, well, you know, I'd be the first bloke to say sorry but it's just the way they came across. It was very sus.

Given that it was after 3am and he had had a very long dramatic day, it probably wan't surprising that Whiteside came up with some contradictory responses to what he had done.

Whiteside: When I look back on it now – I have had a bit of time to look back again – I probably would still have done the same thing, to be honest …

I wouldn't have probably tried to knock their block off or anything like that – which I wasn't intending to till he threw a punch – but

Just Anger

225

probably I wouldn't have gone off. I think I would have just maybe rung the police straightaway and say there are some sus people in the area instead of going chasing them myself. So, I think that was probably the stupidest idea I have ever had … I don't know. To me, mate, I jumped the gun – probably might have. I mean, it seemed very odd, very strange why two people would just sort of run …

I'm not a thug … Whatever's happened, you know, this is going to be a blemish on my record for, probably, the rest of my life and I am not real proud of it … What's happened is a mistake, and that's basically all I can put it down to. It was one of those things that it just got way out of hand …

I'm sorry what happened to that bloke and I mean it 100 per cent. I didn't mean to hurt him and I don't even think Kristian meant to hurt him. I think Kristian would be in the same boat as me. If we could take that last half an hour away … If we had stayed in the pub for another half an hour, none of this would have happened, or if we had left half an hour earlier.

I was just in the wrong place at the wrong time … I was helping out the lady, but.

***

While Dieber and Whiteside tell their stories to police, Mr Hibbins fights for his life. At first, doctors think he will pull through. Once, during his long bedside vigil, Mr Campbell is certain Keitho hears his name and turns towards him. Then on 6 May – 11 days after the bashing – Mr Campbell gets the call: 'Hurry, Keitho's going.' He gets to the hospital just in time for the partner he thought he would grow old with to die in his arms.

***

In the weeks and months after Mr Hibbins's death, Mr Campbell fell into a deep depression. He had post-traumatic stress disorder. A psychologist said of him: 'In all my years of working, I have not witnessed such excruciating suffering in a bereaved person … I have not encountered a more severe grief reaction.' One of Keith and David's many friends, Lindy Marshall, said: 'Keith was so gentle and fun-loving and always wanted people to be the best they could be. He was the sort of person who would lift the spirits of others ... David is so hurt; Keith was his world. It will be very, very hard for David to pick up the pieces and go on.'

In jail, the news of Mr Hibbins's death also hit hard. Dieber and Whiteside were shattered that their misplaced chivalry had ended in the violent death of a gentle man. That, and – when the Office of Public Prosecutions quickly upgraded their 'intentionally cause serious injury' charges to 'murder' – they faced the nightmare prospect of spending a significant part of the rest of their lives in jail. Neither of them was coping well with jail. Whiteside whispered to a visitor that the night before a prisoner had hanged himself. When told Mr Hibbins had died, Whiteside broke down weeping.

Jodi Dieber, a financial adviser, said that when her mother first told her that her younger brother had been arrested for bashing a man, she struggled to believe it – not her quiet, shy, clever little brother; not the brother who had beaten her at chess ever since she taught him how to play. She visited Kristian in jail a couple of days after the bashing.

> *Ms Dieber*: He was extremely shocked – disbelieving of what he had done; the result of what he had done, with such serious injuries. He was very concerned about how Mr Hibbins was going, whether we'd heard any news of whether he was going to be OK.

Ms Dieber said her brother's hopes rose a little when it was believed Mr Hibbins would pull through, but were dashed at the news he had died.

> *Ms Dieber*: He was absolutely shattered. He was shocked and upset, just couldn't believe it ... A few days later ... Kristian asked me whether our family could make contact with Mr Hibbins's family to express our condolences but I thought it was appropriate not to make this move.

***

Just Anger   227

Just days before their murder trial was to start the prosecution accepted Dieber and Whiteside's guilty pleas to manslaughter, accepting that they had not intended to really seriously injure Mr Hibbins. Mr Campbell was devastated, telling a psychologist the decision was 'an enormous breach of trust and a travesty of justice'. It was a major legal victory for Dieber and Whiteside, but they still faced significant jail time – perhaps 10 years maximum with eight years minimum – if Justice Philip Cummins was persuaded that they had committed a 'bad' manslaughter.

Prosecutor Bill Morgan-Payler QC acknowledged that Tsionis's 'state of distress' meant it was reasonable for Dieber and Whiteside to believe she had been raped. He also agreed it was unfortunate but reasonable for Mr Hibbins to wrongly believe Dieber and Whiteside were out to bash gays.

> *Justice Cummins*: The fact that his mistake was reasonable brings shame on us all: shame that our society for so long has been so inept in eliminating violence or the risk of violence against homosexuals, and shame that by our failure homosexuals have become inured to violence or the risk of violence against them.

The prosecutor also acknowledged that Dieber and Whiteside had impressive character references, but said they had lied to police to minimise their roles and tried to put some of the blame on Mr Hibbins. He especially quoted Dieber's 'unquestionably false' claim that Mr Hibbins had said: 'I'm going to kill you, you dobber.'

> *Mr Morgan-Payler*: There is an air about what happened – the ferocity of the assault on the deceased man that was in effect punishment – of almost a sense of righteousness.
>
> What may have commenced with honourable motives degraded into simply a desire to punish. Punishment was inflicted on the deceased in an assault which was brief but furious …
>
> If that be the case, then this offence is a serious example of manslaughter.

228   **REASONABLE DOUBT**

Both Philip Dunn QC for Whiteside and Ian Hill QC for Dieber urged Justice Cummins to reject Ms Skinner's evidence of Mr Hibbins being hit savagely about 20 times. Mr Dunn said what Ms Skinner saw seven floors up out of the window of hospital bedroom of her dying husband must have seemed a 'Kafkaesque nightmare'. He said that in the wrestle with Mr Hibbins his client's shirt was torn and he had broken his thumb. They also urged the judge not to believe that one of their clients had threatened to kill Mr Campbell. Mr Dunn told Justice Cummins he should have 'some misgivings' about Mr Campbell's evidence because he had been 'very distressed, depressed and hysterical'. Both barristers acknowledged that their clients had tried to put themselves in the best light in their police interviews but stressed they had answered questions after no sleep, a traumatic day, and in the very early hours of the morning.

> *Mr Dunn*: What happened on this night was a real example of cruel chance and fate … It was a classic, shocking misunderstanding.

He said when Whiteside had mused to police, 'if only things had been changed by half an hour', he had been 'talking in almost a Shakespearian way about the cruel blows of fate'. Of his client's claim that he was 'just in the wrong place at the wrong time', he said: 'If ever a true word was spoken by somebody at 4 or 5 o' clock in the morning at a police station, that's it.' At this, the judge interrupted.

> *Justice Cummins*: No-one forced him to chase the poor deceased man and to bash *him*.
>
> *Mr Dunn*: No … Your Honour, it was like two cars heading down the roadway in opposite directions to one another on a wet road, on a dark night …
>
> *Justice Cummins*: A car doesn't think for itself. That is not an analogy.
>
> *Mr Dunn*: It's not a good analogy, I will leave it … This is the unintended consequences of what he told police was his own stupidity.

Just Anger 229

Mr Dunn said Whiteside had not been a vigilante but an 'over-zealous … citizen who was trying to do the right thing', but who had overreacted and made a mistake. Mr Hill said it was 'a very sad and tragic happening where best intentions went wrong and it's caused much harm and much tragedy to many people'.

***

In his sentencing of Dieber and Whiteside on 23 June 2000, Justice Cummins told them that they had 'downplayed the extent of your aggressive behaviour and wrongly sought partly to blame the victims', but he said he did not believe they had deliberately tried to mislead the police: 'Rather, you gave your answers as you perceived in your state of high emotion … in the shock of finding yourselves in police custody.' He said he did not believe Mr Hibbins had been hit on the head 20 times but did accept most of the rest of Ms Skinner's evidence of a savage beating. The judge said he wholly accepted Mr Campbell's evidence – that Dieber and Whiteside had been running frantically in the gardens in 'a panic state' and that they were 'very angry' and reeked of alcohol when they confronted Mr Campbell and Mr Hibbins.

The judge said he believed Dieber and Whiteside felt genuine remorse, would not be in criminal courts again and that there was no need to make their sentence stern to deter others.

> *Justice Cummins*: The cruel confluence of events in this case surely serves for general deterrence. If persons are not deterred by this case from taking the law into their own hands, nothing I say and no penalty I impose will deter them.

He said that he felt 'nothing but sympathy for Mr Campbell, a decent and honourable man who has lost his life partner'; and that 'one would have to have a heart of stone not to be moved' by the grief of Mr Campbell, as well as of Mr Hibbins's mother and sister. But the judge said the DPP was right to accept a plea of manslaughter because Mr Hibbins's death 'unintended and unlikely'.

He told Dieber and Whiteside that if they had bashed Mr Hibbins because of his homosexuality, their drunkenness or as vigilantes, they would have been jailed for a long time.

Justice Cummins: This was not a citizen's arrest because you punished the suspect, not apprehended him. But neither were your actions the actions of vigilantes. Vigilante conduct is premeditated, purposive conduct wherein the actor takes the law into his or her own hands having eschewed due process of law. Such conduct should be punished substantially both to uphold the rule of law and to deter others from following such a path. But your conduct was not that of the deliberate, process-eschewing vigilante. Yours occurred because of an unplanned, spontaneous upsurge of emotion in each of you. That immediacy and lack of premeditation distinguish you from vigilantes. Yours was not vigilante conduct ...

Your aggressive and excessive conduct towards Mr Hibbins is to be condemned. It caused the death of a human being. But the categories of manslaughter range widely in culpability. Yours is in the least culpable ...

Yours was the conduct of two young men of good character not looking for trouble, not looking for a fight, not bent upon violence; who truly and reasonably believed a woman had been raped and who without reflection or premeditation sought to ensure the perpetrators did not escape before the summoned police arrived; who then, in a rush of emotion, believing you had found the perpetrators, severely but briefly assaulted the victim. Finally, there is the rare and perverse confluence of events which channelled you towards this tragedy: the false cry of rape, your decent belief in its truth, and the socially induced fear of the victims for which we all share blame. You are, of course, responsible for your actions. No-one suggests otherwise: 'Men at some time are master of their fates; The fault, dear Brutus, is not in our stars, but in ourselves ... '

But you, and the victims, were under a malevolent star that Anzac night.

Just Anger   231

After that quote from *Julius Caesar* – just before pronouncing his sentence – Justice Cummins quoted another Shakespeare play – *The Merchant of Venice*: 'Mercy seasons justice.'

> *Justice Cummins*: Each of you has spent six months in pre-sentence detention: in your case, Mr Whiteside, a period of 165 days, and in your case, Mr Dieber, a period of 193 days …
>
> That is enough detention. I propose to order that each of you be released immediately from further custody … In a few moments you will both be able to leave the court and return to your families.

At the judge's words, Dieber and Whiteside's families and friends hugged each other and wiped away tears of joy and relief. The relief was also obvious on the faces of the two accused. The murmur of joy was such that their actual sentence – three years with thirty months suspended in Dieber's case and 31 months suspended in Whiteside's case – was almost drowned out.

> *Justice Cummins*: Accordingly … each of you is now released from custody to serve the balance of your suspended sentences as citizens in the community. You are free to leave the court.

Outside the court, surrounded by beaming, tearful friends and family, Dieber told the media: 'I just feel sorry for everyone involved.'

***

In the following days, Mr Hibbins's friends strongly campaigned and petitioned for the Director of Public Prosecutions to appeal the leniency of Dieber and Whiteside's sentences. Mr Campbell said: 'I want an appeal because I want justice for my Keith.' Susan McDermott, the general manager of Melbourne Independent Newspapers, where Mr Hibbins worked as the supervisor of the advertising department, told the *Age* that her staff were shocked that Keith's killers had been freed.

Ms McDermott: There's a very strong feeling in the community and people want to have justice prevail in this case. Keith was such a gentle man. Both David and Keith wouldn't hurt a fly and they did not deserve this.

Fellow worker Darren James said: 'It does not seem right that two people who admitted killing someone else can be allowed to walk free.'

***

The Director of Public Prosecutions, Geoff Flatman QC, did not need much persuading. In five weeks – double-quick time for law courts – his appeal against the leniency of Dieber and Whiteside's sentences was being heard by the Victorian Court of Appeal. In Victoria, DPP appeals against the leniency of a sentence are fairly uncommon – there were just 10 others in the year 1999/2000. Appeal Court judges are not supposed to just sentence a person to what they think he or she should have got in the first place. First they have to be persuaded that the sentence is obviously too low, is 'manifestly inadequate'. Then, they must reduce the sentence they would have given if they had been the sentencing judge so the person is not a victim of 'double jeopardy' – being judged twice. Appeal Court judges are also normally more reluctant to change the sentences given by experienced judges such as Justice Cummins.

On 4 August 2000 – six weeks after the sentence – the Appeal Court president Justice John Winneke and two long-serving Appeal Court judges, John D Phillips and Robert Brooking, gave their verdicts to another packed courtroom. Things did not look good for Dieber and Whiteside when the president went against them strongly.

Justice Winneke: Whilst I would normally hesitate to interfere with the sentencing discretion of this very experienced judge – particularly in a Director's appeal – I am satisfied ... His Honour has misconstrued the gravity of the offences ... and, in doing so, has imposed sentences which are so disproportionate to the objective seriousness of these crimes that intervention by this court is warranted ...

Just Anger

The gravity of the circumstances in which the innocent victim was beaten and killed cannot, in my opinion, be obscured by seeking to portray those circumstances as an unfolding tragedy in which the respondents became inevitably entangled. Their final assault on the 45-year-old deceased was, as His Honour found, deliberate and vicious and carried out with a desire to punish. It ceased only when the victim fell senseless to the carriageway of Lansdowne Street. Their acts were not those of well-motivated citizens seeking to apprehend and detain a person whom they had reason to believe had committed violent sexual offences. They had no such reason: they asked no questions and made no investigation. They made no attempt to hold and detain a much older man until the police arrived. They simply concluded guilt because their victim had sought to flee before their patent aggression.

The viciousness of the assault and its lack of foundation, in my mind, smacks far more of a desire to avenge and punish by two persons disinhibited by liquor consumed than, it does of misguided chivalry ... A decent life had been taken because the two respondents, hitherto of good repute, decided to take the law into their own hands and became, without proper justification, the judges and punishers of the deceased. Whatever good intentions may have existed when they chose to remove themselves from their own group and enter the gardens had dissolved by the time they aggressively confronted Hibbins and Campbell and then assaulted Campbell in the park, proclaiming that they were going to 'kill him'. Thereafter, their good intentions were replaced, as I see it, by an unjustified desire to catch and punish.

Any suggestion that they were acting as citizens concerned for the rights of the distressed woman became, in my view, little more than a pale excuse for their unlawful conduct. Although His Honour acquitted them of being vigilantes (in the sense that His Honour used that term), the fact that he found they had taken the law into their own hands, and had acted out of a desire to punish, suggests to me that their conduct did have within it an element of the vigilante as that term is popularly understood. In this regard, it is somewhat revealing that when Whiteside was asked at the scene by Senior Constable Bowman why he had punched the deceased he replied: 'You know, they know' ...

In my opinion, these offences were ... serious examples of the crime of unlawful and dangerous act manslaughter ... The bashing was of an innocent person whom the respondents desired to 'punish'. Such conduct was not the result of a 'cruel confluence of events', but very much of the respondents' own choice.

Things were looking grim for Dieber and Whiteside, but there were still two judges to go. Justice Brooking, however, very quickly snuffed out any hope they had of holding on to their liberty.

Justice Brooking: 'Yours was not vigilante conduct', His Honour said to the respondents. In a sense this was true. The police had been sent for; there was no organised group formed to deal with lawbreakers with entire disregard for the public system of law enforcement. But on the judge's findings – inevitable on the evidence – this was 'vigilante conduct' in the sense that both men were motivated by a desire to punish a supposed rapist. They wanted to administer corporal punishment to an innocent, inoffensive and defenceless man whom they believed (quite unreasonably) to be a sexual offender ... The deceased ... was attacked by two men acting in concert. The victim was 45, with physical disabilities. His assailants were two young men in their 20s, both well built (especially Whiteside), both affected by drink and both out of control.

Vigilante enterprises must be suppressed ...

The ... attack on Hibbins's companion, Campbell, and the angry threat to kill him ... helps to show that both were out to punish from the moment they gave chase.

The judge noted that the defence barristers tried to persuade Justice Cummins not to believe Mr Campbell but did not put their clients in the witness box to face cross-examination.

Justice Brooking: It's striking that so much effort should be directed to putting before the judge evidence of background and character and self-serving, second-hand descriptions via psychologists of the events of the night, but not a word from the respondents themselves about their own state of sobriety and state of mind and their own roles that night ...

It does seem to me that the judge was led into passing altogether too lenient sentences by his strongly held view that the respondents had been borne along by the tide of events and were the victims of misfortune ...

Dieber's claim to police that Mr Hibbins had said: 'I'm gonna kill you, you dobber,' came back to haunt him, with Justice Brooking using it twice to illustrate the 'highly improbable accounts given to police'.

Justice Brooking: Causing death by administering a vicious beating in concert in order to punish an unofficial suspect (unconvicted, un-charged, and not identified by a complainant or by any description) for a supposed crime must be viewed very, very seriously. When it turns out not merely that the victim was entirely innocent, but that the supposed crime had not even been committed, the case becomes very striking.

Justice Phillips made it 3–nil to the DPP when he agreed with the other two judges that the sentences were too lenient.

Disappointed as they must have been at their loss, Dieber and Whiteside's lawyer had probably tried to prepare them for such a possibility. What they almost certainly hadn't been prepared for, however, was what came next.

As Justice Winneke read out the new sentences, six years with a minimum four years before they could apply for parole, Dieber and Whiteside's family and supporters gasped and then sobbed openly – this time from shock and sadness. But, they weren't the only ones: Mr Campbell also wiped away tears.

236   REASONABLE DOUBT

Outside the court, Mr Campbell said he had cried because he heard a woman – a friend or member of the Dieber or Whiteside families – sobbing inconsolably. He was sorry that she had lost someone, too.

Mr Campbell: Nobody won. I do not get my Keitho back and two people were taken into custody. I am not glad it happened, but I wanted it to happen. I don't hate them [Dieber and Whiteside], I don't feel anything for them.

Also outside the court, Whiteside's lawyer said his legal team was considering appealing to the High Court. He pointed out that the new sentence was an extraordinary eight times more severe than Justice Cummins's sentence. The 'double jeopardy' Appeal Court sentencing rule meant that the judges probably thought the original sentences should have been a maximum of about eight years. Dieber's lawyer said his client and the whole legal team were shocked and distressed at the new sentence.

***

Nearly a year later – in June 2001 – lawyers for Dieber and Whiteside got the chance to ask the High Court to grant them a full hearing. The main point their barrister Jeanette Morrish QC tried to get across in the 20 minutes allotted to her was that the Appeal Court should have thrown out the DPP's application without even considering whether the sentences were too short because the prosecution had made a fundamental and unfair change of tactics. She said in the trial the prosecutor had agreed with Justice Cummins that there was no need to make the sentence a deterrent to others, but had told the Appeal Court this is exactly what should have happened. She, however, agreed with Justice Michael Kirby that the prosecution's 'general deterrence' concession at the trial did not deprive either Justice Cummins or the Appeal Court of hearing enough evidence to come up with a just sentence.

Justice Kirby: So … if the Court of Appeal were of the view that the concession was wrong … they were in as good a position as the sentencing judge when they found error to substitute the sentence they thought was appropriate.

Just Anger   237

When Ms Morrish tried to argue that Dieber and Whiteside had reasonably believed a woman had been raped, she had to dodge a barrage of legal bullets from High Court judges Ian Callinan and William Gummow.

> *Justice Callinan*: But Ms Morrish, the big problem about everything you say, it seems to me, is that when one of the victims escaped, the two applicants continued to pursue the unfortunate man who was killed. They pursued him out of the park, into the street, for some considerable distance. He was a much older man who could easily have been restrained; they made no effort to restrain him, they systematically bashed him … It got beyond the stage of being vigilante, it was just a senseless and irrational bashing, far removed from the scene of an imagined crime.
>
> *Ms Morrish*: … We say that to have made such a finding was contrary to the findings of the learned sentencing judge and …
>
> *Justice Callinan*: The learned sentencing judge found, in effect, that it was an almost inevitable consequence of an 'unfolding tragedy'. Now, with all due respect, I find it very difficult to accept that finding.
>
> *Justice Gummow*: It was not inevitable at all.
>
> *Justice Callinan*: It is a perverse finding, I would have thought, and the Court of Appeal was, therefore, entitled to interfere with it. How could you say that it was an inevitable consequence when the man was on his own by this stage and being pursued down the street, held by two much stronger and younger men and senselessly bashed to death? Nothing inevitable about that.

Ms Morrish tried to get her appeal back on track by pointing out that Justice Cummins had said Dieber and Whiteside were responsible for their actions.

> *Justice Gummow*: His Honour fixes on this word 'inevitable'. It is just nonsense, to put it in colloquial language.
>
> *Ms Morrish*: Well, true, His Honour had a particular literary style but His Honour accepted the gravity …

Justice Gummow: It is not a question of literary style. There is much more involved here than literary style.

Ms Morrish: We say His Honour correctly balanced, taking into account the concessions that were made, the factors personal to the accused, against the factors that he was required to take into account under general sentencing principles. That, notwithstanding the gravity of the offence, and … true it is that there was a bashing …

Justice Gummow: It is not a bashing; there was a *killing*.

Ms Morrish: Yes, but the killing was unintended and unexpected and the Crown accepted that … In this case, what the sentencing judge gave weight to was the state of mind, namely why did the applicants do what they did, and they each entertained a belief that the victim had, in fact, raped Tsionis.

The DPP Geoff Flatman QC had a much easier time. Rather than tackling him on why an Appeal Court had given a sentence an extraordinary eight times sterner than the original judge, Justice Kirby even suggested Dieber and Whiteside got off lightly.

Justice Kirby: Upon one view, the sentence imposed by the Court of Appeal in re-sentencing was at the low end of what might have been imposed by a primary judge taking the view of the seriousness of the offences that you are urging upon the Court, and that would be consistent with the principle in Crown appeals?

Mr Flatman: Yes, Your Honour.

It was no surprise when, moments later, Dieber and Whiteside lost their last legal hope of freedom when the judges rejected their applications for a full High Court hearing.

In all, six judges had disagreed with Justice Cummins that at least part of the reason for Mr Hibbins's death was that there was a 'malevolent star that Anzac night'.

SCARE TACTICS

After acting in *Australia's Most Wanted*, the country town police soapie *Blue Heelers*, the courtroom drama *Janus*, and the Jackie Chan 'cops 'n' drug lords' kung fu action film *Mr Nice Guy*, you would have thought Jason Mark Murphy might have been put off crime. He wasn't. From bit parts in these shows, Murphy graduated to the lead villain in a real, ridiculously stupid and very cruel crime ... and, for an 'encore', he offered a *very* difficult to believe excuse.

The 29-year-old was far from your typical criminal. He had never taken illegal drugs, smoked a cigarette or drunk alcohol. He was a fitness fanatic with a dream of being a kung fu stuntman in the movies. The youngest of eight children, he came from a close, law-abiding family – one of his brothers was a policeman. But about 10am on 18 July 2000 – disguised in a balaclava, talking in a deep voice so he wouldn't be recognised and supported by an ex-soldier brandishing a sawn-off double-barrelled shotgun – Murphy kicked in a door and marched into a sleeping man's bedroom.

Murphy: I was going through and opened up the bedroom door and saw him. That's when I grabbed him and flipped him over on his stomach ... He was smiling because he must have thought I was somebody else – I don't know. He must have thought it was a joke at first because even then he had a big smile on his face. Don't ask me why: I would not have a clue ...

I grabbed him and wrestled him ... I had me arm around his neck to stop him shuffling around and then he was handcuffed, but I never touched the handcuffs ... Then I lifted him and took him out to the backyard ... We put him in the boot and then drove to Lerderderg Gorge.

The man Murphy had woken up so terrifyingly and abducted so ruthlessly was 34-year-old Christopher Jewell. After working a nightshift at a printing company, Mr Jewell had just fallen asleep when Murphy stormed into his home. Nicknamed 'Sticks' – because he was tall and skinny – Mr Jewell was popular at his work and as the captain of the North Brunswick Aussie Rules football team. He had been living with his fiancée Malyssa MacKay and her three young children for just over a month. The couple had planned to marry in nine months, and Malyssa was pregnant with Chris's first child.

Chris Jewell had arrived home from work a couple of hours before he was abducted. After a cup of tea with Malyssa, he had gone to bed about 8.15am. He was meant to be woken up about 3.30pm to spend time with Malyssa and the children before going to footy practice but two-year-old Jarod wasn't prepared to wait that long. He insisted on showing his new dad his new trousers, so about 9.30am Malyssa reluctantly let him wake Chris up. After that, she went out so Chris could get some peace.

When Ms MacKay returned home about 2.15pm, she noticed Sticks's car wasn't there and that there was a big crack in the middle of the deadlocked back door, but she didn't panic. It was only when she couldn't contact Chris on his mobile phone and a ring-around of friends proved fruitless that she started to get really concerned. She phoned the police, but they told her to wait 24 hours. Malyssa packed Chris's footy bag and waited, and waited, and waited.

Ms MacKay did not know what had happened to her fiancé, but the man who helped Jason Murphy abduct Chris – Clive Clayton Watson – did. Murphy had met Watson while they worked as bouncers at a nightclub. Watson, 32, was also an unusual robber. About two years earlier, he had retired from the army. He had enjoyed being a soldier but, after 10 years, he had decided acting troop sergeant was as high as he was going to go. Watson did *not* recall Chris Jewell smiling while he was being kidnapped.

Watson: He [Murphy] led the way and went into the bedroom – sorry, I can see the guy's face. He opened the door and he went straight in and he was on top of him and the look on this guy's face was just fuckin' abject horror. So, he got the guy in a headlock and I was standing at the foot of the bed and I had the shotgun in my hand. So, he had the guy in a headlock and the guy went into a semi-faint, and then he just rolled over on top of him on the bed and put the handcuffs on him.

After handcuffing Mr Jewell, the kidnappers stuck tape over his eyes and mouth, stole his mobile phone and wallet, and demanded his bank PIN.

Even though it was a cold day, the kidnappers didn't give their victim a chance to get dressed. They bundled him into the boot of Watson's car dressed only in boxer shorts and a T-shirt. Murphy stole Mr Jewell's car and followed Watson. They drove for about 50km from the Sunshine house on Melbourne's western fringe deep into the 14,250-hectare Lerderderg State Park, which stretches 20km north of the country town of Bacchus Marsh, northwest of Melbourne. Murphy knew Lerderderg well because as a youth he used to go four-wheel driving and motorcycling there with his brothers.

Watson: We actually drove the [Mr Jewell's] car up to the scrub, pushed it down a little bit to, bloody, get it, bloody, out of view of the road and then all I did was reverse up. He popped the boot on the guy's car. Chris Jewell was taken out. By this stage I didn't have a balaclava on or anything and I don't think Jason did either, but the guy was taped up so he couldn't see us. So we popped the boot on Chris's car and walked him over and sit him in there. Then Jason just said: 'Well, yeah, I'll just tape his eyes and his mouth over so he can't talk,' and then that was it …

I don't understand why the guy was doing it because the guy's eyes were already covered and the guy couldn't speak anyway. So I just thought he was being doubly careful, he was just going to tape

242 **REASONABLE DOUBT**

him up and get out of there. I just wanted to leave. I wanted to get out of there because it just means I could go home, forget about having, bloody, this with Jason and then just leave it at that and then not speak to the guy ever again, 'cause it was just out of control …

I went back to the car, started the car up and Jason finished taping him, put him in there and shut the door and then we left.

Murphy told how Chris Jewell was transferred from Watson's boot to the back of his own (Jewell's) car.

Murphy: I opened up the boot and lied him in gently because I didn't want him hurt … He was talking.
Police: What was he saying?
Murphy: He was going: 'Don't hurt me! Don't hurt me! Don't hurt me!' And all that type of stuff.
Police: Was he scared?
Murphy: Oh yeah! Oh yeah!
Police: He wasn't smiling any more?
Murphy: No, no, no!

At Lerderderg, Watson made a scarily stupid attempt to reassure Chris.

Watson: I was just calming the guy down, going: 'Yep, yep. We're just interested in bloody teaching you a lesson,' and bloody, you know: 'We are just interested in, bloody, robbing you. Calm down and relax.' I was calming the guy down and then we put him in the boot of the car.

When they got back to Melbourne, Watson dropped Murphy at the home he shared with his elderly parents in Melton, near Sunshine, and drove on to his unit in High Street, Lower Templestowe, in Melbourne's east.

That afternoon – while Malyssa was phoning around desperately trying to find Chris and packing his footy bag hoping against hope he would

Scare Tactics

walk in the door – Murphy was trying to get an alibi. Soon after being dropped off at his Plover Street home, Murphy went to the home of childhood friend Michael Nedic, gave him a green sports bag and asked him to keep it for a couple of days. He also asked Mr Nedic to 'alibi me'. The green bag had two balaclavas, a pillowcase, gloves, a pair of karate nunchakus, and the sawn-off shotgun used in the abduction.

While Murphy was making his bumbling bid for an alibi, Watson was trying to get $1000 out of an ATM in Templestowe with Chris Jewell's bank card and the PIN the terrified man had given them. He had to settle for $30, however, because there wasn't $1000 in the account.

The next morning, police investigating Mr Jewell's disappearance phoned Murphy. He told them he knew nothing about it, that he had spent the day helping Mr Nedic paint his house.

A few hours after Murphy told this lie, he and Watson returned to the Lerderderg. This time they weren't disguised *and* they had a jerrycan of petrol to torch Mr Jewell's car. Later, Murphy and Watson blamed each other for the burning of Sticks's car. Watson said he decided to return to Lerderderg after remembering he had left things up there that could link him to Mr Jewell's abduction – such as his handcuffs! When he picked up Murphy to go back to the forest, he found him waiting outside his house holding a four-litre jerrycan of petrol.

> *Watson*: He [Murphy] said: ... 'Let's go and torch the car. Just to check ... If he's not there, we'll torch the car.'

Murphy recalled things differently.

> *Murphy*: Clive said he wanted to go back and torch it and I turned around and said: 'Well it's up to you.' I said: 'I want him alive, you know. I don't want him dead.' He goes: 'You've got to come with me,' and I go: 'No, no, no. I'm not coming,' and he went to torch it.
> *Police*: Did you go with him when he torched it?
> *Murphy*: I went with him, but I couldn't do it.

REASONABLE DOUBT

At Lerderderg, Watson went to check on Mr Jewell's car. Murphy said he didn't want to check it just in case Mr Jewell was still there and was dead. He was a bit squeamish because he hadn't seen a dead body before.

> *Watson*: I walked over there and there was a body in the car. He hadn't even made it out … I popped the boot slightly and there was this stench – it smelt bad and he was just like a white-purply colour …
>
> There was a towel draped over him and I pulled the towel back and that's when I saw the black electrical tape covered his entire face … no breathing holes, no eye holes, no mouth holes – no nothing …
>
> I went back to Jason and said: 'What did you do to him?' because I thought he might have stabbed him or something along those lines.
>
> All he said was: 'Nothing. All I did was just tape and stick him in the back – just like I said' … 'I didn't know I covered his nose' … And I went: 'No!' …
>
> So then from there, he [Jason] hopped out of the car with the jerrycan. …
>
> When he returned back to the car with the jerrycan, he was smiling from ear to ear. He had a look of glee – like he'd done so well for himself – on his face. He just had this evil smile on his face and I just started to panic.

Murphy said Watson burnt the car but what he did admit to was even more reprehensible: he confessed to not being sure whether Mr Jewell was dead when the car was set alight. He was not sure whether he had agreed to Chris Jewell being burnt alive!

> *Murphy*: I was just sitting there, sitting shaking my head and scared as hell because … once he makes up his mind nothing stops him … I said: 'No, no, no. Don't do it. Don't do it.' And he goes: 'Yeah, we're going to do it' … I said: 'All right, then do it … Even now, I do not know if the man was alive or dead …

I saw the blaze and that's when I felt really bad, really bad. But I did not get out of the car.

Police: What did you do with that bad feeling that you had?

Murphy: I told Clive, and Clive said: 'Don't worry about it. It'll pass.' He said: 'It'll pass. It'll pass.' He goes: 'Just think, you know, he was an arsehole.' I said: 'Yeah, I didn't want him killed, though,' you know. I didn't want to go that far, you know. And he goes: 'No, it's done now. It's done now. It's done' ... That's all he kept saying: 'It's done.' That's when we drove home back to my place.

About 4.40pm that day a neighbouring farmer noticed the smoke from the burning car and called the Country Fire Authority. Firefighters struggled to find the car in the maze of dirt roads but they eventually came upon a gruesome sight – Mr Jewell's charred body curled up in the back, his hands handcuffed behind him. His body was so scorched a pathologist could not definitely say how he died. He did say, though, that Mr Jewell had not died from the fumes of the fire. He may have been dead before the fire was lit, or – the real nightmare – the fire's heat could have killed him.

When police told Murphy that Mr Jewell's car had just been found burnt in the Lerderderg State Park and asked him if he knew anything about it, he said: 'No. That's a surprise.' Even after Murphy was told that his 'alibi' Michael Nedic had said he had given him a sports bag on the day of Mr Jewell's disappearance, Murphy continued lying.

Police: What's in the bag?

Murphy: I would not know.

Police: Why wouldn't you know?

Murphy: Because I don't think that's my bag, and plus I have no further comment.

When he was interviewed the day after Mr Jewell's body was found, Watson said he had not seen Murphy for about two weeks and had not met Chris Jewell. Both men, however, quickly admitted their lies and confessed to abducting Mr Jewell.

246   **REASONABLE DOUBT**

It turned out Murphy had been spurred into kidnapping Mr Jewell by his obsession with Malyssa MacKay. Murphy and Ms MacKay had had an on–off relationship for about two years until Ms MacKay ended it in February 2000 – five months before Mr Jewell's horrific death. After the split, Ms MacKay moved into a Sunshine caravan park with her children: Sarah, seven; Jordan, five; and Jarod, two. It was there she met Mr Jewell. Despite the end of their relationship, Murphy decided Malyssa and the children shouldn't stay in a caravan park he considered a 'dump' and offered to pay the first month's rent and deposit on a house in Sunshine. Malyssa agreed, but insisted it was not a renewal of their relationship. Murphy even helped Malyssa and the children move into the Sunshine house in April 2000.

As Malyssa's relationship with Chris deepened, Murphy's jealousy ramped up to bizarre levels. He was furious in June 2000 when Chris moved into the house he had helped Malyssa get. Ms MacKay told Murphy's murder trial in the Victorian Supreme Court in August 2001 that in the weeks and months before Chris's death, Murphy constantly talked to her about harming him. She said he often he told her: 'He'd bash him, he'd shoot him, he'd kill him'; constantly he derided Chris as 'just a skinny little cunt'.

> *Ms MacKay*: He'd probably ring every day and each time he rang he'd be on the phone for hours. If I hung up he'd quickly be turning up. So it was either stay on the phone, or put up with him at the front door.

A few weeks before Chris's death, things blew up when Malyssa agreed to Murphy coming over for a visit – if he promised to be 'nice and polite'.

> *Ms MacKay*: He sat there muttering under his breath the whole time … 'Skinny cunt. Going to get you, skinny cunt' … So I asked to speak to him outside … and told him I didn't appreciate him sitting there doing that, and he just went ballistic … Screaming, shouting: he was going to smash Chris's car; he was going to smash

Scare Tactics

the front door; he was going to shoot himself; he was going to shoot Chris. He just went on and on … an hour, two hours.

Murphy only calmed down when a friend knocked 'some sense into him'. Ms Mackay said Murphy even threatened to get someone to injure Chris in a footy game. He also besieged her with pleading letters.

Ms MacKay: All his letters were the same. They all just said how much he loves me; how much he wants me back; how much he's changed; he's realised what he's done wrong – all that garbage.

For a fortnight – every couple of nights in the middle of the night – the family was woken by someone banging on their windows and shining a torch into windows. Murphy denied doing this, but offered a way to stop the harassment.

Ms MacKay: He just insinuated that if I slept with him one more time, he'd leave Chris alone, stop threatening us, stop stalking us and that would be it … He'd say: 'I'd be able to get you out of my system, then I could leave yous alone. I wouldn't need to bother yous any more.'

The harassment stopped after Ms MacKay twice had sex with Murphy.

A few weeks before Chris's abduction, Ms Mackay got a call from Clive Watson.

Ms MacKay: He was ringing up to warn Chris not to go home after work … He said Jason had a gun in his boot and he was going to shoot him. He asked me not to tell Jason he had spoken to me … because Jason used to confide in him and if he knew he'd told me he wouldn't confide in him and he couldn't warn me.

Under cross-examination by Murphy's lawyer David Brustman, Ms MacKay said she hadn't taken Murphy's many threats against Chris seriously because she'd considered her ex-boyfriend 'all talk'. She agreed she saw him as 'nothing but a little wimp', that he was not a violent person. She insisted, however, that Murphy had threatened to kill Sticks – not just to bash him.

Ms MacKay produced one of the trial's biggest surprises when she said she had written many raunchy 'love' letters to Murphy *after* Chris Jewell's gruesome death. She had even proposed marriage to the man who admitted violently abducting her fiancé and suggested naming her and Chris's baby after him. She wrote: 'I am rapt that you accept Crystal Lola May as a girl's name but the boy's name is driving me crazy. What do you think about Mitchell Sean Vincent Murphy? It's just another suggestion.' Ms MacKay said her 'love' letters to Murphy were just a ploy.

> *Ms MacKay*: They are all lies … I wrote what I thought he wanted to hear so he could tell me what happened to Chris. I make out I am close to him: he might tell me the truth … I wanted to know how Chris died. I didn't want to know that it went wrong. I wanted to know how he died.

That it *did* go wrong, that Chris Jewell's death was a tragic accident, *not* a deliberate killing, was what Murphy and Watson repeatedly told police.

> *Murphy*: It's like the old saying: the joke went too far. The joke went way too far … Stupid thing to do. Stupid thing to do. I'll be glad when it's over. One thing's for sure: I didn't kill him … I didn't want him hurt, I just wanted him scared so he would leave Malyssa in order for me to get back with her …
>
> *Watson*: It [Mr Jewell's car] didn't actually have a boot, it was like a hatch. So the impression I got was we were going to leave him there and he was going to climb out over the back seat then make his way home, or do whatever …
>
> I participated in this 'cause as far as I was concerned I am the one who has kept Chris Jewell alive for the last three months …

Scare Tactics 249

I thought my going there was going to be his saving grace … that maybe Jason would have got it out of his system and left him [Mr Jewell] alone …

I thought I was doing the right thing and actually helping this guy by actually being there with Jason and having some sort of, maybe some sort of semi-control over him [Jason] but obviously it has backfired and all I can say is I tried my best to keep this guy out of harm's way.

Murphy denied that he had deliberately suffocated Chris Jewell with electrical tape.

Murphy: I wouldn't bind it so he couldn't breathe. That's one thing I refused to do. I said I wanted him to breathe because I didn't want him to die. No way in the world. No way.

He said the plan had been to call police and tell them where Chris was.

Police: Why didn't you?
Murphy: Well, I wasn't driving so I turned around and said [to Watson]: 'Are you going to call?' and he says: 'No, no, no, no' … I actually thought he was serious when he said we were going to call the cops, because that actually was a relief for me because I didn't want the guy killed. No way in the world. I would never participate in something like that … That's not me: murder. No way. I stay away from that.

Murphy came up with the jaw-droppingly stupid suggestion that perhaps Chris Jewell had not got out because he hadn't wanted to.

Murphy: When I left him he was alive … He was in perfect condition – apart from being afraid. He wasn't injured. He was not struck by us at all. He was handcuffed … I actually thought he would've gotten out …

Police: Why couldn't he have got out?

Murphy: Don't know. I have no idea … Personally myself, I don't think he tried. I mean that's the thing: if he wanted to have got out, he could've. He could've easily. I mean, like I've like mucked around with my brothers in the past and I've had me hands tied up behind me and they put me somewhere and I've gotten out. I've literally gotten out. There was no way in the world he couldn't have gotten out. If he had have tried, he would've gotten out.

At the trial the prosecution made it clear why it thought Mr Jewell didn't escape: he was either dead or very nearly dead; Murphy had murdered him for ruining his chances with Ms MacKay by suffocating him with black electrical tape, and Watson had been his willing and enthusiastic assistant.

Murphy's lawyer, Mr Brustman, told the jury, however, that as outrageous as Murphy's behaviour was in abducting Mr Jewell, he was not guilty of murder or manslaughter because he had not intended killing Mr Jewell *and* had not realised that what he had done could lead to Mr Jewell either dying or being seriously injured.

Mr Brustman: What he intended … was not to kill him, not to hurt him, not to do things knowing it was probable that he would die or probable that he would be seriously injured, but to scare him – to frighten him. We all know with hindsight, of course, that it went dreadfully wrong but murder or manslaughter is not made out by the Crown proving beyond a reasonable doubt that something went dreadfully wrong and someone was tragically dead at the end.

That's not murder. It's not manslaughter. It's nothing. It's bad luck.

He simply wanted to scare him, indeed to scare the hell out of him, scare the wits out of him … This man wanted nothing other than to give the deceased a jolly good fright.

Prosecutor Simon Cooper rejected this, asking why, if Murphy and Watson had only meant to scare Mr Jewell off Ms MacKay, they had said nothing to him about leaving Ms MacKay during the abduction.

Mr Cooper: Why would being a victim of a house invasion, an abduction and an armed robbery scare him out of the relationship with Ms MacKay, particularly when it is not even mentioned ... They wanted to abduct him to kill him.

The prosecutor also asked why – if Murphy and Watson had really wanted Mr Jewell to be found by police alive – they had left his car in such an isolated, well-hidden spot?

Mr Cooper: There was no intention that Christopher Jewell was ever going to leave that scene ... Ladies and gentlemen of the jury, this wasn't 'bad luck' ... this was a calculated plan embarked on by these two men with an express purpose in mind and that was that Chris Jewell be disposed of permanently. The great tragedy is that their plan succeeded.

Mr Brustman said, however, that Murphy's dumping the bag with the goods he and Watson had used in abducting Mr Jewell with the same man he asked to be his alibi showed that far from being a 'cold, calculating ... homicidal maniac', Murphy was an 'just an idiot of the highest order'.

Mr Brustman: You might think that Mr Murphy in this tragic comedy of errors – this horrible, tragic comedy of errors – was nothing other than a fool, and a big one at that. This man lives in what, at the very best ... could be called a fairyland ... This man is half-mad. He's an idiot.

His behaviour was dreadful ... but if you accept that in his own muddled way he did not actually intend to hurt this man, even though we know he did, he's not guilty of murder.

Mr Brustman told the jury Murphy should also be found not guilty of manslaughter – because he hadn't realised his actions could end in seriously

252 REASONABLE DOUBT

injuring or killing Mr Jewell – but he acknowledged it was a 'little bit harder to mount an argument against a conviction ... of manslaughter'.

Watson's barrister, James Montgomery, stressed that his client had no motive to kill Mr Jewell and that he had only agreed to Murphy's plan to 'scare the shit out of' his rival in love after Murphy had nagged him for months. He told the jurors that while they might think Watson's claim to have done his 'best' to protect Mr Jewell had not 'been nearly good enough ... not by a long shot', they should punish him by finding him guilty only of manslaughter, not of murder.

After deliberating for just two and a half hours, the jury on 6 September 2001 found Murphy guilty of murder, but Watson only guilty of manslaughter. This pair of dumb and dumber killers were also, unsurprisingly, found guilty of aggravated burglary, car theft, false imprisonment and kidnapping.

In pleading for a lenient sentence, Mr Montgomery told Justice Geoff Flatman that Watson was 'absolutely horrified at how stupid he was'. Mr Brustman said Murphy was on the border of low to average intelligence and that a psychologist had found he tended to blur the boundaries between fantasy and reality. Mr Brustman said Murphy was 'devastated and deeply disturbed that he contributed in beginning a chain of events that lead to the death of a man'.

> *Mr Brustman*: Notwithstanding his threats, he never intended carrying them out.

On 14 September 2001 Justice Flatman said Murphy's subjecting Mr Jewell to a terrifying death was 'accompanied by extraordinary callousness and lack of remorse' but he said there was hope he could, eventually, be rehabilitated. He sentenced him to 20 years for murder. The sentences for all the other crimes effectively added another two years, taking the overall maximum to 22 years. He told Murphy he could apply for parole in 16 years.

The judge noted that Watson had tried to stop Murphy harming Mr Jewell; that he was remorseful for what he had done; and that he had a

Scare Tactics

good work record, but he said he had 'subjected an innocent man to significant terror over a prolonged period'. He sentenced him to eight years for manslaughter. As with Murphy, he added another two years for the other crimes, taking the maximum overall sentence to 10 years. He told Watson he could apply for parole in eight years.

Just over two years later, the Victorian Court of Appeal was asked to overturn Murphy's murder conviction, or at least to grant him a new trial. The three judges were told Murphy should have been tried separately from Watson because the jury could have been prejudiced against Murphy by some of the things they heard Watson say, even though they had been warned that whatever Watson said could only be used as evidence against Watson and not against Murphy. The court was told there were three things the jury should not have heard: a recorded phone call between Watson and Ms MacKay in which they both called Murphy 'a psycho'; Watson telling police that when Murphy returned from burning the car he had an 'evil smile'; and Watson's description of Mr Jewell's face covered in tape. The judges rejected this argument. Justice Geoffrey Eames said the murder case against Murphy 'was very strong, in that his actions pointed powerfully to the conclusion that it was never intended that Jewell would leave the forest alive'. He said it could not be assumed that the jury had ignored Justice Flatman's repeated warnings not to use evidence against one of the accused men, against the other.

The judges also rejected Murphy's claim his sentence was too long.

Justice Eames: It was a severe sentence but it was a calculated crime and whilst not in the level of a contract killing, but rather more akin to a crime of passion, it cannot be said in my view that a sentence of 20 years for the murder was manifestly excessive. It was a planned killing, carried out in a ruthless fashion, and involved a terrifying kidnapping.

FATAL TAUNT

'Sticks and stones may break my bones, but words can never hurt me.' That's what children are advised to remember when people say nasty things to them; it's what they are told they should say to, or even sing at, their tormentors – a sort of chant to ward off teasing. Jesus 'Jesse' Butay should, perhaps, have remembered that childish chant on 23 June 2000.

About 1½ weeks before that day, Butay had been stunned when his wife Ruth moved out. She left a note saying: 'I have done everything I can but the marriage is over.' Later at a meeting with one of Butay's relatives, she made it clear again that the marriage was finished. Still, Butay wouldn't accept it.

Ruth had not just been his wife for 11 years – Butay had followed her to Australia from their Philippines home. In 1989 at the age of 34 he had left his comfortable life in the village of Ilocano in the Philippines' north – where his father was a community leader and where he was forging a biochemistry career and doing a computer course – to follow 23-year-old Ruth when she migrated to Australia. She had been the only woman he had loved.

Shortly after Jesse arrived in Australia, the pair married. A couple of years later they bought a three-bedroom home in Oriole Drive, Werribee, on Melbourne's western fringe. They both worked for the National Australia Bank, processing and analysing computer information. Every Sunday they went to the local Catholic Church or the Filipino Uniting Church. Often to both.

Butay's conservative Catholic upbringing, as well as the fact he still loved his wife 'very much', made it especially hard for him to accept that she wanted to end their marriage.

Fatal Taunt

Butay: In Philippines it's like … really a big shame to the people who know you … They will laugh at you. I believe in marriage, sir. Marriage for me, sir, is a gift from God.

To try to find out whether there was another man in his wife's life, Butay asked two of their friends who lived nearby to spy on Ruth, to check on her comings and goings. They refused.

After sleeping at a friend's place for a couple of nights, Butay returned home to help get it ready for valuation and sale.

Butay: I am sad, sir, because I leave my house and stay in another place. So breaks my heart.

On 23 June 2000, Ruth Butay suggested Jesse meet and get some advice from one of her work colleagues, Scott Stevenson. She didn't tell him that Mr Stevenson was her lover. Butay did know, however, that his wife and Mr Stevenson were going on a weekend away together the next day.

Butay: My wife told me, sir, that she wanted me to meet her best friend at work who was giving her lots of advices … [I thought] it could be a help, sir, for the marriage.

Butay and Mr Stevenson met in a food court in the Crown Casino Complex. Their 2½ hour meeting was marked by long, uncomfortable silences, even more uncomfortable questions from Butay, and obfuscations and lies from Mr Stevenson. When, for instance, Butay asked where Mr Stevenson and his wife were going away that weekend and what they planned to do, Mr Stevenson just said Ruth was making all the arrangements.

Mr Stevenson: It was kind of strange … All through the conversation he was asking for my help to get back with her. I kept telling him that I didn't think I could help him. He needed to speak to someone who really could help him and Ruth.

REASONABLE DOUBT

Mr Stevenson said that during the long meeting, Butay seemed preoccupied. He often just sort of stared into space and when Mr Stevenson asked him if he was all right, he got no response.

Mr Stevenson did not tell Butay that he and Ruth had had sex the Saturday before and he did not tell him that he and Ruth had been exchanging SMS love letters. One of those was: 'Sleep well, princess and dream of me. I will be thinking of you the whole night. Can't wait to see you tomorrow. Until then, love you heaps, Scott.' Another was: 'It felt good. Your just lucky I didn't make the "hot and steamy" comment I was going to make. Did I make you blush?' Ruth even sent an SMS love note to Scott while he was talking to Jesse at the casino food court. Even while her estranged husband was naively asking his wife's lover how to fix their marriage, Ruth messaged Scott: 'I'm never going to love you less than I love you now, Ruth.' Mr Stevenson fudged when Butay asked him whether he was Ruth's boyfriend.

> *Butay*: Scott asked me what I meant by 'boyfriend' … I asked him whether or not they had sex and he said, 'No' … Scott just told me that it's only a business relationship they were having …
> *Stevenson*: I told him that apart from some kissing and cuddling, it had gone no further than that …
> *Butay*: I was so glad to hear from him that he was not my wife's boyfriend … because, of course … I want to save our marriage and, yes, I can ask him to help us.

During this meeting between two rivals in love – one lying about his relationship and the other seemingly not wanting to pick up the obvious clues – Ruth Butay phoned her husband and asked him to hand the phone to Scott. After his long talk with Mr Stevenson, Butay returned home. He denied he was angry after the meeting. After the long drive to Werribee, Butay said he walked in through his front door calling out: 'I'm home, Ruth' – just like a normal day; just like his life wasn't about to change; just like he wasn't about to bash his wife to death with a claw hammer.

Fatal Taunt

257

Butay: She didn't answer me, so I went closer to our bedroom and said it again. 'I am here now, Ruth ... She told me: 'You can't come in right now because I am having a shower.' ...

Mr Stevenson later said that he had phoned Ruth not long after Butay had left him. He said their conversation ended with Ruth telling him: 'Jesse's home. I've got to go.' Those were the last words he heard his lover speak. Butay said while he waited for his wife to finish her shower, he stretched his sore back on a couch.

Butay: After a while my wife called to me that: 'All right, I am finished now. You can come in.' I went into the bedroom. She asked me: 'How was your meeting with Scott?' I went in front of her and dropped to my knee and beg her not to leave ... My hands were together. As if I am praying ... I said: 'Don't leave. Have pity. If we have to go to a priest or a marriage counsellor.' ...

My wife just laugh at me and answered me in a loud voice that those people can't help us because she doesn't believe those people ... She doesn't believe in marriage because it's only written in a piece of paper ... She doesn't care what people say.

I am begging her ... that we got to work it out in the marriage ... I don't want our marriage broken ... because she doesn't give me any reason why she is doing that to me ... I said to my wife that she should consider my health ... She laugh and told me: 'I don't care about you. Even if you cry now and tears with blood, I won't change my mind and if you get even heart attack or die now, I will turn my back on you.'

Butay said while his wife was saying all this she was laughing and he was crying.

Butay: My wife told me ... that she's no longer 'Butay' and even at work ... and her friends know about that already ... I was really broken-hearted ...

258 REASONABLE DOUBT

He said then his wife got really personal and nasty, comparing Butay to her younger boyfriend Scott.

> *Butay*: Ruth told me that he's a horse. 'He's a horse and you are a turtle.' ... It's just like she was stepping her foot on your head and just keeps you to the ground. She was riding an aeroplane and I was like riding a donkey.
>
> After that ... she told me: 'You are no better than dirt.' 'I won and you lose and you are always a loser' and that's what she told me ... Laughing and, you know, yelling ... My wife told me that Scotty was her boyfriend and lover ... She compare me with Scotty ... My wife told me that they are having sex already for a fortnight ... and he's better than me and he's more meatier than me ... And Scotty is younger and at his peak ...
>
> She told me that she's got a lot of sexy scanty things she can wear [on the upcoming weekend away]. That can make her man, you know, horny ... She told me ... I cannot wait to have sex in front of the fireplace.' ... 'Stop ruining my weekend trip.' ...
>
> She told me: 'You dickhead ... You cannot perform like Scott, you're useless and you better cut off your dick,' and she pushed my head back ... very hard ... She told me, sir, that she doesn't want to see my face and to turn it away from her ... She told me ... that she can do anything what she want to do and she can now fuck around because she won't get pregnant and she's safe.

Butay said when his wife said she had been having sex with Scott he had appealed to 'heaven and earth' and felt devastated. He said when she pushed his head, Ruth was 'still saying a lot of words'.

> *Butay*: A lot of talking ... very insulting and even laughing and yelling at me and I can't feel my body – something like a strange feeling. Something like hot and cold over my body and then after that, sir, just a loud pop in my head and my ears filled with water and they wouldn't clear out and I was drowning, sir.

Defence barrister Michael Bourke: Do you remember what happened after that?

Butay: No, sir.

Mr Bourke: What's the next thing that you remember?

Butay: Yes, I saw my wife on the floor, sir ... I was shocked, sir. I was confused. I just can't believe what was happening to her. I said: 'Ruth, what happened, please.' I said, 'Ruth' ... I just said, 'God please help me. I don't know, I don't know what to do.' And I ask her again, 'Ruth, please, what happened? Answer me.' And I pray even more.

Mr Bourke: Do you remember doing anything like checking her pulse?

Butay: No.

Mr Bourke: Do you remember any towels?

Butay: No.

Mr Bourke: Dou you remember leaving that bedroom?

Butay: No, I can't. No, sir.

Mr Bourke: Do you remember a hammer?

Butay: No, sir.

Mr Bourke: Do you remember leaving a hammer in the laundry?

Butay: No, sir.

Mr Bourke: There is evidence that you rang some people.

Butay: I can't remember, sir.

Mr Bourke: Do you remember any alcohol?

Butay: No, sir.

Mr Bourke: Do you remember the police on the Westgate Bridge?

Butay: No, sir.

Butay said the next thing he remembered was seeing police officers at the station and then waking up in hospital to a visit from a friend.

The prosecutor John Dickson QC tried to prompt Butay into remembering the night he bashed his wife to death. After taking him through what Butay said were the last of his wife's insults: 'You dickhead, you

260   **REASONABLE DOUBT**

better cut off your dick … You are just useless … ' Mr Dickson asked: 'Is that when you went to get the hammer?'

Butay: I don't know, sir.

Mr Dickson: You can remember all that [the alleged insults] yet you can't remember getting the hammer?

Butay: I can't remember, sir.

Mr Dickson: You hit her from behind, didn't you?

Butay: I don't know, sir.

Mr Dickson: And she bled all over the bookshelves, spraying blood on the bookshelf and the walls, hadn't she?

Butay: I don't know, sir.

Mr Dickson: And you just kept on hitting her with the hammer. That's right, isn't it?

Butay: I don't know, sir.

Mr Dickson: When did you buy the bottle of tequila?

Butay: I don't know.

When the normally reliable Ruth didn't turn up for her nightshift a couple of hours later, her worried workmates raised the alarm. When someone went around to her home and saw lights on and her car in the driveway but got no answer at the door, police were called. After breaking a window to get inside, police found Ruth Butay's bloody body lying on the floor in the bedroom dressed in white tights and black shirt. Her head was wrapped in two blood-soaked towels – a pink one and a white one. A hammer indentation in one towel indicated she had been hit at least once *after* her head was wrapped in a towel. A pathologist said Ruth Butay's head had been hit at once with a hammer while she lay face down on the floor. Police found runners stained with Ruth Butay's blood and, in the laundry on top of a basket of clothes, they found a bloodstained half-kilo claw hammer. In the bin they found a torn-up note in Butay's handwriting. Part of it was: 'I'm willing to compromise … You have given me hope. I believe in you as a partner.'

About 11.45pm, Ruth Butay's mother Erlinda Amores in New South Wales – still unaware her daughter had been bashed to death – got a strange call from her son-in-law. Slurring his words, Butay asked his mother-in-law why Ruth wanted to separate from him. During the strange and unsettling one-hour call, when Ms Amores managed to interrupt Butay's drunken ramblings, she asked him where her daughter was. He told her she had gone to work. Butay repeatedly, drunkenly declared his love for Ruth. He told Ms Amores: 'Ruth can't leave me. Ruth is my treasure and not even you as a parent can get Ruth back from me.' Finally, he told Ms Amores: 'I love her,' and hung up.

Just after that phone call – about 1.30am on June 24 – Butay called Ruth's supervisor and told her: 'Scott says he's going to kill me. I just want you to know that,' and then hung up.

Almost 12 hours later a daughter of a friend of Ruth and Jesse Butay happened to be driving over Melbourne's massive West Gate Bridge when she recognised Butay's car parked on the side. Police found Butay sitting locked inside his car. Eventually they managed to persuade him to get out and then realised he was very, very drunk. On the passenger's seat they found a one-litre bottle of tequila with just 100 millilitres left. They also found a note: 'Goodbye, I'm tired, I want to rest forever.' It was next to a crucifix and a photo of Butay's parents. There were also some fresh flowers, with another note in Butay's handwriting. It said: 'For you, love. I love you.'

High up on that big bridge, Butay told police: 'Can you do me a favour? Can you please shoot me? I just want to rest forever. I am a very bad person.'

***

At his murder trial in the Victorian Supreme Court in September 2001 – a year and three months after he killed his wife – Butay claimed he wasn't guilty of his wife's murder because Ruth's torrent of insults had provoked him into losing self-control and killing her in a blind, mindless fury. Eventually, the jurors agreed or, at least, agreed they could not discount the reasonable possibility that Butay had snapped and lost his self-control when he bashed his wife to death with a hammer and found him only guilty of manslaughter.

REASONABLE DOUBT

In the pre-sentence plea-hearing, Mr Bourke pleaded for leniency, saying Butay was deeply remorseful for what he had done; was being treated for depression when he killed his wife; was continuing to suffer depression; would have a difficult time in jail with his family living overseas, and had not committed a crime before.

The prosecutor, however, called for a stern sentence, saying the killing of Ruth Butay was a particularly serious manslaughter.

In sentencing Butay on 2 November 2001, Justice Geoff Flatman told him his wife 'had clearly decided to leave you, but that she wanted the separation to be as amicable as possible'. He said Butay refused to accept that. The judge said Butay savagely struck his wife's head at least five times with a hammer when she was vulnerable and defenceless. He said he had found it difficult to accept that Butay felt genuine remorse for what he had done.

> *Justice Flatman*: Even accepting that you have no recollection of the attack you made on your wife, you say you became aware at some stage that she was seriously hurt. You did nothing to assist your wife, the woman you say you loved, after you came to your senses.

But the judge said he noted that on the West Gate Bridge, Butay told police: 'Shoot me. I am a bad man.' He told Butay this seemed to show some remorse and that he was prepared to accept 'you are sorry your wife is dead'.

After all the claims Butay had made against his estranged wife, Justice Flatman was keen to balance up the ledger.

> *Justice Flatman*: It is clear that Ruth Butay was a much-loved daughter and sister. She was described by her sister as a person respectful of others. She was a caring, considerate and courteous person. Her mother described her as a respectful, well-spoken and caring young woman ... She was highly regarded by her workmates.

The judge noted that Ruth Butay had not only asked a relative of her husband's to help him come to terms with the end of their marriage, but she had been embracing Butay while trying to discuss the marriage break-up. The judge said that Ruth Butay's family had been shocked by what he said she told him just before he killed her.

> *Justice Flatman*: From their perspective, just as Ruth was unable to defend herself from your violent and savage attack with the hammer, equally she was unable to defend herself from your allegations as to her use of provocative and abusive words ... I would emphasise to Ruth Butay's family and friends ... the jury verdict means no more than ... that the jury could not exclude, beyond reasonable doubt, the possibility of those words being said.

Even though a jury had found there was a reasonable possibility it was enough to cause him to lose self-control and kill, the judge told Butay the 'degree of provocation was not great'.

> *Justice Flatman*: There was in my view, assuming the provocative words were said, a real question for the jury to find that an ordinary man in the same circumstances as you were in might lose self-control. The allegation really came down to the proposition that you lost self-control because your wife used insulting and abusive words and you felt you had been lied to ... The degree of violence involved was excessive ...
>
> In the end, we are faced with the fact that a very decent young woman has had her life cruelly cut short as a result of a brutal attack ...
>
> I have decided that the appropriate sentence to be imposed upon you is one of imprisonment for eight years. I fix a nonparole period of six years.

BEDSIT TRAGEDY

In a tiny flat in Cartwright – a struggler's suburb of Sydney – 59-year-old Jeffrey Dunn and 41-year-old Jacqueline Dowd played out the classic flat-share nightmare. For four months, in the claustrophobic confines of their bedsit – lounge/bedroom/kitchen and a bathroom/toilet – the former workmates tested their friendship to the limit. Unemployed and with money tight, it was next to impossible to avoid each other.

They were a very odd 'couple'. Jackie was quite gregarious; Dunn was quiet. She liked watching television and doing crosswords; he liked reading (even though he had battled dyslexia) and motorcycles. He liked country music; she couldn't stand it. Dunn grew up in a happy, close family in a village in Wales; Jackie had a nightmare childhood of abandonment and abuse in Sydney.

When they met while working in a BHP factory in the early '90s, about the only thing Dunn and Ms Dowd had in common was that their hearts had been broken.

When he migrated from Wales as a qualified motorcycle mechanic with his wife and five-year-old daughter and three-year-old son in the early '80s, things had looked promising for Dunn. A few years later, however, his life started unravelling when his homesick wife returned to the other side of the world with the children. Bitter and hurt, Dunn stayed behind, vowing not to risk falling in love again. He did not hear from his ex-wife or children again.

Jackie's marriage also broke up after she had two children, but the split wasn't nearly as complete as Dunn's. She kept in contact with her children – and with her nephews, nieces and grandchildren. Jackie wasn't as lonely as Dunn but she never escaped the horror of her childhood. Her older sister Maureen Brincal told how her baby sister's troubles started.

Ms Brincal: Grandfather came to the house when I was five years old. Jackie was six weeks. I was placed in the back seat ... Jackie was tightly wrapped in a flannel blanket and was placed on the seat snuggled up against my leg. The car did not stop until we got to Coonabarabran (450km northwest of Sydney).

Outside the hotel my mother got out. She said she had to go to the toilet. After a while when she had not returned, I was sent to find her. I asked a man in the beer garden: 'Have you seen my mother?' 'Yes, she hopped into a semi for Sydney.'

Jackie's fate was sealed from that moment.

Jackie was sent to one aunt and I went to another ...

Jackie was brutalised from Day 1. She would be tied to the clothes line with a piece of rope around her neck and thrown scraps of bread ...

Her past was so cruel she was not able to speak of it for the memories brought on tears.

This is just a brief insight into her life of hell.

In late 2003, Jackie accepted Dunn's offer to stay with him: she had found it a bit crowded living with her daughter, son-in-law and grandchildren in a three-bedroom home. She moved out of Dunn's flat a couple of times when the close-living friction got too heated, but each time Dunn coaxed her back.

To avoid explaining that they were 'just friends', Jeffrey and Jackie took to calling each other 'brother' and 'sister' and, despite their frequent verbal stoushes, Dunn saw Jackie as 'more or less the sister I left behind' in Wales.

Along with their broken marriages, what Dunn and Ms Dowd also had in common was the way they dealt with their woes – by drinking lots of alcohol.

In the four months before 12 March 2004, most days in their little flat they drank at least a four-litre cask of cheap wine and that last day was no different. By 5.30pm on that day, Dunn and Ms Dowd had been drinking wine for eight hours. Also, like most days under the big, yellowing Harley Davidson motorcycle poster of an eagle on the wall, Ms Dowd, with her long straggly dark-red hair, was sitting on a battered brown-check op-shop couch, smoking a cigarette. She was wearing tracksuit pants and a 'Come on Down to South Park' T-shirt. She was half doing a women's magazine crossword and half watching *Deal or No Deal* on the tiny television perched on a rickety table in the corner. On the couch next to her was a full ashtray and the well-thumbed hardcover *Macquarie Dictionary* she used for her crosswords. Dunn was sitting on an equally well-worn lounge chair.

Dunn: We were talking, drinking and she started arguing, pushing shit on me … She was goading, goading, goading. She's pushing. I tried to go to sleep and she turned the telly on, then she turned the stereo on. I asked her not to but she kept it up, laughing – 'Ha, ha, ha' – the way she used to … and I said: 'Look, Jackie, if you don't shut up, I'm gunna come over and kill you' – which, at that particular time, was a joke but she just kept on and on and she bugged the shit out of me.

So I went to the kitchen … and got two knives and I walked down and I said: 'Which one do you want, Jackie?' And she went: 'Go for it!' So I did. And believe me, man, I am sorry as a shithouse – but she was fuckin' goading me into it …

I'm the fuckin' little shit that killed her – but I loved her. She was the greatest person in the world for fuck's sake and I end up here with you guys 'cause I fuckin' knifed the bitch …

Believe me man, I'm fuckin' sorry. I'm gunna pay for this for the rest of my life. I might even stab meself if I can get hold of something. Believe me, man: don't let me out on me own.

Police: Do you remember where you stabbed her?

Dunn: Of course. Right in the guts. Straight in her stomach … She

Bedsit Tragedy   267

lasted about three fuckin' seconds … And the first thing I did was
call the fuckin' ambulance …

With Jackie bloodied and unconscious next to him, her cigarette still in
her hand slowly burning down, Dunn told the ambulance dispatch operator: 'I've killed me sister … She was mouthing off and I, and I took the
knife and actually stabbed her in the guts. She's bleeding.' Following the
dispatcher's instructions, he pressed a towel on her wound but then admitted it was useless.

Dunn: Look, look she's not all right … She's dead. I know that for a
fact. There's no point in me doing anything else. She's gone.

He later told police: 'I put a towel on her and tried to press and stop the
fuckin' blood flow. Didn't work. She's gone.'

Dunn: I tried … I did the wrong thing to start with but I did try to
stop it. That's not going to help me anyway, is it? … She looked at
me and said: 'Why?' and that's it …
Police: Did you answer her when she said: 'Why?'
Dunn: No, I was too busy ringing the fuckin' ambulance … Charge
me. Put me away for life. Why should I try to get out of it? The fact
is it's done. It's gone – finished. I am guilty and I will go to court
and fuckin' plead guilty OK? … I don't need this fuckin' shit, man.
Yous are doing the right thing, guys, but, please, what do I have to
do to plead guilty … She's dead. I am the biggest sorriest person in
the fuckin' world but there is nothing I can do to change that, apart
from spending the rest of my fuckin' life in jail – hopefully not, but
it's gunna happen 'cause I killed somebody … She goaded me. She's
done that for a long time. Goad. Goad. Goad. 'Try to fuckin' shut up,
Jackie.' She's always pushing me.
    She's pushed me too far this time and look where I am: sitting in
the fuckin' cop shop talking to detectives and the poor bitch is dead.

268   **REASONABLE DOUBT**

Do you think I am happy about that? No, I am not fuckin' happy, Bill. No way in the world …

It's my place – or it was, 'cause I won't be there again – and she couldn't handle it and she pushed me too fuckin' far. I have threatened her before, but never done anything about it. Never even fuckin' hit her. This time: yes. So you've got it on tape. I'm as guilty as fuck, so you don't have to ask me any more questions. Lock me away … Unless I get me a good solicitor to get me out of it, but I don't think so. There's a knife with fingerprints on it and they're mine …

I don't know why you have to go through all this process when I am admitting the bloody fact.

Police: All right.

Dunn: Just lock me up.

Police: OK, all right, that's what we're gonna do.

Despite telling police he was as 'guilty as fuck' and urging them to lock him up, Dunn pleaded not guilty to Ms Dowd's murder. His excuse was that Jackie Dowd goaded him into losing control. The second act of this tragedy was played out in June 2005 in the New South Wales Supreme Court.

Defence barrister Richard Button: Is there anything you want to say to Ms Dowd's family?

Dunn: Only that I am extremely sorry for what has happened because, obviously, a lot of harm has been done …

Mr Button: You told police that you, in effect, loved her?

Dunn: As a sister she was a really good sister to me, and I loved her dearly for that reason …

Mr Button: How do you feel about what has happened?

Dunn: I feel disgusted with myself …

Mr Button: Was there a common theme that Ms Dowd would return to when these arguments became heated? …

Dunn: The fact that I don't have a family and my prowess as a

Bedsit Tragedy

male ... I couldn't get a female. I was hopeless.

Mr Button: If we can go to the 11th and 12th of March 2004. Do you have any memory of the events of that day?

Dunn: No.

The prosecutor Paul Conlon SC tried to prompt Dunn into remembering something.

Mr Conlon: Do you still regard her [Ms Dowd] now as the greatest person in the world?

Dunn: Oh, yes I do.

Mr Conlon: I want to suggest to you that when you were living together with Ms Dowd, you would have liked for there to have been more to the relationship.

Dunn: I would have liked, yes.

Mr Conlon: The fact that your affection for her was not returned was a disappointment, wasn't it?

Dunn: Slightly, yes.

Mr Conlon: Did you come to regard her as a bit of a nagger?

Dunn: Yes.

Mr Conlon: Did you feel that she used to pick on you?

Dunn: A little ...

Mr Conlon: I want to suggest to you, Mr Dunn, that on this day – 12 March 2004 – you just had enough of the continual bickering between yourselves, and you decided to put an end to the situation.

Dunn: I don't know. I can't answer that question.

Again and again the prosecutor tried to get Dunn to say what happened on the day he killed Ms Dowd, but he repeatedly said he couldn't remember anything – not the stabbing, not the hours before the stabbing, not even the interview with police after the stabbing in which he begged to be locked up. A psychologist told the court that although Dunn was of average intelligence, years of drinking too much alcohol had severely impaired his memory.

270 REASONABLE DOUBT

Mr Conlon urged the jurors to find Dunn guilty of murder, saying no ordinary person could have been provoked by Ms Dowd's taunts into losing control and killing her.

Mr Conlon: You might think it's a little bit like two kids bickering over childish issues ... An ordinary person with ordinary powers of self-control could have said ... to her: 'I want you out of here tomorrow. I've had a gutful of you. This is my place.'

He said the stabbing was not an uncontrolled, furious action. He reminded the jurors that Dunn had warned Ms Dowd: 'Look, Jackie if you don't shut up, I'm gunna come over and kill you,' walked to the kitchen, picked out two knives, returned, showed them to Ms Dowd and asked her: 'Which one do you want, Jackie?'

Mr Button hit back.

Mr Button: Not every loss of self-control involves running down the street screaming maniacally. There are many ways to lose self-control – some obvious, some less so; some wild, some not.

The fact that the accused man got the knives and was able to talk – drunkenly – to the deceased for a few seconds before stabbing her certainly does not demonstrate that there was no loss of self-control ...

Everything you know about the accused man, about his way of living, everything you know about the injury and everything you know about how it came to be inflicted ... demonstrate that here, in this flat, on 12 March 2004, there was a loss of self-control ...

Two weeks earlier she had told him: 'You're not a man at all' ... Here is a man who hadn't had a kiss or a cuddle for five years – those words were deeply painful ... She was screaming the fact that ... she was going out with her daughter and that Mr Dunn had no-one who loved him. That was very painful. Why? For the simple reason that it was true ...

Bedsit Tragedy

271

These words were screamed moments before – moments before – the accused man stabbed the deceased. Can there be any question … but that loss of control on the part of the accused was caused by the conduct of the deceased, including by her grossly insulting words?

A couple of days later, after deliberating for about three hours, the jury found the man who had told police he was 'guilty as fuck' not guilty of murder. He was declared only guilty of manslaughter.

On 13 September 2005 – about 1½ years after Mr Dunn killed his 'sister' – Justice Megan Latham gave her judgment. In another 'win' for Dunn's defence she found that he had been provoked into trying to injure Ms Dowd, not into wanting to kill her, even though that's what he told her he would do.

Justice Latham: There is no basis upon which I should reject out of hand his statement to police that his threat to the victim was just a joke. That said, this was an objectively serious offence. The victim was a defenceless woman, sitting in a chair, smoking a cigarette when the prisoner stabbed her. The prisoner's resort to the use of knives to silence her was cowardly and brutal … Whilst he was affected by alcohol, he was nonetheless capable of acting rationally …

She recognised a key thing about house-sharing: silly sleights, insults, irritations and spats can build up to a serious explosion in the pressure cooker of a small 'nowhere to hide' flat.

Justice Latham: I would not regard the degree of provocation offered by the victim as significant; however, the prisoner had endured her jibes for some years … so the cumulative effect of the provocative conduct was triggered on this particular evening.

The judge noted that Dunn's loss of control was 'relatively brief'; that he had become socially isolated and emotionally detached after his wife and his children left him; that he was tackling his brain-damaging alcoholism; that he was deeply sorry for killing Ms Dowd; and that he was 60 and had not been in prison before. She sentenced him to a maximum eight years' jail, saying he could apply for parole after five.

Outside the court, Ms Dowd's son Robert Thorne was furious.

Mr Thorne: It sucks ... I've lost me mum over nothing ... He told her he was going to kill her and he did.

ONE BODY, THREE BURIALS

For almost 20 years, Venda and Dennis Hunter's three daughters – Deborah, Dianne, and Jennifer – thought their mother had left them in the middle of the night; they thought she had driven away with a man they had never met.

Their brother, David, thought that too, but he never got the chance to find out what really happened. In another sad twist to the Hunter family tragedy, when David was 16 – five years after his mother apparently ran away on a rainy night in October 1981 – he was stabbed to death on Melbourne's bayside St Kilda beach.

In 2002, 33-year-old Deborah vividly remembered as a 13-year-old waking up and, with 11-year-old David, looking in vain for her mother. Nine-year-old Dianne was away at school camp, and Deborah and David did not know that two-year-old Jennifer had already found out their mother was not there.

Deborah: My brother and I woke up and we couldn't find Mum, so we went looking for her in the washhouse because she was normally in there washing clothes or she was outside hanging clothes on the washing line … We asked Dad where she was, and he just said that she left during the night … that she had gone with another man in a car during the night.

As a 30-year-old, Dianne remembered returning from school camp and having to wait for hours with a teacher because her parents had not turned up. Eventually, she got a lift home with a classmate's parents.

Dianne: When I walked inside, Dad was on the couch, crying with his head in his hands and I knew something was wrong, but I wasn't sure … He told me that mum had left us that she had taken off with somebody else … After he told me, I didn't believe him, and then he told me that, well, she was gone and, 'Go and have a look in her cupboards,' and I went and had a look and I saw some of her clothes had been taken and some of her possessions weren't there as well … He said it happened during the night. He was woken up by a car and then by the time he got up and looked out the window, a car was taking off.

Dennis Hunter told a neighbour of their Furlonger Street home, in the industrial Victorian town of Traralgon, that his wife had 'shot through with her boyfriend and will never come back'. The day his mother disappeared, David phoned one of her best friends, Yvonne Gentle, to tell her. He passed the phone to his father.

Ms Gentle: He said that they had a fight, that he had gone to bed and that Venda had got up and rang somebody she knew, that she had gone off with this guy in the middle of the night and that he heard the car doors bang … I asked him … 'Did she take her car? And he said: 'No'. I asked him if she took her handbag … She didn't even take her handbag … I asked him about Jenny … I was just so shocked because I couldn't believe that she could go anywhere without Jenny … or her car, or her handbag.

Dennis Hunter also explained Venda's disappearance to her professional soldier brother John Holtman.

Mr Holtman: A rainy night, nonidentified motor vehicle, Venda barely said any words, went out into the rainy night, into the unidentified motor vehicle with a strange man, and drove off into oblivion …

I was told by Dennis that $12,000 had been whipped out of the bank accounts of the children very close to the time that Venda disappeared ... He claimed that Venda had taken it when she left.

Years later, Hunter explained his first wife's disappearance to his de facto wife, Frances Medley.

Ms Medley: He said that there was an argument and he went to bed ... He got up at three o' clock in the morning when he heard car doors slam and went out and he saw the car take off.

That wasn't all. According to her husband, Venda Hunter made several mysterious reappearances after walking out on her family.

A short time after that wet October night in 1981, while Dennis Hunter was driving Dianne in a nearby town, he told her he had just seen her mother drive by. He asked her if she had seen her too. Dianne hadn't. About three years later, when the children returned from a day-long picnic to the picturesque country Victorian town of Walhalla with their stepmother, Hunter told them their runaway mother had visited.

Deborah: Dad said Mum had been and we had just missed her ...
She'd come to see us kids.
Dianne: He said they had got into an argument because she wanted to come and collect us kids ... and Mum had hopped into the car and taken off and ... Dad had hopped into his car and followed them.

The saddest sighting Dennis Hunter reported of his wife was in 1986. He said she was seen at the gate of the cemetery when David was being buried.

All of it was nonsense. For almost 20 years, Dennis Hunter lied to hide a terrible secret.

Persistent questioning by Venda's brother, lingering suspicions of others, a renewed missing persons investigation after Venda inherited some money and inquiries by the police department's new cold case unit eventually led to police arresting Hunter in May 2001 and charging him with murdering his wife 19½ years earlier.

He quickly confessed.

Hunter told police he had killed Venda by hitting her two or three times with a stick at about two or three o' clock one morning in October 1981. He couldn't remember the exact date, describe the stick, or say where he had got it from. He also wasn't sure whether he had bashed Venda in the lounge or in the hallway.

Hunter: I just hit her with whatever – I can't remember what – was near me at the time, just killed her … It just happened so fast …

Police: How hard did you hit her?

Hunter: Must have been enough to have killed her and the blood to have come out.

Police: A fair bit of blood?

Hunter: Yeah … Just bloody went down like a bag of spuds …

Police: Where did you hit her?

Hunter: Her head, I think … two or three times …

Police: When did you know she was dead?

Hunter: When she started bleeding and I started freaking. I didn't know what to do … I think I rolled her up in something … a quilt, a blanket or a sheet, I can't remember … I carried her to the back door, put her in a wheelbarrow, I think … That's how I done it. I put her in the shed … then I cleaned up the mess and went back to bed. I woke up about six or seven, or something like that.

Hunter said he hadn't planned on telling his children anything but then two-year-old Jennifer toddled through, wanting to see her mother.

Hunter: Young Jenny … She just wanted to know where Mum was, and I said she was in bed asleep. I said, 'Don't go in there, Mummy's had a hard night and she wants … to be left to sleep.' … But she

One Body, Three Burials

went in there and that was when I broke down ... I think I told them she took off in the early hours of the morning ... Took some of her clothes and left in a car.

When his children had gone to school, Hunter said he 'dug a big hole out the back' in the garden shed and 'put a lot of wood and that in it'.

Hunter: I dug the hole about four – maybe five – feet deep, probably as long as this table ... Put timber down, paper down, then put her down there, put timber on top – anything and everything I could get ... Put petrol in it and set it alight. Let it go all day – kept stoking it ... When I ran out of fuel for it, I just filled the hole in and left it there.

He laid a brick floor over his incinerated wife's secret grave. Hunter said that 12 years later, in 1993, he decided it would be best to move Venda's remains to a garage he was building.

Hunter: What was left of Venda, I just put under a [concrete] slab in the shed ... I just put it [Venda's remains] in a plastic bag and buried her under the slab ... I dug a hole and just put her ... planted her ... in there, and slabbed her.

At the end of the interview, Hunter with astonishing naivety asked police: 'My kids aren't gonna get to know about this, are they?'

Hunter: I don't really want my kids to know about it. I don't want it to go in the media. I don't want it to go anywhere, not past these four walls.
Police: The kids have probably got a right to know what happened to their mother.
Hunter: I can say that to 'em in me own time ... I would rather tell my kids.

Shortly after that interview, Hunter did fess up to his three daughters, as well as to his new wife, when they visited him in his police cell. At her father's murder trial more than a year later, Deborah wept as she recalled the day her dad admitted he was a killer.

Deborah: He told me that he'd killed Mum, that he had hit her with a stick and then cremated her …

Defence barrister Julie Sutherland: Did he say to you that he was sorry that it happened?

Deborah: Yes.

Ms Sutherland: Was he crying when he was telling you what occurred?

Deborah: Yes.

Dianne also cried as she told of her dad's confession.

Dianne: He told me that he did it … that he murdered Mum … He was very distressed … His first words were: 'I did it.' And he was saying 'sorry'. He just kept repeating himself that he was sorry and told us how much he loved us and we just hugged and cuddled and kissed …

Jennifer: He said that he killed her and he was very sorry. He didn't mean to do it …

Ms Medley: He said: 'I have got something to tell you.' And all I could say was: 'You did it, didn't you.' He said: 'Yes, I did.' And he just kept repeating: 'I am sorry.'

But, while Dennis Hunter admitted killing Venda – and lying for 20 years about it – he denied murdering her. He said it had been self-defence.

Dianne: He basically said that they were fighting and Mum had come at him with a knife and it all just happened from there. He said he had to defend himself …

One Body, Three Burials

Jennifer: He told us she was chasing him around the house with a knife and he couldn't do anything ...

Hunter also told police he had been trying to defend himself from an angry, knife-wielding Venda.

Hunter: As usual, we had a blue and she went at me with a knife and I just bloody killed her. I just beat her to death ... The kids, they were in bed, it was about two or three in the morning, thereabouts ... I think we might have been watching TV or something ... I was a shift worker at the SEC at the time ... and as I said we were blueing and I killed her ...

I don't know. It's a long time ago. I just don't know. I didn't even know I was going to kill her until it happened ... We were arguing about something. I don't know what it was ... Well, I think I went to the loo and when I got back she had a knife then ... I just hit her with whatever, I can't remember what, was near me at the time – just killed her ...

The second time she came at me, that was it: I just let her have it ...

Police: She had a knife?

Hunter: Yeah. She sort of came towards me with it ... I was just bloody petrified, scared, bloody crying ... I shit meself, like I always did. How would you like somebody coming at you with a bloody knife? She called me some name. I think I hit her with a stick. Yeah, I think I hit her with a stick. She went down and I think it sort of dazzled her. I didn't hit her that hard ... I think the second time [I hit her] and that was just – that was it.

Police: Did she manage to stab you on this night?

Hunter: Nearly, but I think I got in first.

According to Hunter, Venda's threatening him with a knife was far from being a surprise.

Hunter: And then she came at me with a knife and that was the last straw because I was sick of her coming at me with a knife. I just couldn't take any more and the kids couldn't take any more … There's been times … I'd even have to shut my bedroom door so I'd know she wasn't going to kill me because she was always threatening me with a knife, always threatening me life …

[She would] just pick up the knife … Just reckoned she was going to kill me. 'You bastard,' she'd say, 'I just hate you and blah, blah, blah.' Always on with the hate …

Police: Has anybody ever seen that?

Hunter: There's only ever been me and the kids there. People don't realise what goes on between four walls of your life of your family. You love, you like, your wife so much but the last 10 years of our marriage – just wasn't anything there. I couldn't afford to move. I just wanted to be with me own kids. I didn't want her to take my kids because I know she could never have looked after 'em 'cause of the abuse and that, they used to get. David, she hated so bad it wasn't funny. Anywhere and everywhere I went I was allowed to take David 'cause she just couldn't stand David being around. I was never allowed to take the girls …

I didn't want to leave her with the kids. I just hoped to hell she'd up and go. She wouldn't up and go. She always abused me kids – that used to get on my nerves …

I love my kids so bloody much and they just went through hell and misery – I felt sorry for 'em … [Hunter breaks down weeping.]

Hunter said that for 'years and years' he had tried to persuade Venda to get psychiatric help but she had refused, saying he was 'the idiot'. He admitted to police that at the time he drank a *lot* of alcohol. He and a mate would sometimes finish off five *slabs* of beer in a day. Hunter said he told Venda that they both should get help 'because we got kids, for Pete's sake'. She eventually agreed to go to see a psychiatrist – but only if Dennis went to see one as well. They let the experts decide which of them had the 'problem'.

One Body, Three Burials

Hunter: I was all right, but we found out she was schizophrenic. And I didn't know what the hell that was and that freaked me out. I said, 'Can she be helped?' then they said, 'Yeah,' and I think they put her on valium or something, I don't know. I just don't think she wanted to take 'em any more, and I think the last 10 years of our marriage was the worst I ever had …

Police: When you say that on other occasions [when she came at you with a knife] you had just taken off, why didn't you take off on this night?

Hunter: I don't know … I think I just got jack of it all at the finish … Always getting the kids abused and bloody bashed, I think it just got to me all at once … I think I just had a gutful of it. I think it was just really pissing me off. I think it was just a spur of the moment. It happened, and I just freaked … It just got the best of me. I just couldn't handle it any more … I didn't even know I was going to kill her till it happened and she came at me with a knife and that was the last straw 'cause I was sick of her coming at me with a knife.

After Venda 'went down like a bag of spuds', Hunter said he had mixed feelings.

Hunter: At the time I wasn't happy, [but] I was happy. It was going to relieve me. It was going to relieve me kids. I was just freaking …

Police: Why didn't you contact police or an ambulance?

Hunter: Dunno. I was scared, petrified.

Police: Of what?

Hunter: I dunno. I didn't contact police. I didn't tell anybody … I just kept it to myself.

Police: Do you think you would have been in trouble with the police if you had rung them?

Hunter: Possibly. No doubt.

Police: 'Possibly' or 'No doubt'?

Hunter: I'd say yes.

REASONABLE DOUBT

Police: Why was that?

Hunter: Dunno – 'cause of what I'd done …

Police: What was your reason for killing Venda Hunter?

Hunter: I think I was just sick and tired of the way the kids were getting treated, the way I was getting treated. I don't know. It just happened.

Hunter was then told he was going to be charged with Venda's murder, and asked if he had anything to say.

Hunter: No, except that I don't know how me kids are going to react and I am sorry I done it, but it just happened. It wasn't meant to, but it did.

I just wish to hell it hadn't have happened. I just wish to hell she hadn't have pushed me …

He told the police that even though he hadn't told his second wife, Vicky, that he had killed Venda he had warned her not to push him too far when they started having a relationship a couple of years after Venda died. Dennis and Vicky's happy marriage ended when she died of breast cancer in 1993. To help his wife fight the disease, Hunter took voluntary redundancy from the state electricity commission in 1992 – after 24 years.

Hunter: The day I wanted a relationship with Vicky, I said: 'Vick, don't ever push me to the extreme. I want to be happy. I just don't want to be abused or a blue if I dropped that and made that mess …' you know, and we had a beautiful relationship and I am having another one now …

Hunter's daughters strongly backed their dad's claims of Venda's abuse.

Prosecutor: How did you get on with your mum at the time you moved to Traralgon?

Deborah: I didn't. I was scared to come home from school because she always ... belted into us. We were scared to come home from school in case we copped it again.

Prosecutor: Did you ever tell anybody about what your mother did?

Deborah: We weren't allowed to tell anyone, not even Dad.

Prosecutor: Why didn't you tell your father?

Deborah: 'Cause if we did, we would have copped it again from Mum.

Prosecutor: ... How did your mother treat Dianne?

Deborah: She did the same to her, just belted her up as well.

Prosecutor: What about David?

Deborah: The same.

Prosecutor: Jennifer was only a baby?

Deborah: She was only a baby, she didn't cop anything ...

Prosecutor: Did your father tell you why he hit your mother [on the night he killed her]?

Deborah: Just to save us from all the beltings that we were getting and so we could have a better life.

Deborah told the trial that a bashing from her mother once left her with a bad cut on her head but that she hadn't told her teacher the truth about how she got it because at the time Venda was a cleaner at the school. She and Dianne agreed their mother had a Jekyll and Hyde personality: she appeared meek and shy in public, but flew into violent, unexpected rages at home.

Dianne: Mum was very cruel. There was no love, affection. She used to beat us around a lot [but] she was pretty good with Jennifer ... I was very scared of Mum. We never could talk to Mum. There was just nothing there ...

Once Mum was bathing me ... I was five or six ... when and – I don't know what I did wrong, you didn't have to do anything wrong sometimes – and she just grabbed me by my hair and slammed my head on to the bath tap and she cut above my eye and the scar is still there ...

I was told to say [to the doctor and nurses] that I had fallen off the swing ... I also wasn't allowed to tell Dad what had happened. I had to tell him I had fallen off the swing as well ...
I remember Dad asked me – when it was just Dad and me on our own – what had happened and I couldn't tell him and he begged me to tell him, and eventually I did, but I also begged him to please not tell Mum because I knew exactly what would happen.
Barrister: Was she particularly vicious to David?
Dianne: Yes.
Barrister: She seemed to dislike him intensely?
Dianne: Yes.

Dianne said Venda would use belts, brooms, dusters, hoses – anything she could lay her hands on – to throw at and beat her children with, particularly David. Even when Venda wasn't being violent, she was hard to live with.

Dianne: We would be sitting down watching the TV ... and she would just call out: 'One of yous pick the skin off my toes,' and we used to do that – we were all scared of her. And we used to scratch her head and scratch her back and hold her mouth if she had a tooth-ache and we would be standing there it seemed like hours doing it.

Deborah and Dianne both said that they would often hear their mother talking to herself.

Dianne: It was mainly while she was washing dishes or washing out in the laundry, she would be talking to herself and because we were so scared of her we used to always think she was talking to us and we were always like: 'Pardon, Mum?' ... because if she called us we basically had to run because if we weren't there when she wanted us –

she didn't like to call a second time … but she would just be talking to herself and she would always tell us where to go … I know I was very young but I saw my friends' mums and I knew my mum wasn't right.

Deborah and Dianne both agreed their father had drunk a lot of alcohol when they were children but said he had been a 'happy drunk', a gentle giant. They said that although he had punished them, it had always been for a reason – unlike what they endured from their mother. They also agreed that after Venda's disappearance, the family had had a relatively peaceful time. They had got on well with their stepmother Vicky, and – after she died – with Norma Medley.

One of David's childhood friends, neighbour Darren Hilsey, backed the Hunter family's claims of Venda's violence, particularly towards her son.

Mr Hilsey: I was actually over there and David and I were just mucking around and he must have been in trouble for something or other, and she [Venda] actually hit him across the head with a broomstick – snapped the broomstick over his head …

Another time, I don't really know what David had done wrong, but Venda was belting into David in the dining room and, basically, you could hear him being thrown into the wall.

Mr Hilsey also said that when he was around at the Hunters playing with David, Venda Hunter had called his 12-year-old sister a 'slut' and a 'harlot'.

But not everybody thought Venda Hunter was the villain of the 16-year marriage. Yvonne Gentle said the Venda Hunter she had known for many years was 'very timid, very withdrawn'.

Ms Gentle: She was a simple person. She seemed meek and mild.
Prosecutor: Did you see Venda threaten the children?
Ms Gentle: She was fine with them. I never saw anything untoward.
Prosecutor: How did Dennis Hunter treat his wife?
Ms Gentle: When we first knew them they seemed, well, distant.

286   REASONABLE DOUBT

They didn't talk a lot but they seemed to get on all right but as the years went by the relationship deteriorated a lot. A lot of the time Dennis ignored Venda, didn't talk to her … When he spoke to her, it wasn't very nice. He said things I used to get embarrassed about … Things like: 'Why don't you do this like Yvonne does it?', 'Why aren't you dressed like that?' … I felt embarrassed because I just felt for her feelings because, you know, it was so cruel, I thought.

She said that Venda seldom wore make-up, cooked very simple food and wore very simple clothes. She said she sometimes felt as though Dennis Hunter was flirting with her in front of his wife. This claim was vigorously tackled at the trial by Hunter's barrister, Julie Sutherland.

Ms Sutherland: In fact it's nonsense, I suggest to you it's nonsense about my client flirting with you … He has never flirted with you, madam. What do you say about that?
Ms Gentle: Well, that's not true.
Ms Sutherland: You were flirting with him and he told you to stop it. That's the truth, isn't it?
Ms Gentle: That's not true.

Venda Hunter's brother John Holtman said his sister had grown up in an orphanage for 'underprivileged children' in Melbourne's working-class suburb of Sunshine. He said he had largely lost contact with Venda while he fought in Malaya and in Vietnam, and then was posted to Queensland. He said that on a visit to his sister in Mt Beauty in 1970s he had found a 'feeling of tension' between his sister and her husband. He said there didn't appear to be any 'affection or love' between the two. He said that he had heard of his sister's 'disappearance' in a letter from Dennis and that he had been 'tenacious' in quizzing Dennis about the circumstances of her disappearance – particularly when he came down to Melbourne for David's funeral. Under cross-examination by Ms Sutherland, Mr Holtman agreed that the 'orphanage for underprivileged children' his sister went to was a 'sort of remedial institution'.

Mr Holtman: She did have some problems associating with reality in her daily life.

The prosecution's point was that Dennis Hunter's 20 years of lies showed that his self-defence claim was nonsense – most people who kill while defending themselves call an ambulance or the police after they fatally fell their attacker. They don't bury them in the backyard. They don't tell their children their mother has run away in the night. Even those who panic don't make up lies about seeing the person over the years. They certainly don't dig up their bones 12 years later, rebury them in a garage and pour concrete over them.

Prosecutor Colin Hillman SC: The accused's conduct was consistent only with him having murdered Venda Hunter. Why otherwise would he make up the story that he did and continue with that story for such a long, long time? ... If Mrs Hunter did come at him with a knife, he killed her under the pretence of self-defence and not in genuine self-defence ... It is, I suggest, abundantly clear that he wanted to get rid of Venda Hunter and that the relationship between Venda Hunter and the accused man was one which was as far from a happy marriage as you can get ...

By killing Venda Hunter, he got what he wanted: she was gone and he was left with the children. I say that concealing the body overnight; putting the body in the earth floor of the shed; adding paper, wood, petrol; setting it alight; allowing the fire to burn; filling in the hole containing the burnt remains; and bricking over the floor of the shed, all display a consciousness of guilt of murder.

Mr Hillman told the jury that it wasn't a case of manslaughter, that Hunter had not been provoked into even temporarily losing self-control. He pointed out that after bashing his wife to death, Hunter went outside to smoke a cigarette.

288 REASONABLE DOUBT

Mr Hillman: This is as clear a case of murder as you can get. Self-defence has been excluded. There is clearly an intention to kill or inflict really serious injury, and provocation is excluded. I suggest you will be satisfied beyond a reasonable doubt that in fact he did not lose his self-control but rather took advantage of the situation and decided to kill Venda Hunter.

The defence put the spotlight on the victim.

Ms Sutherland: Can I start by saying this about Venda Hunter: there probably weren't too many people who got a glimpse into the upside-down world that she occupied. There was probably no-one who could even begin to penetrate the unfathomable spaces which her mind occupied.

Was she desperately unhappy? Probably.

Was she a frightening sight to those who did see her in full flight? There would have to be no doubt about that.

Was she scary, unpredictable? Could she fly off the handle into an uncontrollable rage? You have evidence of that before you …

To live with this woman must have been a terrifying ordeal at times – not knowing what you could do and what you couldn't do, when she would lose it …

He [pointing at Hunter in the dock] hit her to protect himself. Should he have waited until she killed him? He was confronted with an abnormal situation: a person in a rage with a knife. He says: 'I shit meself. How would you like it, a person coming at you with a knife.' …

Ms Sutherland denied that what Hunter did in the moments – and decades – after killing his wife showed that he had a guilty conscience, that he felt guilty about murdering his wife.

Ms Sutherland: What can you say about his subsequent conduct? It was utterly, utterly macabre … bizarre even, wrong, immoral but, to state the obvious, Mr Hunter is not here, in this court, because he acted immorally, in a macabre fashion or a bizarre way. He is here to face the most serious charge that the state can bring against any individual ... that is a charge murder ...

He panicked. He freaked.

Then Ms Sutherland carefully approached the issue of provocation. The risk was that by explaining to jurors how they could find Hunter guilty just of manslaughter – because he had been provoked into losing his self-control when he killed his wife – she could undermine her claim that he had been defending himself. She could, of course, have not mentioned the provocation defence, but that would have also been risky. If the jurors were not prepared to let Hunter off completely, if they didn't accept there was a reasonable possibility he had been defending himself, they might think they had no alternative but to find him guilty of murder.

Ms Sutherland: As to provocation manslaughter. It's not something I ask you to do ... Again, I stress that I am asking you not to ... but you may say that what happened here is that he acted under provocation, he acted because he was provoked to the point where he lost self-control.

She ended with a plea to the jury to find Hunter not guilty because he had only killed to defend himself.

Ms Sutherland: What you have before you is, is a peace-loving, ordinary, decent fellow – an ordinary man who was put into an extraordinary situation.

After deliberating for about three and a half hours, the jury announced its verdict in April 2002 – 20 years and six months after Dennis Hunter killed his first wife. As he was declared 'Not guilty' of murder, Hunter appeared to relax ever so slightly, his daughters had relieved expressions and the beginnings of smiles, but then came what few were expecting: the

290 REASONABLE DOUBT

jury found Hunter guilty of manslaughter – the charge both the defence and prosecution had all but ignored and had argued against.

Hunter hardly showed any emotion but his daughters cried for their dad. John Holtman was angry for his sister.

At the pre-sentence plea-hearing, the prosecution urged a stern sentence, stressing to Justice Bernard Teague that Hunter had burnt Venda Hunter's body *and* hidden his crime for 20 years. The judge was told that in 1981 the maximum term for manslaughter in Victoria was 15 years (it was later raised to 20 years).

Ms Sutherland called for a merciful sentence. She told the judge that Dennis Hunter was 57 and had led a faultless life except for one 'fateful, regrettable and tragic night almost 21 years ago'. She said given his horrific childhood, it was amazing that Hunter had become such a loving, gentle father.

> *Ms Sutherland*: He tells me that he was tortured by his stepfather …
> by being stripped naked, tied up to a post and systematically
> beaten … One of the most vivid memories of his childhood is having spiders thrown at him by his stepfather.

She said that because of his stepfather's abuse, Dennis was put into a boys' home from the age of seven to 11. When he was returned home, he ran away and survived in a refuge. She said that despite his horrific start, Hunter eventually managed to get a job at the SEC, where he stayed for 24 years until taking voluntary redundancy in 1992 to care for his cancer-stricken second wife.

> *Ms Sutherland*: You have a peace-loving, even-tempered, wonderful
> father before you who comes to be sentenced at this time for, really,
> what was a momentary total loss of control.

In sentencing Hunter on 14 May 2002, Justice Teague noted a sad coincidence – he was the judge who had sentenced David Hunter's killer, also for manslaughter. The judge noted that as well as his turbulent first

One Body, Three Burials

marriage, and the deaths of his son and second wife, Hunter had had to cope with an intellectually disabled son. Justice Teague said it was a tribute to Hunter that none of his children had given evidence against him.

> *Justice Teague*: You have clearly cared for your children and that is shown in their loyalty to you.

But the judge told Hunter that what he did after he killed his wife must increase his punishment.

> *Justice Teague*: A covered-up killing can impose a continuing burden on those close to the person who has seemingly just disappeared. The process of grief and closure and the like are suspended ...
>
> I take account of the circumstance that your younger children will suffer particularly from the absence of your stabilising influence. Your knowing that will mean your time in prison will not be easily served ...
>
> Mr Hunter, I sentence you to seven years' imprisonment. I fix a nonparole period of four years and six months. The prisoner may be removed.

Outside the court, Mr Holtman had a very different opinion of the man who had killed his sister.

> *Mr Holtman*: How does an ice cube like that walk around watching the children of his second marriage play on the bones of his first wife? How do you do that?
>
> He burnt that body in the backyard and a great pillar of filthy, flesh-infested smoke rose into the atmosphere and nobody even rang the fire brigade.
>
> I have a horrible feeling that if I had not come down there her remains would have laid there until Furlonger Street, Traralgon was levelled for a football field and he would have died with that secret.

TEACHING A TODDLER WHO'S BOSS

For two-year-old Lewis Blackley, Haemon Gill was like a fun dad. They had been pals since Gill and Lewis's 27-year-old mum Daisy De Los Reyes started a passionate relationship in August 2001. Three days a week, often more, Gill, 28, would stay over at Daisy's home and he and Lewis would often be seen playing together in the front yard. Lewis had so much fun with Haemon that he would whinge when he had to leave him to go to crèche, even though he had lots of friends at crèche.

Lewis's mum and his new 'dad' had both been buffeted about a bit by life.

Daisy had had a few mental breakdowns. Her battles with internal demons and with illegal drugs had triggered violent, unpredictable outbursts. Once, she told Vaughan Blackley, Lewis's father, that her aunt had bought him a T-shirt and she wanted to put it on him. She asked him to close his eyes and to kneel on the floor. Then, instead of taking a T-shirt out of the bag, Daisy took a large kitchen knife. Luckily, Mr Blackley hadn't trusted his unpredictable girlfriend and had only half shut his eyes. He saw her take the knife out of the bag, jumped at her, grabbed her hand and wrested the knife out of her grip. When Daisy and Vaughan split three months after Lewis was born, Mr Blackley wanted custody of his son. He was told, however, that mothers almost always won custody of their children. Despite the knife attack, Mr Blackley became more confident his son would be safe with his mother when Daisy started having monthly injections. They reduced her unpredictable outbursts. She was

Teaching a Toddler Who's Boss 293

also heeding the advice of childcare nurses on how to deal with Lewis's tantrums. When she couldn't control or cope with his screams and head-banging, she put him in 'time-out', locking him in the lounge while she stayed in the kitchen or her bedroom until he calmed down.

Gill had also had troubles. He had finished Year 10 by correspondence after 'minor skirmishes' in the playground led to him being suspended a few times. In his first job – at his father's clothing firm – he discovered a flair for art and clothes designing, but his ambitions were dashed when he injured his hand in a machine. He then drifted from job to job: brickie's labourer to carpenter, bottleshop attendant to forklift driver to carpet maker. On the side, he kept on drawing, painting and designing clothes. From the age of 20 to 24, Gill worked on a garbage truck. The work kept him fit and gave him time to design clothes for skateboarders and surfers. Things started to look up when he returned to work as a clothes designer for his father but that soon ended when he clashed with his dad over the clothes' style and quality. Gill then ricocheted to a falling-out with his mother, with whom he had been living since she and his father divorced when he was 13. In 2001, she accused Haemon of pawning her jewellery to buy drugs, chucked her 27-year-old son out of home … and took out an intervention order against him. Gill moved in with his 'nanna', but soon he was spending most of his time at Daisy's.

So, in August 2001, a couple of life's lifeboat clingers in the working-class Geelong suburb of Norlane found each other.

Daisy, a life model for art students, had found somebody she could have fun with, smoke some pot with, drink some cheap booze with, as well as someone who was fit and good-looking. So had Gill. Daisy had also found someone who made her baby laugh.

Gill would give his little pal 'zerberts', blowing 'raspberries' on Lewis's belly. 'Here comes the zerbert! Watch out! Prrrrrp. Here comes another one.' Sometimes, Gill would tap Lewis's head with a video cassette. Tap – 'Where's the video?' – tap – 'Does Lewis want to watch this video?' – tap – 'Well, come on then, champ, come and get it!' – tap. Then there was the throwing-Lewis-on-the-bouncy-bed game. Lotsa laughs with that one, too.

294   REASONABLE DOUBT

But on the morning of 11 November 2001 the laughter ended in tears –
lots and lots of tears.

About 6.30 that morning, a half-awake Gill walked through the lounge
to the toilet, past Lewis lying on the couch. That's where the boy normally
slept because he slept better there than in his own bed. He was sort of
wedged down the back of couch. Gill felt the boy's head. It was cool but
it was a cool morning, so he didn't worry too much about that. He also
checked that the boy was breathing. He was. On the way back from the toilet, he nicked Lewis's pillow – he wasn't using it anyway – and went to bed
and to sleep. The next thing he knew Daisy was screaming. It was 9.40am
and she had found her baby dead on the couch – cold, stiff, blue and dead.

> *Ms De Los Reyes*: I found Lewis facing the other way [to the way
> she left him] on the other end of the couch and he was very cold
> and his face was all blue … I cried, I tried to shake him a little bit;
> carried him into the kitchen and carried him back and forth in the
> loungeroom … I nursed him. I didn't know what I was thinking …
> I called Mark and Rose Shuttleworth [neighbours] and said that
> Lewis had passed away and he told me to call an ambulance.
> *Prosecutor*: It was obvious to you that Lewis had passed away. Is
> that right?
> *Ms De Los Reyes*: He, he was stiff and cold.
> *Prosecutor*: What about Haemon Gill? What was he doing?
> *Ms De Los Reyes*: He tried to call his nan but no-one was home. He
> just didn't say a word. He was shocked.

Daisy thought maybe her son's head-banging tantrum the night before –
the tantrum she had punished him for by putting him into time-out – had
proved fatal: that her two-year-old might have accidentally killed himself.

Gill didn't tell his girlfriend that the night before he had hurt her son,
his little mate … very, very badly.

***

Teaching a Toddler Who's Boss

On 10 November 2001, Lewis had been 'whingey'. His mother remembered him: 'Grizzling and asking for lollies ... trying to get us to be attentive to him and everything.'

> *Ms De Los Reyes*: ... I couldn't understand why he was whingeing a lot ... Cry and whingeing.

Lewis might have been whingeing that day because he had not fully recovered from the diarrhoea he had had a couple of days earlier. During his nap from 12.30pm to 3.30pm, Daisy and Gill grabbed their chance to relax by smoking a few bongs of marijuana. When her son woke, Daisy took him grocery shopping.

> *Ms De Los Reyes*: He jumped in the pram. He was quite happy about it. So, he likes to go out all the time and go for walks. So, yes, he's fine.

About 5.15pm Gill's mother, Sarah Kilburn, drove over to check whether her son and his girlfriend had voted that day in the federal election – they risked a fine if they hadn't. They hadn't, so she drove them through the heavy rain the few minutes to a shopping centre polling booth. Because of the rain, Ms Kilburn stayed in the car with Lewis while Gill and Daisy went to vote. Lewis was not happy to see his mother leave him – he was being a real mummy's boy that day.

> *Ms Kilburn*: He became quite distressed, actually, because his mother was leaving and he started crying quite a lot. It distressed me considerably because I am a grandmother ... He continued crying until ... I sat in the back seat with him. I pulled him on to my lap, cuddled him, held him, tried to play with him – just to soothe him, so he would take his mind off his mother being gone.
>
> *Prosecutor:* Did he settle down?
>
> *Ms Kilburn*: He certainly did. I was playing little games with him to keep him occupied and he seemed fine ... I was playing a game with

296   **REASONABLE DOUBT**

putting a lolly into his pocket which had Velcro on and I was pulling the pocket open and tucking a lolly into it …

Prosecutor: Did you see any bruises on his face?

Ms Kilburn: I didn't notice anything except his little tears rolling down his face. He was distressed.

She said when Lewis saw his mother returning, he started to cry for her again but that he settled down when she was sitting next to him.

Ms Kilburn: He just wanted his mum.

When they got home, while making dinner, Daisy and Gill drank from a cask of Lambrusco and smoked more marijuana bongs. Lewis whinged and tantrumed.

Ms De Los Reyes: From the minute that we got back … he would not stop crying and asking for lollies and because it's dinner time and I don't want him to have lollies before he eats. So I close the loungeroom door, which the nurse advised me to do – if he's really having a tantrum like that to let him go for a little and let him cry … I tried to calm him down and he wouldn't stop … I just had enough so I closed the door [to the lounge] – time-out for me.

She said that while Lewis was in his lounge time-out tantruming – hitting the door, crying, screaming – for about 30 minutes, Haemon checked on him a few times. Gill tried to entertain Lewis out of his whingeing. He gave him a few zerberts and played the video-tap-on-the-head game and the throw-Lewis-on-the-bed game. Daisy wasn't impressed, however, with one version of the throw-Lewis-on-the-bed game.

Ms De Los Reyes: When he didn't stop crying, so he [Gill] – like all of a sudden – went just like that over his shoulder and he [Lewis] landed on his head on the bed … He cried a bit … I said: 'Don't do it again. He doesn't like it.'

Teaching a Toddler Who's Boss 297

Frustrated, Daisy even called Lewis's father in Sydney, telling him their child was 'driving her nuts', that he was 'whingeing all the time'. She asked him to give her a break and take Lewis for a holiday. Mr Blackley – a driver on the docks – said he would happily take his son in a couple of months when he could get time off.

> *Mr Blackley*: I have always wanted him [Lewis] to come up to Sydney with me for a holiday or, actually – initially – for good.

Mr Blackley excitedly told his friends that his son was finally coming to Sydney. He didn't know that within hours his celebrations would prove to have been sadly premature.

> *Mr Blackley*: The way she spoke I couldn't tell that Lewis was in any harm.
>
> *Gill's barrister Gavin Silbert*: I put it to you that she sounded frustrated … ?
>
> *Mr Blackley*: She sounded like a mother that needed a break from her kid.
>
> *Mr Silbert*: In fact, she asked you to take him away for six months, didn't she?
>
> *Mr Blackley*: Well, it was from a general conversation she said that, you know: 'He's whingeing a lot. Can you come and get him?' She says: 'Oh, can you take him for six months' but … She was sort of laughing at the same time as she said it, so I didn't take her seriously that Lewis was in any harm … She wasn't being serious. It wasn't like a full-on serious conversation … She was just being her normal 'la la' sort of dizzy self.

At 7pm, Lewis had a good meal of fried rice, feeding himself in his high chair. About 9pm, his mum finally managed to settle him down to sleep on the couch. Gill and Daisy had planned to watch a video then, but Daisy said she was too tired and went to bed about 9.30pm, leaving Gill with her sleeping son. The only person who knows what happened after that is Gill – and he's not so sure.

**

About a week after Lewis died, Gill admitted to police that the night before the boy was found dead, he had hit him on the head a few times with a video cassette. But Gill said he was sure this did him no harm. He also admitted that when he threw Lewis over his shoulder on to a double bed, the child had landed awkwardly and hard on his head, but Gill said he also believed this hadn't injured him.

> *Gill*: He landed hard. He came down on his head ... His entire body just flopped.

He acknowledged he had been angry with Lewis that day.

> *Gill*: He was clingy to Mum. I think it offended me a bit with the fact that he just did not stop crying. He didn't stop crying and ... I tried to comfort him and he just didn't want a bar of me and I think it offended me, and I just reacted.

Gill admitted that in his anger, he may have hit Lewis's head a bit harder than he normally did with the video cassette, and a few more times than usual – maybe 20. He also admitted that a zerbert he intended giving the boy had turned into a bite. He said he bit the toddler on his hip and then felt so ashamed of what he had done, he rubbed the mark to try to make it go away. He could not explain how Lewis's right leg had a spiral fracture – as if it had been twisted.

Later that day, police secretly recorded Daisy asking her boyfriend: 'You tell me the truth, Haemon: Did you touch him?' and Gill lying: 'No'.

> *Daisy*: [crying] Why did you touch him while he was sleeping?
> *Gill*: They're saying all sorts of stuff. I told you everything that happened that day.

Teaching a Toddler Who's Boss   299

Daisy: Oh, well what happened to him, Haemon? He's got a broken leg. They told me … that someone broke his leg that night.
Gill: I don't know … caught in the couch. They're saying that to me. They're saying it's a twisting thing.
Daisy: [inaudible] … It's murder. He was killed that night.
Gill: How did he die?
Daisy: Someone killed him that night. Who done it then?
Gill: [inaudible] … What you want me to say?

A few days later – after he had been charged with Lewis's murder – Gill contacted police saying he had more to tell them.

Gill: So far, I, I've told the truth but there are issues, or, or parts of what has happened that I haven't completed. [Pause] I bel … [pause, deep breath] *I believe Lewis's death is the fault of mine* … I believe the death of Lewis Blackley is a result of some actions that I've taken.

Before going into the details of a tale that horrified even him, Gill listed some of his excuses. His 'confession' was mixed with self-pity, self-centredness and a readiness to deflect blame.

Gill: In no way have I intended the death of anybody … I'm horrified with this … I actually want to tell you this so that I may be able to get some help in some way as I'm not 100 per cent sure of my actions at the time. There are things I do know of but, as I say, there's things that you police have told me that have just horrified me and, if I'm to blame for those things, I'd rather get some sort of help … I have been told I have a borderline personality disorder and I believe I was overcoming that …

I haven't been happier in my life – with the time that I spent with Daisy and … if something has happened because of a disorder of some sort … I'd rather get it fixed up …

With the … personality disorder I've been given, I'm very easily influenced. I haven't had good people around me for many years and so my life hasn't been great. It hasn't been going in the direction I wish it was and that is just to be a good person – a good, hard-working family-type person. And over the last, say six months … I've had great people around me. I've had fantastic situations around me … magnificent. Up until the night of Lewis Blackley's passing – death …

On the night in question, my girlfriend Daisy had gone to sleep roughly at 9.30. We had been drinking … Daisy had gone to bed because she was quite intoxicated, couldn't have any more drinks.

She went to sleep. I stayed up for quite some time in the kitchen drinking. We had a pretty hard day: Lewis was crying all day … and I just wanted to escape. I used the alcohol as a bit of an escape. I just drank and drank and drank.

He said he probably had about 10 bongs of marijuana and drank 24 glasses of wine to Daisy's seven – that he had just drunk himself 'stupid'.

Gill: I had a video to watch, so I went from the kitchen – I'm not 100 per cent sure what time, I'd say about 10.30 to 11ish – to start watching this video. I was in a real intoxicated daze, so I could barely watch the video …

And I was sitting on the couch with Lewis at one stage and he started crying and it certainly amused me that you couldn't hear him because he was muffled. He was already slight, part of the way into the couch. I don't know, as I say, I was intoxicated, and I am not 100 per cent sure of the order or whatever but I – and this horrifies me – have bitten him and bitten him hard … on the hip there …

Just seeing exposed skin … I used to give him zerberts, which is [Gill blows a zerbert on his arm] on his belly … I know I would have started off like that and then I have just bitten him. To me it's a disgrace, to anybody that's just a disgrace. Daisy's bitten him out of fun and I have bitten him out of fun and left no marks but I know I gave him a decent, reasonably decent bite. I could do it on myself, if you want to see.

Teaching a Toddler Who's Boss

Detective Jon Woodyatt: No, that'll be fine. Why did you bite Lewis?

Gill: I have no idea. I really don't know why. To me, that's just shocking. It's an appalling thing to do. It's off!

Det Woodyatt: What did Lewis do after you bit him?

Gill: Probably cried.

Det Woodyatt: Do you recall what he did?

Gill: No. Yeah, actually he may have kicked me and that's why I got on to giving him a Chinese burn on the leg.

Det Woodyatt: After you've bitten him. Did you take a look at what you had done?

Gill: I did, actually, 'cause I knew I'd left a decent mark on him.

Det Woodyatt: Why did you start rubbing the area where you'd bitten Lewis?

Gill: [Going to bite his own arm] I just do this for my own satisfaction.

Det Woodyatt: Hang on. I don't want you to hurt yourself …

Gill: The mark. See the mark?

Det Woodyatt: There's no need for you to injure yourself.

Gill: No. I'm not hurting myself. That hasn't hurt. That didn't hurt me. That's lesser than what I would have done to Lewis. I didn't want to – I had no goal – in harming that boy. [Breaks down weeping] There's nothing to gain. I had everything to lose. There's nothing for me to gain in telling you this. I've got everything to lose. I just want to tell the truth as I know it. [Cries again]

Det Woodyatt: Well, just try and calm down a bit. Are you happy to go on?

Gill: Yeah.

Det Woodyatt: Are you sure?

Gill: [Weeps] I'm just scared of what I have done. I am shocked at what I've done. I don't know why I've done what I've done. As I say, there was a [bite] mark there … I was shittin': 'Oh! Got to get rid of that.' I don't know if it was gonna bruise … I've got a thing when I'm drunk [weeps] of just tensing up. I don't know if I have grabbed him and held him. [Breaks down and weeps] …

302   REASONABLE DOUBT

Det Woodyatt: Do you think that biting Lewis in that way, you did cause him pain?

Gill: Minor pain. Minor pain. Except, I have thought about it since … He was a delicate child. He was a two-year-old for God's sake. [Breaks down weeping] And he was delicate. I'm shocked and I frightened myself … I may have ruptured something inside. That's my thinking now …

Det Woodyatt: Why did you hit the area [of the bite]?

Gill: … I don't know if I was mad, angry, sad – what – but … I knew I'd caused him some harm, some sort of pain – slight, major or otherwise – in that spot … I'd rather have a bruise there than a bite mark. Bite's just strange. It's just strange … I'm trying to cover something up.

Det Woodyatt: How hard were you hitting him?

Gill: I don't know. He was a two-year-old. I don't normally hit the boy hard … I do not know.

Det Woodyatt: Can I ask you what you were trying to achieve by hitting where you'd bitten him?

Gill: I'll repeat myself for about 18, I don't know how many times. But that night and leading up to that night – Saturday the 10th – he's pissed me off, he'd pissed his mum off, he'd pissed us off. On thinking – I don't know – but I'm thinking – [pause] I've lost it … I intended to hurt the little sh … in some way … I intended to hurt Lewis. I would rather hurt him in one spot than hurt him all over …

I intended to hurt him – hurt, but not maim, injure, kill … I was, yeah: 'Little shit'; 'Cockroach'; 'What do you think you're doing, turd?' I was just flicking him but, on the grog, I can't say how hard it was. I'd done a week's worth of extensive workout with weights and things and I'm a reasonably solid, heavy bloke so it may be harder [Gill hits the table] than what I'm showing at the moment.

While admitting he hurt Lewis, Gill strenuously denied inflicting the massive head injuries doctors believed killed the child.

Teaching a Toddler Who's Boss   **303**

Gill: I believe there's injuries to Lewis's head that may have caused his death. I honestly don't believe I've hit Lewis in the head because he used to do quite a lot of damage to himself. He'd bang his head and he's crunched his head and he certainly hit it on floors and walls and things. So, as from knowing myself, I don't believe I would have hit him in the head. I don't believe that because he already had lumps on his head from bruises and things. I used to call him 'Lumpy Head' …

Det Woodyatt: Is it possible you could have hit him in other areas apart from the hip?

Gill: It's possible but I did not know. I do not know. Honestly, I do not know.

Det Woodyatt: What was Lewis doing when you were hitting him?

Gill: I do not know. Crying. Muffled crying.

Det Woodyatt: Did that worry you?

Gill: I know it did enough for me to stop and go to bed when I went to bed.

Gill admitted twisting the toddler's leg in a 'Chinese burn' after Lewis 'in distress during whatever I was doing' kicked him. He said he grabbed the boy's leg with two hands and twisted it, and that Lewis must have been 'very fragile' with bones 'like chalk' for what he had done to have snapped his leg.

Gill: I thought it was superficial … I've heard legs break. I've felt broken bones. I had no idea if I'd broken a bone.

Det Woodyatt: What did Lewis do after you gave him a Chinese burn?

Gill: I really don't know his reactions. I know he was crying and he may have been crying from start to finish, just crying. That's it.

Det Woodyatt: How loud was his crying?

Gill: Not loud enough to wake his mum up. He was muffled. I didn't do that. I know he was muffled already.

304   REASONABLE DOUBT

Det Woodyatt: At what stage did you go to bed?

Gill: … When I felt he'd had enough. I intended to harm him in a way – 'harm' is a harsh word. I intended to hurt Lewis because he hurt us throughout the week with just his actions, his reactions – his behaviour, his misbehaviour.

Again, Gill's extraordinary and cruel immaturity spilled out.

Gill: I intended to hurt him physically. I copped fuckin' heaps when I was a kid. I copped bashings, beltings, thrown across the room. I got all sorts of stuff. I intended to make him know – this is just come to me, I haven't thought about this: *I intended to let him know who's boss 'cause he was a little shit.*

He, he was demanding. He was terribly demanding: demand, demand, demand. Just cry, sook, try to get his own way and usually Daisy would give up and give him his own way.

Det Woodyatt: Whose child is Lewis?

Gill: Daisy's. I will not say the father's name because he had nothing to do with her and I intended to be a stand-in father. I honestly wanted to make us a family unit …

It was Daisy's job to discipline Lewis. At times, I would – and she wouldn't mind – yell at him when he's going to grab something that he shouldn't … I wasn't rough … I'm great with kids and I don't want to hurt them. Yeah, I wasn't overly rough with him at any stage.

Det Woodyatt: Before that …

Gill: Up, up until that night. I know I have done something wrong and I can't help it.

Det Woodyatt: Before you went over to that couch, had Lewis done anything to warrant you disciplining him?

Gill: … He probably started crying … I really do not know except for the fact that he was being a cunt – I'll say that. He was being a cunt that week and I just wanted him not to be such a prick to his mum and not be such a prick – I don't care about me but he was hurt-

Teaching a Toddler Who's Boss   305

ing his mum that week. She was in tears at stages through that week. We had big discussions about it. We'd rung the father, at some stage, to pick him up and he said: 'We'll organise it tomorrow' …

Det Woodyatt: When you went to bed, did you wake up Daisy at all?

Gill: It was about the only night since I have been with Daisy I haven't had sex with her. I know consciously, subconsciously – whatever it is – I knew I'd done something terrible. Same with the things I'd done – I don't know if I did it consciously, subconsciously. I don't know. I went to sleep. She was bombed that night. She's had a big week and it was a shit of a day. She was bombed; I didn't want to wake her up.

This answer seemed to sum up the conundrum of Gill. He admitted knowing he had done something terrible – even if only at a subconscious level – but seemed to think a good indication of his revulsion at what he had done was that he did not have sex with the child's mother.

Det Woodyatt: What was Lewis doing when you left him to go to bed?

Gill: Lying on the couch. Dunno if he was awake, asleep, crying. I don't know. I do not know.

Det Woodyatt: Did it concern you, how he was?

Gill: I knew I'd hurt him more than I aimed to. I knew that.

Det Woodyatt: When you went to bed, did you go straight to sleep?

Gill: I think I sat up for about five minutes – at most.

Det Woodyatt: What did you do in that time?

Gill: Showed some concern for my actions 'cause I knew they were … beyond what I aimed to do.

Det Woodyatt: What concern did you show?

Gill: Worry in the head.

Det Woodyatt: Did you do anything to try and help Lewis?

Gill: Well … I knew he was breathing … I stayed up a while concerned that: 'Shit, I've hurt this kid.' Him being my girl's [son], I had thoughts in my head: 'Oh shit, you know should I wake Daze

306   REASONABLE DOUBT

and maybe check him out?' I laid there and just worried. I didn't hear much noise out of him, so I just went to sleep. And that's it, that's as far as I know.

What does one make of someone who says he was worried about a toddler he had just hurt more than he 'aimed to', but that he worried for 'at most' five minutes and then went to sleep because he didn't hear much noise from his victim?

Det Woodyatt: How did you check [the next morning] that he was breathing?

Gill: Could hear him. I went past. I felt his head. It was cold but that didn't worry me because it was a cold night and I could hear him breathing. I, I had no thoughts whatsoever that the actions I'd taken had hurt him to the extent of death. So, he may be cold, but it's not a problem. He were breathing. I thought: 'You beauty. He's, he's OK. I'll talk to Daisy in the morning about what I've done, or whatever.' Up comes the morning, the boy's blue: I can't believe it. I don't know what to do except be there for Daisy. I've looked after her. I have no intentions of hurting her. I love Daisy and I did want to love Lewis. I had all the intentions of making a family life with the two of them.

Det Woodyatt: Did you tell Daisy what you'd done to Lewis that night?

Gill: … She has no idea. She has not a single clue … Nobody except for you guys have any idea. It's burning me up … I can't believe what's happened. I can't believe I'm the cause of somebody's death …

Det Woodyatt: Was Daisy present when you inflicted these injuries?

Gill: As far as I know she was asleep.

Det Woodyatt: As far as you know, did she have any knowledge as to what you were doing?

Gill: No, none whatsoever. I, I broke down at the funeral because all I wanted to do was tell everybody that I was sure it was my actions that had led to that boy's demise.

Teaching a Toddler Who's Boss

Gill said that when Daisy found her son dead, he wasn't certain his actions had killed the boy.

> *Gill*: I wasn't 100 per cent sure because of the way he was in the couch. He was pretty much in there when I left him. I thought he'd suffocated … I've never seen a dead figure, body – whatever – before. I thought Lewis had suffocated. I really did. And that stressed me out to no end because I'm sure I'd seen him earlier breathing … when I got up … muffled but breathing. My thoughts actually in the morning were: If he's died of suffocation throughout the night, I could have stopped that from happening. I could have pulled him out of that part of the couch.

Gill explained why he had not told police the whole truth in the first interview.

> *Gill*: I wanted to deny it for my sake that I have done this stuff because I can't believe I've done it. It's shocking. It's appalling. It's horrific. There's that reason but also Daisy doesn't really have anybody … I love her and I want the best for her. I had to be there for her for a while at least until she could have some sort of support. She's living with my family at the moment. I know the law will stand in my way [but] … I wanted to look after Daisy for the rest of my days. I owe her now. I owe her so much. I remember before that 'cause she helped me get my life happy again. [crying] I was happy. It's a lose, lose situation for me.
>
> I've got so much to offer this world. I've got so much to live for. I've got things going so well. I had up until, you know … I wanted to try and move on and I would have had to live with me killing a child for the rest of my days.

But why did he go to the couch Lewis was sleeping on at all?

Gill: Just restlessness. I probably went over there just to say, 'Good night' to Lewis and … in a drunken stupor it certainly amused me that you could hardly hear him. He was crying as he usually does but he was muffled and it seemed … I love that kid. I was trying to make a future with Daisy and Lewis.

When asked the question again, Gill repeated he was 'probably' just going to say, 'Good night' but then he came up with another extraordinary outburst.

Gill: I honestly loved that – he gave me the shits. The kid gave me the shits but I loved the life we were having and there's a no-win situation in me killing that kid. I got scared. My girlfriend which I still love and I'll probably lose because of this, these actions …
Det Woodyatt: Why didn't you just say, 'Good night' and go to bed?
Gill: I don't know. I don't know. I don't know.

When asked if he wanted to say anything about being charged with Lewis Blackley's murder, Gill said: 'Yes. As far as I'm concerned, as far as I knew, murder was something that you think of, and this child's death is because I *wasn't* thinking … To me murder is when you pre-plan, you got the notion: 'I'm gonna kill this person, whatever.'

***

In March 2003, a Supreme Court jury in Geelong was asked to decide whether Gill had murdered his little mate. It heard and saw not only evidence but some peculiar antics from Gill and Ms De Los Reyes. Frequently Gill smiled at and mouthed, 'I love you' to Ms De Los Reyes … and she smiled back at him. She smiled back at the man who admitted to hurting her baby boy; who told police Lewis was being 'a shit', 'a cockroach'; who was on trial for murdering her son. The mutual smiling and mouthing of sweet nothings across the courtroom continued even after Gill's barrister in his opening address tried to cast suspicion on Ms De Los Reyes. Mr Silbert told the jury that Gill had made 'extremist attempts to exculpate

Teaching a Toddler Who's Boss 309

her of any involvement in the death of Lewis'. The pair even made eyes at each other – like a couple of teenagers – while the jury looked at heart-wrenching pictures of Lewis's body. During breaks in the trial, Ms De Los Reyes chatted with Gill in the dock. Once she showed him her newly polished nails and asked him what he thought. Daisy's evidence and performance on the witness stand was also extraordinary.

Mr Silbert: You were very much in love with Haemon Gill?

Ms De Los Reyes: Yes.

Mr Silbert: You still are?

Ms De Los Reyes: Yes.

Mr Silbert: He is very much in love with you?

Ms De Los Reyes: Yes.

Mr Silbert: You were very much concerned that the relationship would continue?

Ms De Los Reyes: Yes.

Mr Silbert: You wanted it to go on?

Ms De Los Reyes: Yes.

Mr Silbert: You still want it to go on?

Ms De Los Reyes: Yes.

Mr Silbert: You continue to visit Haemon Gill in jail?

Ms De Los Reyes: Yes …

Mr Silbert: You have said that you believe he should not have been charged?

Prosecutor Michele Williams: What's the relevance of that, Your Honour? Quite frankly, it's outrageous.

Mr Silbert: As to her state of mind only, Your Honour.

Justice John Coldrey: I think that it may open other matters; I will allow it.

Mr Silbert: You have said to various people that he should not have been charged?

Ms De Los Reyes: No, not to murder.

Mr Silbert: You have said to people that he is innocent?

310   REASONABLE DOUBT

Ms De Los Reyes: Yes.

Mr Silbert: You still think that?

Ms De Los Reyes: Yes.

She agreed that Gill had told her he had given Lewis a Chinese burn.

Ms De Los Reyes: He did say that but he said that he has done it softly. I suppose he didn't realise how much strength he gave to that … He told me he didn't think he had hurt him. He was just playing around that night.

Daisy said her son and Gill had been fond of each other but she agreed that Haemon would occasionally get a little jealous when Lewis took too much of her attention. She said Lewis would often bang his head when having a tantrum and that he had banged his head several times on the day before she found him dead.

Ms De Los Reyes: Head injuries … stupid kid.

She said that on the last day of her son's life she had slapped him a couple of times on his face after becoming fed up with his continual crying. She agreed that Lewis had been an unplanned baby and that she once told Haemon she wished she had never had him. Ms De Los Reyes agreed she had been taking monthly injections after having a few mental breakdowns, but denied they were to control paranoid schizophrenia.

While confirming that she had attacked Vaughan Blackley with a knife after telling him to close his eyes and kneel down, Ms De Los Reyes smiled. She smiled again when asked whether she had tried to 'glass' another former boyfriend with a broken beer glass.

Ms De Los Reyes: No, it wasn't a broken beer glass.

Mr Silbert: What was it?

Ms De Los Reyes: It was a glass with beer in it.

Mr Silbert: It was the stub of a glass with beer in it, I put it to you?

Ms De Los Reyes: No, it was not a stubby. It's just a pot.

Mr Silbert: Did you actually break that glass?

Ms De Los Reyes: [Grinning broadly] Yes.

Mr Silbert: You did break the glass?

Ms De Los Reyes: [Still grinning] Yes. I didn't break it. It breaked on his face.

Maternal and child health nurse Julene Barnes said that when she saw Lewis Blackley three weeks before he died, he appeared to be a very happy, cheeky little boy keen to be out playing with his friends. She said a small bruise on his forehead was a normal bruise for an active toddler and had not noticed any other bruises on him in eight visits. Ms Barnes said she considered Ms De Los Reyes a 'caring and interested mother'.

Forensic pathologist Dr Matthew Lynch said he believed Lewis died from one of five recently inflicted injuries to his head that had been hit with 'mild to moderate' force. He also found a recent bruise to the boy's right hip, that his right leg had been broken shortly before he died, a recent bruise on his left thigh, and some 'old' bruises around his body.

The trial came down to whether it was reasonably possible that Lewis had unwittingly killed himself by banging his head in a tantrum earlier that day, or whether his frustrated mother's slaps combined with what Gill had done to him could have unintentionally injured him so badly that he died. Could Lewis have been fatally injured before a drunken, stoned, childish, jealous and frustrated Gill twisted his little mate's leg until it broke? Could Gill have failed to notice that the toddler he was hurting so badly was already mortally injured – was dying? This would only have been possible if Lewis was having a 'lucid interval'. In most cases, children are knocked immediately unconscious when they get a fatal blow to the head but, very occasionally, the swelling of the brain will cause them to have a 'lucid interval' – to seem all right for a short time – before dying.

Dr Lynch said he did not think that Lewis could have had a lucid interval after his fatal head injury, but he said he was not an expert and a neurosurgeon should be asked.

REASONABLE DOUBT

The senior neurosurgeon at Melbourne's Royal Children's Hospital, Geoffrey Klug, hit the defence case for a proverbial six. Mr Klug said it was highly likely Lewis would have been knocked unconscious by the blow that killed him. He said even if the boy had had some sort of a lucid interval, it was very unlikely he would have been able to talk normally or feed himself. Mr Klug said he believed Lewis's fatal injury would have been caused by more than one 'severe' blow. He said he did not believe those blows could have been inflicted by a tantrum, or by a video cassette being tapped on his head, or even by him being tossed over a man's shoulder onto a bed. The killer blow or blows, he said, would have been akin to Lewis falling out of a window, or over a stair banister and hitting his head on a hard surface – or being hit with a brick.

Gill's antics continued, even as his trial drew to its close. He interrupted the prosecutor's final address, calling out from the dock: 'I can't listen to her. She's lying, she's blatantly lying.'

In his closing address, Mr Silbert acknowledged that what his client had done to Lewis on the night before he was found dead was despicable, but he said that did *not* mean Gill had inflicted the fatal blow or that he had intended to kill or even to really seriously injure his little mate.

But on 14 March 2003 – after deliberating for three hours and sleeping on their decision overnight – the seven men and five women on the jury declared Gill a child murderer. As the verdict was announced, Gill took his hands out of his pockets, rested them on the dock and shouted: 'You've *got* to be joking!' The newly convicted murderer's father broke down weeping. His mother stared straight ahead. Daisy wasn't there.

***

Six months later, things were very different when the case moved to Melbourne for Gill's pre-sentence plea-hearing.

Gill had morphed from a pretty-boy, floppy-haired yuppy look to a muscle-bound, close-cropped, pony-tailed tough. Was this a reversion to the real Gill, a dropping of a facade put on for the jury; was it a tough facade to make it easier to cope in jail; or was this 'chameleon' Gill, once again being easily influenced by those around him?

Teaching a Toddler Who's Boss 313

The other big change was that Daisy no longer loved the man who had admitted cruelly hurting her baby, who had been found guilty of murdering her toddler son. In her victim impact statement, Ms De Los Reyes wrote that because of Gill's 'evilness' and betrayal, she had come to distrust men.

Gill's new barrister, David Brustman, called for the sentence not to be 'crushing', saying his client had 'very much loved' Lewis. He said Gill had only had four hours' sleep in the 72 hours before Lewis's death, that the boy had been killed after 'nerves became frayed' during a frustrating day and that the killing had not been planned. He also handed up nine glowing character references in which Gill was described as soft and charming, loving, caring, polite, well-mannered, pleasant, fun-loving and artistically talented. Mr Brustman said that while in jail, Gill had painted the portraits of many inmates' loved ones.

Prosecutor Michele Williams called for a long prison term, saying the murder was a serious example of the murder of a two-year-old and that Gill had expressed no real remorse.

Outside the court, as he was being led away in chains, Gill looked at me and pleaded: 'Write the truth: I'm not a murderer.' I did not reply and certainly didn't feel any pity. I just watched him being led away, looking plaintively back at me: a child–man still playing a childish game despite facing a very adult punishment for a very bad crime.

A month later, in sentencing Gill, then 30, Justice Coldrey said he accepted that the killing of Lewis had been unplanned and that Gill had been shocked by what he had done. He said Gill had fatally hurt Lewis in an extraordinarily immature explosion of violence fuelled by frustration, alcohol and drugs.

Justice Coldrey: You, as a grown adult, wanted to show a two-year-old who was boss … A further distorted train of thought which emerges was that you were, in effect, punishing Lewis out of concern for the distress he was causing your partner, Daisy.

He noted that a psychologist believed Gill had had a childlike dependency on Daisy, that he had tried to stop Lewis crying to protect his relationship with her and that Gill felt he was competing with Lewis for his mother's affection.

> *Justice Coldrey*: Whatever the motivation for your behaviour, it represents a grave abuse of the position of power and control that you held over this young child. Instead of the care and protection to which Lewis Blackley was entitled, he received aggression and violence and pain and suffering. On any view, your conduct constituted a grave breach of trust ...
>
> I have no doubt that you regret the death of Lewis Blackley, but your primary concern is the destruction of your relationship with Daisy De Los Reyes and your own situation of incarceration. Indeed, despite comments you made to police ... you refuse to accept responsibility for Lewis's death. Consequently, your state of mind falls well short of genuine remorse.

The judge said Ms De Los Reyes's change of heart towards Gill since the trial showed she had gradually accepted 'the reality of what befell her child at your hands'. He said Lewis's death had also traumatised the boy's father and his grandmother, Kathleen Thompson.

> *Justice Coldrey*: Mr Blackley is faced with feelings of depression and – on such occasions as birthdays, Christmas, Father's Days and long weekends when he and Lewis were together – that depression is exacerbated. Additionally, there are understandable feelings of guilt at not being able to be with Lewis at the time. Mr Blackley writes that he has gone from being an outgoing and gregarious person to a person with minimal social interaction with the everyday world and one who had been undergoing psychological counselling ...
>
> Like her son, Mrs Thompson has ceased to be an outgoing person and is struggling to get on with her life and find some happiness.

During Justice Coldrey's sentencing remarks – like a naughty schoolboy having to listen to a boring lesson – Gill muttered to himself, looked up

Teaching a Toddler Who's Boss

at the ceiling, shook his head and gazed at those in the court; sometimes quizzically, sometimes blankly, sometimes plaintively, sometimes defiantly. When the judge talked of him losing the love of Ms De Los Reyes, he bowed his head and wiped away a tear. He wept when he heard of the suffering of Lewis's grandparents and shook his head furiously when the judge said he still failed to accept full responsibility for the boy's death. Finally, however, he was still when Justice Coldrey came to announce his sentence.

> *Justice Coldrey*: Mr Gill, I have determined that you should be imprisoned for a period of 19 years. I fix a period of 14 years before you become eligible for parole ... Remove the prisoner.

Still Gill was still. Finally, perhaps, grim reality was sinking in.

Afterwards, on the steps of the court, Lewis's dad struggled to hold back tears as he declared the man who killed his son: 'Just a scumbag.'

> *Mr Blackley*: Lock him up and throw away the key ... Lewis would be four now and doing all the stuff four-year-olds do ... There will always be dates, anniversaries and reminders of what should have been.

Mrs Thompson said she and her husband, Don, had flown from their home in Dunedin, New Zealand to see the trial and sentencing of the man who had hurt her happy grandson so badly he died. She said she still woke in the middle of the night thinking about Lewis's agonising death; she hadn't had a full night's sleep since her grandson's death.

> *Mrs Thompson*: Sometimes, I feel as though I am wearing a mask to the world. I don't think I will ever be the same again.

Nearly a year and a half later – when Lewis should have been preparing to go to school – his murderer's appeal was heard.

One of the reasons Gill's lawyers claimed his trial was unfair was that Mr Klug had been allowed to give evidence. Justice Coldrey had let the prosecution call Mr Klug after Dr Lynch told the court he was not an expert on 'lucid intervals'. Normally the prosecution is not allowed to add witnesses during a trial – accused people have a right to know everything about the prosecution case before their trial so they have every chance to mount a successful defence. The problem was that the only witness asked to deal with the crucial issue of whether Lewis could have had a 'lucid interval' before he died – Dr Lynch – had said he wasn't expert enough to answer the question. Justice Coldrey's solution was to let the prosecution call Mr Klug but to adjourn the trial for a week to give the defence a chance to quiz him before the jury got to hear what he had to say – so they knew what he was going to say and could, if necessary, try to find a way to counter his evidence. At the appeal, the defence said the judge should have aborted the trial, saying the delay would have made it hard for the jurors to remember all the evidence to properly decide the case.

The appeal court was also told Gill's trial had been unfair because the judge had failed to emphasise enough to the jurors that they had to be convinced that Lewis had *not* inflicted his own fatal injury in a tantrum; the judge should have warned the jury that Ms De Los Reyes's schizophrenia might make her an unreliable witness; and the jury had not been warned strongly enough against assuming that because Gill had inflicted some of Lewis's injuries, he had inflicted the fatal one.

Gill's lawyers also claimed his sentence was much too harsh for someone who had killed after temporarily losing his self-control.

In April 2005 – three years and nearly four months after Lewis was killed – the Victorian Court of Appeal roundly rejected Gill's appeal.

The three judges accepted that Mr Klug's evidence would have been devastating to Gill's hopes of being acquitted – particularly the surgeon's denial that Lewis could have inflicted the fatal injury on himself and that it was very unlikely the fatally wounded boy could have had a lucid interval. They denied, however, that it had been unfair of the judge to let him give evidence, pointing out that Gill's lawyer had introduced the 'lucid interval' issue in cross-examining Dr Lynch. They also said the issues in the trial were relatively simple so the short adjournment would not have made it hard for the jury to properly consider the evidence.

They denied that the judge should have warned the jury about the reliability of Ms De Los Reyes's evidence, pointing out that her evidence was substantially the same as Gill's.

The appeal did not even come close to succeeding.

Justice Stephen Charles: There was ample evidence to support the verdict. It seems to me that the Crown case was a very strong one. The evidence of Mr Klug was damning to the applicant, whose statements in his second record of interview could also be taken by the jury as a complete admission to his having struck the blows to Lewis's head which led to his death.

As for Gill's sentence, sometimes appeal judges will say that a sentence was stern, that they might have given a lighter one if they had been the trial judge but then note that they can only change sentences they consider are 'manifestly' unfair. The opposite was true here.

Justice Charles: The applicant … used a very substantial amount of force in the infliction of the fatal injury and had grossly abused a position of trust and his position of power and control over a young child. In my view, the sentence was plainly within range. Furthermore, the nonparole period is very short and, indeed, lenient.

Gill had not only lost his appeal, he had come very close to getting more time in jail.

BACKYARD BONFIRE

Everyone was ready for the mountain of old, unwanted furniture to burn. Beers were in hands, seats were positioned. There's nothing like a bonfire to get people together – more interesting than television, more spectacular than a barbecue. When the smelly old couch was finally heaved atop the pile of old chairs and other junk, the bonfire lighter, Graham 'Scotty' Watson, stuck a blazing sword of paper into the pile. And … nothing. He tried again; this time … nothing again. Finally, there was a little flame but it looked like it could die any second. The bonfire party was turning into a fizzer but then, despite an afternoon of drinking alcohol, Scotty had a brainwave. He ran inside and got the can of whipper-snipper petrol.

Scotty the bonfire saviour splashed some of the petrol on the dying flame and – Hey presto! Whoosh! Shoom! – it sprang to life.

> *John Kercheval*: It reacted … into a fireball. I was standing fairly close to the fire when he threw the fuel on and I had to get out of the way of the flames.

At first Scotty's de facto Helen Forsyth was also impressed. She got the camera and took a photograph of the inferno but then she started to get nervous. The backyard of the Lewis Street flat she shared with Scotty in the outer bayside Melbourne suburb of Frankston, was not very big.

> *Ms Forsyth*: It started to get pretty high and I was a bit worried about the wooden fences catching fire, so I grabbed a hose and was wetting down the fences to keep them from catching fire.

Backyard Bonfire 319

The problem was that the hose wasn't long enough and for Ms Forsyth to wet the fences she had to spray over the flames. The bonfire watchers, especially Scotty, were not impressed. Annoyed and drunk, he splashed some petrol on his girlfriend and when she went inside to change, followed, still berating her for dousing the fire.

Their friends Mr Kercheval and his de facto Louise Dart stayed outside. They tried to mind their own business but they could see the silhouettes of their warring hosts on the bedroom curtain. When the smoke alarm went off, they decided to *make* it their business.

Mr Kercheval: The first thing that went through my mind was that the smoke from the bonfire had set off the alarm, so I was going in to tell them to turn off the alarm, but that wasn't the case ... I went in ... smoke was coming from ... towards the bedroom and then I walked down ... The fumes were pretty bad ... I nearly choked myself. I saw Helen on the ground in a pretty bad way ... Graham was there ... I could see that she'd been burnt.
Prosecutor: What did it look like?
Mr Kercheval: Horrible. I turned around and told Louise to get out, that she didn't need to see it. She just looked black ... She was gasping for air ... I tried to reach down and grab her but at the same time I abused Graham ... I just said: 'What are you doing? What the hell have you done?' ... 'It's about time you started picking on blokes and stopped getting into girls' ... He told me to leave her, just let her die.
Prosecutor: Leave her, just let her die?
Mr Kercheval: And mind my own business.

After being told he was allowed to repeat swear words in court, Mr Kercheval was again asked what Watson told him.

Mr Kercheval: I think the exact words were: 'Let the fucking dog die,' or 'She's a dog, let her fucking die' – something like that ... He said: 'Do you want to have a go?' and then he punched me in the mouth.

320 REASONABLE DOUBT

*Prosecut*or: What did you do?

Mr Kercheval: Fell over.

Ms Dart later remembered seeing Helen 'laying on the floor screaming and choking and spluttering and choking'. She said Scotty had told them: 'Let her choke.'

A policeman said Watson drank beer even as ambulance officers treated his unconscious girlfriend.

Sen-Constable Steve Peck: He was reluctant to put the beer down. He just seemed uncaring.

After that disastrous backyard bonfire night on 9 September 1999, 39 per cent of 40-year-old Helen Forsyth's body was burnt. Her face, ears, neck and the upper part of her legs were scarred. When she gave evidence at Watson's trial about a year later, she was still wearing a pressure stocking. Speaking barely above a whisper, she said she was just about to have the little finger on her left hand amputated and told of her daily pain.

Ms Forsyth: I get a lot of pins and needles in my legs and a burning sensation, and just, it's uncomfortable.

She told the court that after a five-year, on-off, often drunken relationship, she had moved in to live with Watson just a week before he set her alight. Of the night she was burnt, Ms Forsyth said she remembered trying to hose down the fence and then 'trying to really get away from Scotty because I had petrol on me'.

Ms Forsyth: He'd thrown petrol on me.

She said 'because of the trauma' she couldn't remember most of that night but she remembered Watson 'following me with a can of petrol, abusing me'.

Backyard Bonfire

Ms Forsyth: I changed my clothes and then he came into the bedroom ... put more petrol on me and then lit a cigarette lighter and set me on fire ...

I just sort of yelled at him to put me out.

Prosecutor: ... What did he do?

Ms Forsyth: He said: 'Die bitch. Burn. Die.'

As she said this, Ms Forsyth broke down and wept and the court adjourned for lunch.

Prosecutor: What was the next thing you remember?

Ms Forsyth: Trying to put myself out with doonas.

Prosecutor: Did he do anything to help or hinder?

Ms Forsyth: I can't remember ... I blacked out ... I just felt a feeling of choking, burning, and then I must have passed out.

A couple of hours after setting Ms Forsyth alight, and then punching Mr Kercheval, Watson, 33, was interviewed by police. He told them he was still a bit drunk.

Watson: It was an accident. Me and her had an argument ... For some reason I've gone – I must admit, I will, yeah – at some point in time, I poured petrol around the corner and some of it got on her ...

Police: Who lit the petrol?

Watson: I think it was a smoke at the time, or something. A smoke or a lighter.

Police: Did you light the petrol?

Watson: No, I did not. No.

Later he gave a different answer to the same question.

Police: Did you light the petrol yourself?

Watson: I might have done, yeah.

322 REASONABLE DOUBT

Police: What were you trying to do? Scare her?

Watson: Joke. It was just a joke … Dumb thing to do. Didn't realise the consequences …

If it wasn't for me she'd probably be dead. Then again if it wasn't for me, she wouldn't be burnt … I agree it was my fault. I wasn't going for her … It was just a little shit stir … I was pissed off with her … I didn't realise how it would flare up … Suddenly it's gone, 'Shoom!', big flames everywhere and I was trying to put her out … Some flames were there and then all of a sudden they were all over her.

A flame would be here and a flame would be there and fly over there. A flame would be out and I start getting up and the flame would appear here for some reason … I was giving her a cuddle – 'What's wrong?', 'What's the problem?' – then I realised the burns on her face. That spun me out actually. I didn't realise what had happened until I was giving her a cuddle and I saw her face … Burn marks all over her face. Just spun me out. I didn't really expect to see that.

Police: I put it to you that because you were angry you wanted to hurt her by throwing petrol and possibly kill her?

Watson: No. Load of shit. That's a load of shit … If I want to kill her that much or hurt her that much, why did I put her out right away as soon as it happened?

Didn't realise it would catch fire. I thought: Yeah, a little fire and that's it … It all happened … Bang! Like that. Spur of the moment … 'Fuck, what's going on?' … It's an accident, that's the honest truth. It wasn't no malicious intent.

Police: You know what happens with petrol.

Watson: Yeah, but I didn't realise it was gonna happen with Helen like that.

Police: Why would it change? …

Watson: Well, I never set fire to a human being in my entire life, have I?

He said he tried to put the fire out on his girlfriend with doonas and a pillow. She had, he said, 'started whingeing about pain, the pain or

Backyard Bonfire

something. I dunno'. Watson said he hadn't called an ambulance because the 'other guy said he had'.

Police: Who was that?

Watson: Probably the guy I punched before – John …

Police: Why did you punch him out?

Watson: Being a smart-arse.

Police: How was he being a smart-arse?

Watson: He was saying I did it on purpose … He came at me and wanna blue me. I said, 'Bullshit. I didn't. Fucking, it was an accident' …

Police: I put it to you that when John came in after hearing you and Helen fight, he saw you standing over Helen and you said to him: 'Leave her alone and let her die.'

Watson: That's a load of shit. I totally deny that, whatsoever. That's bullshit. I'll say that right now. I swear on my life. I swear on my parents' life … Ask Helen what I said. I guarantee it won't be that.

He also strongly denied Louise Dart's claim he had said: 'Let her choke.' Finally, it was brought home to Watson just how much trouble he was in.

Police: Graham, at this stage you are going to be charged with the attempted murder of Helen Forsyth.

Watson: Attempted murder? … Attempted murder?!

At his trial in the Victorian Supreme Court in September 2000, Watson pleaded guilty to recklessly causing serious injury but *not* guilty to intentionally causing serious injury or to attempted murder.

His barrister David Drake tackled Mr Kercheval's claim that Watson said: 'Leave her alone. Let the fucking dog die,' by pointing out that he had only told police and the pre-trial magistrates' court hearing that Watson had said: 'Leave her alone. Let her die.' He accused Mr Kercheval of trying to make himself out to be a hero and that his role in the events

324   REASONABLE DOUBT

had 'grown in your imagination'. Mr Kercheval denied this and said he only had not said that Watson had said 'Let the fucking dog die' because he believed you weren't allowed to use swear words in courts.

Mr Drake attacked head-on Ms Forsyth's claim that Watson had told her: 'Die, bitch. Burn. Die,' while she was being burnt.

> *Mr Drake*: You said before lunch: 'He said: "Die, bitch. Burn. Die." '
> That's a lie, isn't it.
> *Ms Forsyth*: No. It's not.
> *Mr Drake*: Something you would never forget?
> *Ms Forsyth*: I'll never forget it.
> *Mr Drake*: Remember it forever?
> *Ms Forsyth*: It will be in my mind forever.

Mr Drake pointed out, however, that Ms Forsyth did not tell this 'memorable phrase' to police when they interviewed her about two and a half months after she was burnt, or to the pre-trial committal hearing more than four months after that. Ms Forsyth said that at first she had struggled to remember the day she was burnt and later that she hadn't thought to mention it. She denied that it was a lie or something she had come to believe happened after talking to other witnesses. Ms Forsyth also denied that Watson had saved her life.

> *Mr Drake*: I put it to you that the person who put you out was the accused.
> *Ms Forsyth*: No.
> *Mr Drake*: You don't have any memory …
> *Ms Forsyth*: I know that Graham was not going to put me out. If someone wants you dead, they make sure you die.

***

On 30 September 2000 – after deliberating for three hours – a jury found Watson not guilty of attempted murder but rejected his claim that he had not meant to hurt his girlfriend, finding him guilty of intentionally causing serious injury. Upon hearing the verdicts, Watson betrayed no emotion but in the public gallery, hiding behind big sunglasses, Ms Forsyth gasped a gasp of deep disappointment. She was clearly distraught when she left the court. Outside, with her voice breaking and her hand shaking as she tried to light a cigarette, she said she did not want to say what she thought.

∗

Watson's pre-sentence plea-hearing heard that the 34-year-old pastry chef's practically tea-total parents were devastated at their son's descent into alcoholism after they migrated from Scotland when he was 16. Mr Drake pointed out that Watson had put out the flames of his victim and that while awaiting trial he had done an anger management course. Prosecutor Joe Dickson QC said Ms Forsyth had been 'scarred for life'.

In October 2000, Justice Teague told Watson that he had shown a 'curious ambivalence' towards his victim after setting her alight.

> *Justice Teague*: At times you were supportive and accepting of blame. At other times you were abusive, callous, uncaring and dismissive.

He accepted, however, that Watson felt some remorse and noted his plea of guilty to recklessly causing serious injury.

> *Justice Teague*: Mr Watson, I sentence you to six years' imprisonment. I fix a period of four years before you will be eligible for parole.

The judge also ordered Watson to pay $80,000 compensation to Ms Forsyth but he said he realised it was 'highly unlikely' that Watson would be able to pay any of this, noting that his 'personal belongings' were of 'relatively little realisable value'.

ALREADY DEAD

The 'unusual' death of Lindsay Jellett – a brain-damaged man who died while on a walk to find pink golf balls for his twin sister – turned out to be a bizarrely tough riddle for the justice system.

Mr Jellett's bloodied and crushed body was found on the grassy edge of a dirt road about 2km from his home in the western Victorian town of Ararat. Someone had dragged him off the road and *then* reversed a car over him – *twice*.

Lindsay's body was found on 11 May 1994 – the morning after he failed to return from his walk in time for dinner at the house he shared with four other intellectually disabled people.

Before setting out on his fateful walk, Lindsay had kissed his twin sister Judith Anne Cengiz goodbye. They had just spent a happy five hours together – lunching, playing the pokies, shopping, and going to two meetings to discuss Lindsay's progress. As she usually did on her six-weekly visits, Cengiz had brought her brother clothes, cigarettes, lollies and drinks. During her visit she bought Lindsay arch supports to ease the pain of walking. She also forked out the $30 he blew on the pokies, and gave him another $25 cash. The very different twins returned to Lindsay's home about 3.30pm and a few minutes later Lindsay set off on his walk.

Cengiz: I was standing there talking to Rod [a staff member at the community services–run unit] and Lindsay kissed me goodbye and said he was going to the golf course. Lindsay goes to the golf course all the time in order to collect golf balls and he later sells them. I remember he told me he was going to get me some pink golf balls …

I gave Lindsay a bottle of Coke, a jar of Nescafé and chocolate-chip biscuits, and he put these in his room and left … That would have been about 4pm …

Lindsay seemed to want to get away as soon as possible and that was the last I saw of him. I spoke to Rod for about five minutes and then drove to Melton.

Cengiz refused a staff offer of a cup of tea, saying she needed to get back home to pick up her seven-year-old son and three-year-old daughter.

About four hours later, a worried worker at the Ararat home phoned Cengiz at home to tell her that Lindsay had not returned from his walk. Nobody answered the call and she left a message. Half an hour later – about 8pm – Cengiz got home and returned the call. She phoned several times that night asking if Lindsay had been found and suggesting where he might have gone.

Cengiz: I was very worried and hadn't hardly slept and I thought he may have gone to Aradale [the Ararat institution Lindsay had recently moved from] and she told me to wait and they would notify me when he came in.

***

Just before he died, things were looking up for Lindsay Jellett. For the first time since his brain was injured at the age of two when a car crashed into his pram, the 41-year-old was getting the chance to live in a house instead of a big institution. He could not read or write, but had learnt to feed, dress and shower himself. He could also go on long walks by himself, safely crossing roads. He had epilepsy but that was controlled with twice-daily medication. Lindsay's share in the house was going to cost him $15,000 but that wasn't a problem for him. He still had $105,000 of the compensation he was awarded after the car crashed into his pram.

Even though everybody praised Cengiz as a caring sister, police quickly suspected she killed her twin to inherit his $105,000 – that she had been spurred into homicidal action when she feared her inheritance

328 REASONABLE DOUBT

was about to be cut by $15,000. Cengiz had made it clear to her eldest son Greg that she felt entitled to inherit her brother's money. She told him she planned to buy a new car with it and when the 25-year-old asked if she could also buy him a $10,000 car, she said: 'No. It's my money.'

Detectives believed that after kissing Lindsay goodbye, Cengiz picked him up a few hundred metres into his walk. An Aradale nurse who knew Lindsay well told them that about 3.45pm on 10 May 1994 he saw Lindsay get into a Ford car with an LPG sticker on its number plate – Cengiz's car was a Ford and it had an LPG sticker. The nurse, however, also said the car was blue or brown and the woman driving it had dark hair – Cengiz's car was 'burgundy and champagne' and she has fair hair. Police, however, put these discrepancies down to typical mistakes made by witnesses.

Detectives also suspected Cengiz of murder because of the long time it took her to get back to her Melton home on Melbourne's western outskirts. Sticking to the speed limits, the 170km trip can be done in about two hours, but on 10 May 1994 it took Cengiz 4½ hours to reach her Dunvegan Drive home. She later explained that her car had overheated on the way back from Ararat and she had had to wait for about 40 minutes to let it cool. A car expert said Cengiz's car would have been prone to overheating.

Cengiz also said that before going home she had picked up her two young children and put the car through a car wash. She denied doing this to remove evidence of running over her brother, saying she usually washed the car after visiting Ararat. Greg Cengiz, however, did not back this claim. He said that while his mother was awaiting trial, she said to him: 'You know I always wash my car, and I wash underneath the car when I return from seeing Lindsay.'

Greg Cengiz: It was like she was asking me to confirm that.
Prosecutor: Did you know anything about her usually washing under the car after she went to visit Lindsay?
Greg Cengiz: No.

Despite the car wash, investigators found human blood, human hair and bits of fabric on the underside of Cengiz's car. The hair was the same colour as Lindsay's, the fabric matched his trousers, and DNA tests of the blood and hair found that the chance of them coming from anybody other than Lindsay Jellett was one in 4500. At her trial the only answer Cengiz's barrister Daryl Wraith had to the DNA evidence was to warn the jury that DNA examiners had made mistakes.

Mr Wraith also told the jurors that even if Cengiz's car had run over her brother, they should not assume she was driving it at the time. Greg Cengiz told the court what his mother suspected might have happened.

> *Greg Cengiz*: She told me that she thinks someone had taken her motor vehicle from the driveway and driven it to Ararat and did what they decided to do, and then returned the car back to her driveway.

Mr Cengiz, however, said he had fitted an alarm in his mother's car, which turned on 30 seconds after the ignition was turned off and the doors were closed – even if they weren't locked. Prosecutor Colin Hillman derided this stolen car theory as 'absurd'. He said even if someone had taken Cengiz's car without triggering the alarm and without her realising it had gone, by the time they had driven it to Ararat they would have to have found – and reversed over – Lindsay Jellett while police and about 15 other searchers were combing the area.

For police, it looked like a clear case of murder by a greedy sister fed up with caring for her brother.

Then came the bizarre twist: the pathologist found that Lindsay Jellett had died *before* a car was reversed over him. The injuries caused by the reversing car *would* have been bad enough to kill him – but they *hadn't*. The car had twice reversed over a dead man.

The pathologist could not say how Lindsay Jellett had died.

Still, Cengiz was charged with her brother's murder.

In opening the prosecution case at Cengiz's trial in the Victorian Supreme Court in August 1996, Mr Hillman told the jury: 'What she did to kill him is not known, but kill him she did.' He said the prosecution did not have to prove how Mr Jellett died, just that Judith Cengiz had killed him.

330 REASONABLE DOUBT

Mr Hillman: The evidence will establish that after this charade of
saying farewell, Ms Cengiz received her twin brother Lindsay into
her car and ... took a sinister diversion onto a lonely country road
and killed him ...

When the car was used to run over his body, Lindsay Jellett was
already dead. Either she was following through with her murderous
plan to kill him, or she was masking what she had already done to
make it look like a motor-car accident.

He said a pathologist would not have been able to detect how Mr Jellett had
died if, for instance, he had been smothered with a pillow.

The prosecutor said that if Mr Jellett had died as a result of his epilepsy
and Cengiz had realised this, she would have taken him to hospital – not
'run over the body and then lie about the last time she had seen him'. He
also said it was 'stretching human experience too far' to believe that Mr
Jellett had 'conveniently' died naturally just before his sister, not realising
he was dead, reversed her car over him.

Mr Hillman: The use of the car to run him over ... is only explicable
upon the basis that she did kill him, and that she intended to kill him.

In his opening address, Mr Wraith warned the jurors it was a 'highly
unusual' case. He stressed that Cengiz denied driving over *or* killing her
twin brother but told them that even if they were convinced she drove
over Lindsay's body, that did not mean she murdered him. Mr Wraith
said there was a very real possibility Mr Jellett died of a well-known
complication of epilepsy called 'sudden, unexpected death in epileptic
persons', or SUDEP. After the prosecution ended its case, the trial really
did become 'highly unusual' when Justice Tim Smith ordered the jury to
acquit Cengiz of murder.

The judge said that even though it would have been a 'remarkable coincidence' for Mr Jellett to die of epilepsy just before a car was reversed
over him, the jury could not rule it out. He said the incidence of epilepsy

Already Dead

331

sufferers dying suddenly and unexpectedly was frequent enough for it to be a recognised syndrome.

It was not, however, a complete win for the defence. Justice Smith said the jury could still consider whether Cengiz was guilty of attempted murder. In a ruling that was not heard by the jury, he said the jurors could still decide that Ms Cengiz had *tried* to murder her brother and had only failed because he died just before she could succeed. He said that as unlikely as it was that Mr Jellett was alive when he was dragged to the side of the road, but died naturally in the time it took the car driver to go back to the car and start reversing over him, it was 'bordering on the fanciful' to think his killer knew he was dead and thought dragging his body off the road and reversing over it twice would make it look like a hit–run.

The ruling turned the trial on its head. It led to the prosecution trying to persuade the jury that Cengiz had *not* killed her brother and to the defence highlighting the possibility that she *might* have killed him (even though she denied it). It opened the way to an extraordinary defence: 'You can't find me guilty of *attempted* murder because *I may have murdered him.*' In a perverse way, if the jury thought there was a reasonable possibility that Ms Cengiz had killed her brother before running him over, it would have to acquit her of attempted murder. People don't *try* to kill people they *know* are dead. No-one tries to kill a corpse.

The prosecution had a big problem. It had opened the case strongly arguing that Cengiz had killed her brother and then run over him to try to hide what she had done but, after the judge's ruling, it had to make sure the jury did not believe this – or even accept it as a reasonable possibility. In his closing address, Mr Hillman had to convince the jury that the possibility he had called 'stretching human experience too far' in his opening – that Cengiz tried to kill her brother by reversing over him because she hadn't realised he had 'conveniently' already died – was, in fact, what happened.

Mr Hillman: The running over of the body only makes sense if it was done with the intention to kill him, and being unaware that he was already dead.

REASONABLE DOUBT

In his closing address, Mr Wraith told the jury they had to be convinced beyond a reasonable doubt that 'whoever drove the car over that dead body at that time believed it was alive'. He highlighted how the prosecution had changed its argument.

> *Mr Wraith*: If the Crown doesn't really know what happened in Down Road and doesn't really know what was in the mind of the driver of the vehicle, then why should you? ...

He stressed that his client denied killing *or* driving over her brother but told the jurors the case was far from over even if they thought she did.

> *Mr Wraith*: You may ... find the conduct of driving over a dead body is abhorrent and despicable but ... despicable conduct is not a legal offence.

He said that as odd as it might seem, they would have to find Cengiz not guilty of attempted murder if they thought there was a reasonable possibility she *knew* her brother was dead before reversing over him because she had just killed him.

On 26 July 1996, after deliberating for about seven hours, the jury tackling this topsy-turvy trial decided Cengiz had tried to kill her already-dead brother and declared her guilty of attempted murder.

A few weeks later, Justice Smith acknowledged Cengiz had overcome an 'appalling' childhood (including a stepfather who tried to gas her in a murder–suicide attempt) and three violent marriages to become a caring mother of four. He said for many years she had also helped Lindsay. He said, however, that she had done all she could to kill her vulnerable brother for the basest of motives – greed. He jailed her for at least six years and set a maximum term of 10 years.

Almost a year later – in June 1997 – Victoria's Court of Appeal rejected Cengiz's appeal against her conviction and the length of her sentence. Her lawyer's main argument was that the jury should not have ruled out the possibility that Cengiz might have known Lindsay was dead before running him over. Not only did all three judges reject the appeal against her conviction, two said they thought that Cengiz was lucky Justice Smith had ordered the jury to acquit her of murder.

Justice William Ormiston said he did not believe it was completely fanciful that Cengiz may have killed her brother and then dragged him to the side of the road and reversed over him to make it look like a hit–run. He said this would have been irrational behaviour but one should be 'cautious … to impute an entirely reasonable or logical chain of reasoning to a person involved in the killing of a relative'. He said, however, that he did not believe the jury had been wrong to find that it was not a reasonable possibility.

Justice Ormiston: Indeed, commonsense suggests that their conclusion on this issue was entirely appropriate.

The judges all also rejected Cengiz's appeal against the severity of her sentence. Justice David Harper noted that Mr Wraith had told them the sentence was one of the highest in Victoria for the crime of attempted murder.

Justice Harper: This appears to be true, but the applicant would be guilty of murder had not death intervened.

Unlike most of the other accused people in this book, Cengiz not only continued to say she was innocent of the crime she was convicted of, she continued to claim that somebody else had done it. She denied that she had been interested in inheriting her brother's money, pointing out that a few years before her brother died the Guardianship and Administration Board had offered her control of her brother's money but she had refused the offer because she hadn't wanted the responsibility. She also told *Herald Sun* reporter Geoff Wilkinson that if she had really wanted to kill Lindsay she had had plenty of chances to do so in 'much simpler and less suspicious circumstances'.

Cengiz: We used to go for walks in Lerderderg Gorge. I could have easily just pushed him over a cliff and said it was an accident.

Lawyers campaigning to have Cengiz freed called on a coroner to re-open an investigation into Mr Jellett's death, saying new evidence cast doubt on the DNA tests linking Cengiz's car to the running over of Mr Jellett. They also claimed a violent man who knew of Cengiz's movements, had spare keys to her car and had moved interstate could have killed Mr Jellett and 'set up' Cengiz as the killer.

In March 2000, however, Coroner Iain West refused to re-open the case, saying it was an abuse of process. He pointed out that even if the DNA testing of Cengiz's car was discredited it would not help him find out how Mr Jellett died, because everyone agreed he had died before being run over. Before being taken back to prison, Cengiz hit out at the judge's decision.

Ms Cengiz: I don't believe it. I've been accused of abusing the system, but it's the system that's abusing me. I think it's wrong. It's so unfair.

INSANELY HOMESICK

Winning a promotion and getting the chance to see the other side of the world did not prompt the sort of reaction Gerry Skura thought he would get from his wife. There was no: 'Oh, wow, honey. That's great. Congratulations. That'll be exciting. I have never thought about living in Australia. We'll miss our friends and family, but it'll be an adventure and it won't be for ever.' None of that. Instead, Marie Skura struggled to hold back the tears when her husband broke the news in July 2001. Gerry, however, did not let his wife's teary response stop him accepting the transfer. He thought she would get over it.

He could not have been more wrong.

The Skuras' move down-under would turn out to be a bizarre journey into darkness; it would shake the seemingly ordinary family to its core; it would show them what they were capable of – the good and the very, very bad.

Gerry (early 40s, successful businessman, married for almost 20 years to an equally successful businesswoman, no children) and Marie (early 20s, single mother of a young daughter, living from pay cheque to pay cheque) met at a work cocktail party in the early '90s while working for different importing/exporting companies. After a couple of years, they started seeing each other more than just at cocktail parties. Gerry would drop around on Saturdays after golf, and on Fridays – when his wife was out of town working. In January 1996, Gerry ended his 22-year marriage and moved in with Marie and five-year-old Alexa. At the end of that year, Marie persuaded a reluctant Gerry to try marriage again.

Things were going well for the Skuras. Marie was quickly rising through the ranks in her company and they had a nice house in Vancouver.

REASONABLE DOUBT

Gerry saw only two problems: his wife was drinking a little too much on the cocktail 'circuit', and the grain-shipping industry was going through tough times. So in July 2001, when he was offered the position of general manager of the Australian arm of the company, he grabbed it. It was a slight promotion and a chance for Marie get off the cocktail party merry-go-round before alcohol became a real problem.

In April 2002, Marie and Alexa joined Gerry in Melbourne. It was a big move for a woman who had not lived outside a small part of Vancouver. That's where she had endured a troubled childhood – she said her father was a 'raving alcoholic' she never saw sober, and her stepfather sexually and physically abused her for 12 years until she was 18. She said he even beat her if he saw her with other boys. (A few years after they left home, Marie and her sister told police they had been abused. Their stepfather was charged but a judge ruled that after such a long time there was not enough evidence to be able to find him guilty beyond a reasonable doubt.) Vancouver was also where Marie had battled through as a young single mother, and, finally, where she had found her way to a happy family life and a satisfying career. Still, at first, Gerry thought things would be OK in Australia.

Gerry: Marie seemed happy enough when we first arrived; however, I know she wasn't completely happy.

It wasn't long before Marie made her feelings clear to her husband.

Gerry: About three weeks after we arrived, Marie collected me from work. She was to the point of tears and told me she couldn't take it any more and she wanted to go home.

Gerry gently refused and suggested his wife join some clubs to make new friends; that she give Australia, as the locals put it, 'a go'. Over the next few months, Gerry slowly realised that Marie had no intention of doing anything of the sort.

A few days after Marie's tearful plea to go home, Gerry Skura got food poisoning – something that had not happened to him before. He had to

Insanely Homesick

go to hospital and spent two hours being fed intravenously. A few weeks later, Marie gave her husband what she called a 'natural remedy'. Gerry complained that it tasted awful but she urged him to finish it, saying it was a mixture of vitamins and would help relieve his stress. The next day Gerry kept falling asleep and his fingers and toes tingled. He lost that day; he could not remember it at all. His wife later told him that he had had a nosebleed and that he had fallen in the shower. Various tests in hospital, such as a CAT scan, didn't pick up anything, but a few hours later, back at home, Gerry started stuttering and Marie called an ambulance. A blood test found sleeping tablets in his system.

Gerry: I was shocked because I have never taken sleeping pills. Marie did take them and there were some in the house, but I had never had them.

Marie told her husband that he had got up in the middle of the night with a headache and must have mistaken her sleeping pills for headache tablets. Gerry didn't buy this: the sleeping pills were much smaller than the headache tablets and were in a bottle about half the size.

Gerry: The conclusion I came to was the sleeping pills were in the mixture Marie gave me.

Gerry's suspicion that his wife was trying to poison him mounted over the weeks. An open bottle of Powerade in his office smelt so bad he threw it out and he found an open box of rat poison next to the stove – they did not have a problem with rats or mice.

Gerry: I blew my cork on the week of June 17 when I found prescription drugs and all sorts of drugs around the house … and when I was looking through a drawer I found a syringe with blood in it … Marie made the excuse that it was used on her cat in Canada and it inadvertently was shipped in the move. I didn't believe her but I didn't know where it was from.

338   REASONABLE DOUBT

In June, Gerry's run of foul-tasting drinks and food troubles stopped when he went on a business trip to Bangkok and Singapore. A few weeks after his return, however, his Aussie bad luck continued when a poisonous white-tailed spider bit his foot and he found himself back in hospital.

On 21 November 2002, things got really heated.

Gerry: Once again I was tired and kept falling asleep ... The only other time in my life I felt like that was when I believe Marie gave me an overdose of sleeping pills in the 'natural remedy'. I was asleep in the master bedroom when the fire broke out there. Marie had told me that she was going to Southland [shopping centre] to get some Christmas presents. She received a call on her cell phone from the fire brigade telling her that the house was on fire and that I was being rushed to hospital by ambulance with smoke inhalation. I was suspicious ... but couldn't prove anything.

The fire destroyed the bedroom. Soon after that mysterious blaze, Marie and 12-year-old Alexa returned to Canada for a holiday.

Alexa: When we were in Canada, my mom told me that we were going to stay and we were not going back to Australia. She told me not to tell anyone. She said that because we missed all our friends and family and stuff in Canada.

I wanted to come back to Australia a little bit, but I missed friends and stuff over there. We did end up coming back though, because Uncle Jim really wanted to come.

Gerry not only feared his wife was trying to kill him, he also suspected she was secretly spending thousands of dollars. After months of denials and obfuscation, she admitted she had done exactly that. She said she had lost it on gambling and promised to go to Gamblers Anonymous and to Alcoholics Anonymous. What Gerry did not know was that his wife and her daughter had long been plotting their escape from Oz.

Alexa: Mom started telling me about moving back to Canada again. She said she would try to get a flight home and stuff like that. I was happy that she was trying and I told her that I wanted to go home really badly.

Mom told me that there was a flight on Singapore Airlines every night, so I would ask her every night. She would always say that they had been cancelled. When she told me this I didn't feel good because I wanted to go home.

Mom told me a while ago that she put $40,000 into another bank account. Mom told me that this money came from Dad's account. She told me not to tell anyone that. She told me that she didn't want Dad to know about it. Mom told me that this money was to get our life started in Canada.

Mom told me that there was a ticket organised for her and I to go together to Canada. Mom told me that her and I were going over to Canada first, and that, hopefully, Dad would follow us a little later on.

I didn't think there was anything strange happening. I just thought that Mom was trying to get organised to go back to Canada because we were both homesick.

I know Mom didn't like it over here. She said she hated it here.

In the 10 days before he went on a business trip to Canberra on 4 March, Gerry once again felt uncharacteristically ill – his food tasted 'a little off'. In Canberra he felt better.

Upon returning to Melbourne on 6 March, he rushed home and changed his clothes because he had been offered a ticket to the Australian Formula 1 Grand Prix. Marie dropped him off at the big race.

A few hours later, the Skuras' lives crashed.

Gerry: At approximately 2pm, I was informed by police that my wife had been arrested for incitement to murder. The target of this murder was to be me.

Gerry broke the news to Alexa.

Alexa: Dad told me that Mom had been arrested for trying to kill Dad and was in jail. I was pretty mad at her for trying to kill my dad.

Alexa was soon to learn that for months – while she was at school and her dad was at work – her mother had been living a very strange, secret life.

***

Around Christmas 2002, at a pub in the nearby well-to-do suburb of Brighton, Marie was having a smoko while playing pokies when she was noticed by a group of unemployed men. On a day out from their modest lodgings in Noble Park, they were looking for some 'uptown' bayside fun. The smoothest talker among them – Darren – decided to have a go at chatting up this good-looking 'sheila'. One of his mates – Christopher Brett Duke – remembered.

Mr Duke: We were just having a good time looking at the girls on the beach and having a few drinks. We went to the hotel but we weren't dressed proper and they wouldn't let us in. Outside the pokies area we saw an attractive blonde woman, sitting having a smoke. She was on her own and Darren went up to her and sort of struck up a conversation.

The next evening Darren came back to the boarding house with Marie in her white BMW. She brought a slab of beer and a cask of wine. She stayed a good two or three hours and left on her own.

Darren said that he had sex with her the evening before. Marie would come around to the boarding house just about every day. Each time she came around she'd bring alcohol – normally a slab of beer, and wine for herself.

Marie had found some local 'friends'. They were not, however, the sort her husband had urged her to find, and she had certainly *not* found them to cure her homesickness. In her desperation, she also badly misjudged her new 'Aussie mates'.

Insanely Homesick

Mr Duke: Darren told me that Marie wanted someone to kill her husband. He told me that he had no intention of killing anyone but that he'd string her along to try to get some money out of her.

Darren's scam worked a treat: after a couple of months Marie gave him $10,000 – and her wedding ring – to kill her husband, but instead of doing that, instead of keeping his promise, Darren and his girlfriend promptly disappeared. Despite this treachery, Marie kept visiting the boarding house nearly every day. She continued her quest for a husband-killer.

Mr Duke: Marie told me one night that she wanted her husband out of the picture. She told me that she had embezzled money from him and that he'd found out about it. Each time I spoke to her she kept saying she wanted her husband out of the way. She became more and more specific about it and went on to say that she wanted her husband dead. I then commenced having a sexual relationship with her ...

She didn't say how she wanted her husband killed, just that she wanted it done. I had no intention of killing her husband, or anyone else for that matter. I was happy to get free grog from her and the occasional $50 and $100 from her, but I was never going to kill anyone.

I had no doubt that she was serious about having her husband killed. She definitely wasn't joking.

In February 2003, Mr Duke finally stopped stringing Marie along.

Mr Duke: Marie asked me to get her ... heroin. She told me she wanted to put it into her husband's food.

By this stage, I was getting a bit worried about how serious things were becoming. I didn't want to get into any trouble. I eventually told her that I wouldn't kill her husband. This didn't seem to upset her at all. She just went to speak to Alan ... [another of the Noble Park group] and asked him the same thing.

Alan wasn't interested in killing anyone but told her he knew someone who could.

342   REASONABLE DOUBT

***

So on 4 March 2003, Marie continued her bumbling *'Double Indemnity* meets the Three Stooges meets *Eyes Wide Shut'* trip into what she must have imagined was Australian's psychopathic underworld.

At the Elsternwick Hotel in Elwood, on Brighton's northern border, Alan introduced 'Jason' as her hitman. Anyone eavesdropping on the start of this meeting would never have guessed the pretty blonde in the brown floral summer dress and the fit young 'baby-faced' man were meeting to discuss the contract killing of her blameless husband.

Alan: Jason.

Marie: Pleased to meet you.

Jason: How are you? What's your name?

Marie: Marie.

Jason: Marie. Pleased to meet you.

Alan: Want a beer, mate?

Jason: Yeah. Get me ... Have they got a Stella on tap or, oh, whatever ...

Jason [to Marie]: Didn't hold you up too long, did I?

Marie: No. Did you have a hard time finding it? ...

Jason: I'm from the other side of town.

Marie: Where?

Jason: West.

Marie: You have to forgive me. I'm not from Melbourne. So when I hear west it ...

Jason: Over the West Gate is out west.

Marie: OK, the West Gate Bridge is towards the airport?

Jason: Yes. You go over it ... Where are you from?

Marie: Vancouver.

Jason: Oh. OK.

Marie: And we actually live in Brighton now.

Jason: You haven't been here long, have you?

Marie: Actually, almost a year ... but it's been really up and down. My husband got bit by one of your spiders. He got bit by a

Insanely Homesick

343

white-tailed spider … It was a hole about that big and it went past his tendon … We're not familiar with your spiders.

Jason: Oh. OK.

Marie tells the men the spider's toxicity depends on what sort of other spiders it has eaten recently. She doesn't mention that she wants to kill one of her own. When Alan goes to get beer, Jason asks Marie where her husband is. She tells him he's in Canberra but still doesn't mention wanting him killed. They talk about anything but Gerry's murder: Marie reckons the Australian shipping industry is 'male-dominated'; she doesn't agree with the war in Iraq ('I don't believe in war, period. I don't believe it serves any purpose other than population control'); and she believes China is the world's biggest threat. Finally, Alan cuts through the chitchat and political debate.

Alan: Talk to him seriously.

Marie: I don't know what to say to him.

Jason: I've got a few questions for you to start with.

Marie: Oh.

Jason stresses that after this meeting it will be just him and Marie. Marie tells Alan: 'OK, that's fine because I like him.'

Jason: You gotta understand. What I'm doing here, there's a lot of risk … So the least amount of people that know anything the better.

Marie: That's fine. No problem. I understand.

Jason: Well, tell me, tell me the situation. I have got to know …

Marie: I don't know you from Adam …

Jason: Yeah, well we have got a mutual contact in Alan … All right, I won't bullshit you. I don't know him that well.

Alan tries to reassure Marie.

Alan: This man is a hitman. A professional hitman. He will do the job for you … This man does not muck around or fuck around.

REASONABLE DOUBT

They get down to business.

> *Marie*: What happens now?
>
> *Jason*: Well, I ask for a deposit.
>
> *Marie*: OK.
>
> *Jason*: … We will negotiate the price. We negotiate first of all what you want done.

Marie still has doubts.

> *Marie*: You don't have a wire on, do you?
>
> *Jason*: No.
>
> *Marie*: I'm sorry. I have to ask.
>
> *Jason*: That, that's insulting me …
>
> *Marie*: I'm sorry, you know, but you have to be careful, as well I have to be careful.
>
> *Jason*: Why do you think I did two laps around here before I walked in? This is safe … All I need to know is how you want it done.
>
> *Marie*: I prefer an accident like a car accident, or something. If that's not possible you have to tell me, otherwise that would be my preference.
>
> *Jason*: I need to have a photo, I need to know his movements and I don't need to know this now. OK? I want you to go away and then I will give you a few things I need from you, and the next time we meet …
>
> *Marie*: How long is this going to take?
>
> *Jason*: Well, it depends. Is there a time limit?
>
> *Marie*: I'd prefer that it be done sooner rather than later. I want to go home.
>
> *Jason*: Well, from my point of view, I'll tell you, I don't just go in cold. I need to know who it is. I do a bit of watching myself first … What do you want to prove that it's done?
>
> *Marie*: You don't have to prove to me that it's done. I mean, Gerry not coming home is going to be proof enough.

Insanely Homesick

Jason: Normally, people would ask for a finger, people have asked for his balls, or they want something.

Marie: No, no, no, no I don't want …

Jason: 'Cause generally I get a deposit, then I do the job, and then I'd show you that the job's done, and then I want the money within 24 hours. OK?

Marie: Well, that can be a problem.

Jason: Why's that?

Marie: Because I don't have … How much money do you want?

Jason: What do you want to pay? What do you think's fair?

Marie: I'd like to pay $25,000.

Alan: Nah.

Marie: No?

Alan: It should be nearer 50.

Marie: I'll try.

Jason proves more reasonable than Alan.

Jason: Marie … I don't want to agree on a price that you can't *deliver* … You've just said 25 then …

Marie: That's my preference …

Jason: … I want cash. No cheques.

Marie: It can't be in cash because, personally, I don't have that much.

Alan: Darl, this man is a good man, don't fuck him around.

Marie: I understand. I'm not fucking him around … I want to be very honest …

Understand my point of view. I don't want to pull out $25,000 and have my husband die and then have the cops looking for me … They are going to come looking for me because I am the only one that has any advantage with him dying. I am the one that is getting all the insurance policies. I am the one that gets the house.

Jason: So that's the reason, yeah?

Marie: I am the one that gets everything …

Marie: If I fuck you over, what would you do to me? …

Jason: Let's not talk about what's gonna happen if you don't pay because …

Marie: I would assume you would kill me if you don't get paid.

Jason: What I am saying, though, is that I don't just go and kill someone unless I know I am going to get paid …

Marie: You're going to get paid and what I am doing is trying to mitigate any of us getting caught.

Jason: Exactly.

Marie: Exactly. So it will have to be done over a certain period of time … I have already determined how to do it. What you have to do is set up a business here in Australia and I will transfer that money to your account at the business. And it will be done.

Jason: And what if you get asked … ?

Marie: I am investing in your business. You're somebody I met here that had a viable business opportunity, and I am investing in it.

Jason: What sort of business do you think?

Marie: Pools. A new way of cleaning pools, an ecologically friendly way of cleaning pools.

Jason: Yeah, no, that might work.

Marie: Without the chemicals.

Jason: Might work, too.

Marie: All right. And I will transfer that money into that account …

Jason: How long is that gonna take?

Marie: I suspect it's gonna be about six months before I get paid out on the insurance, possibly less …

Jason: So, are you gonna stay in Australia until you get …

Marie: I'm not. I'm going back to Canada.

Jason: When?

Marie: As soon as this is done, I'm going back to Canada …

Jason: So you are asking …

Marie: I am asking you to trust me, yes.

Jason: … me to do the job and then you go away to Canada …

Insanely Homesick

Marie: Yes, yes.

Jason: ... and then transfer the money?

Marie: Yeah, yes.

Alan: That's a big ask.

Jason: It is.

Marie: It's a big ask, but I am being very honest with you and I am telling you what I am doing ...

Jason: I'll probably need a couple of days to think about it ... I just need his movements. Where he's going to be ... Just rough, you know.

Marie tells Jason what Gerry will be doing when he returns from Canberra. Her mobile phone rings: it's Alexa.

Marie: Hi Lexi. What you doing? ... Oh, not too much. I'm going to be home in about half an hour ... OK, hon. All right, baby ... All right. Sit and watch TV and enjoy yourself ... All right, I'll talk to you real soon. Love you. Bye sweety ...

Jason: So, I just want to be clear. So, you want it done straightaway.

Marie: Mmm.

Jason: And why? Why haven't you got time?

Marie: Because – I mean, I'm being completely honest with you – I took some money from my husband. I have already tried to have this done. I paid $10,000 to a person that took the money and ran ...

Jason: So you've been fucked around by someone.

Marie: By over $10,000 and Gerry knows that money is gone and he's questioning me every day as to where the money's gone.

Jason: What did you tell him?

Marie: I am playing dumb and crying and going: 'I don't remember' – and it's not going to work ...

Marie: That's why I want it done sooner rather than later.

Jason: 'Cause he's giving you grief over the ten grand.

Marie: 'Cause he's giving me grief over the ten thousand.

REASONABLE DOUBT

Marie tells Jason that her husband is insured for $250,000.

Marie: And if it's a car accident – you know what? – I also collect on car insurance.

Jason: OK.

Marie: And that means more money. If you can actually make it like a car accident, $50,000 … and we'll look at a bonus on top of that … I'm not out to screw you. I want this done …

Alan: Hold your end up girl.

Marie: OK. Is this the point that I am supposed to get pissed? … I've told you time and time again.

Alan: I want you to be serious about what you are talking about.

Marie: I'm absolutely fucking serious about it. Dead serious about it.

Alan: Well, get serious about it.

Jason: No Alan, mate – it's all right. Just, I just have a few more questions.

Marie: I apologise.

Jason: No, that's fine and like I said, Alan: after this, mate, you're out of the picture … All right, I need a couple of details. If you write it down now. The car: I need the rego, make, model ra ra … An accident: well, the problem there … I don't want him having an accident and killing a carload of people and then it gets looked at.

Marie: And I don't want my daughter involved in any way, shape or form …

Jason: Well you've gotta write down for me where she's going to be … You may have to have her with you … at the time.

Marie: Fine. I will make sure she's with me.

Jason: When it happens, you have to be with someone else, you know.

Marie: To cover my butt …

Jason: Once I get a deposit …

Marie: What deposit?

Jason: Just something to show you're fair dinkum. All right, that's up to you.

Marie: But … Gerry knows $10,000 is gone … He told me to tell him what I did with that money.

Alan: You're gonna have to come up with a story.

Marie: I know. I've been working on that. I've come up with gambling but I'm not a gambler … But if it's done in a very quick period of time, I do not have to come up with any more stories: that's what I'm saying. That's why I am asking for it to be done quickly, as opposed to not quickly.

Jason: Well, when do you have in mind?

Marie: My preference is tomorrow.

Jason: You are asking me to kill your husband tomorrow without … That's a big ask, you know. How about I meet you on Thursday in a couple of days, you give me all the details I need and I'll try, I'll try and do it by the weekend? I just gotta cover my arse.

Marie: I know, but …

Jason: Big, big ask. I'm leaving myself wide open … Give me till Thursday …

Marie: OK. This is a very rude question but are you capable of doing this? The baby-face that you have, are you actually capable?

Jason: Who is capable, Marie? Who's capable?

Marie: I'm not. That's why I'm hiring you.

Jason: I am. There are certain things that I do, that I do not want to tell you about. So don't ask too many questions. I really don't know too much about you.

Marie: Even.

Jason asks some more about Darren duping Marie.

Jason: How did you pay him? Cash?

Marie: Cash. Cash! Fool! Fool! Fool! …

Jason: Oh well, you live and learn …

Alan: You're playing a different league now. Play this game.

Marie: Do you believe I am playing?

Jason: I don't think so. I think if you paid someone, you are obviously pretty keen, pretty keen to get it done.

Marie: I am very keen … I will tell you one thing. He [Darren] has my wedding ring and that's totally exclusive to me …

Jason: Hang on. You gave him ten cash and the ring?

Marie: Yeah, and the ring was made for me totally – totally. That's completely and utterly irreplaceable.

Jason repeats that he's concerned that a car accident may risk other lives.

Marie: I'm a cold-hearted bitch, that doesn't concern me … I want it to look like an accident so that nobody comes looking afterwards. Nobody comes looking for anybody.

Jason: All right.

Marie: We all walk away scot-free. That's what I want: we all walk away scot-free.

Jason: And so you can go back to Canada.

Marie: I want to go back to Canada, and have my life.

Jason: And you won't come back to Australia?

Marie: Nope. I will never come back to Australia …

Jason: You realise it's a big thing you're asking.

Marie: And it's a big thing you're asking that I trust you. I've already been screwed for $10,000.

Jason: Yeah.

Marie: I think you are actually the real thing … I have never wanted anything more than I want this. So, you're going to have to trust me.

Jason: So, you've thought it through.

Marie: I've thought it through, and want it done.

Jason: And when it's done, how are you going to feel afterward?

Marie: I'm gonna feel like shit, you know.

Jason: So, all right. So, you know that.

Marie: Yeah, I know that I'm going to feel like shit, but, you know, I'll get over it.

Jason: OK, just so long as you know that and there's no turning

Insanely Homesick

back. Once it's done, it's done.

Marie: I'll get over it. Once it's done, it's done.

Jason: It's done. It's final. That's it.

Marie: Final. Absolutely.

Jason: All right … So, what sort of deposit can you give me?

Marie: I have no assets.

Jason: None?

Marie: None … Actually that's not true. Al, go get $900 out. Here's my card.

While sitting in the car in the hotel car park waiting for Al, Jason has to contend with another surprise proposition.

Marie: Would you, would you take exception to the fact that I would like to feel your body?

Jason: Yeah, I would because there's someone sitting right there.

Marie: I wouldn't take exception for you to feel my body.

Jason: Someone's sitting right there. Do you know that man?

Marie: Nah …

Jason: You've got me a bit spooked, I tell ya now. The reason being … Can you see it from my point of view?

Marie: Can you see it from my point of view?

Jason: I can, I can.

Marie: You could be a cop, for all I know.

Jason: … I'm not a cop. I wouldn't be doing this shit if I was.

Marie: No. I have to tell you: if you're a cop, this is entrapment.

Jason: Exactly. Oh well, you know the law. I don't know about entrapment but I just know what I know … I'm in it for the cash, OK. It's the cash that I want and I don't want to get caught and I don't want any trouble down the track. That's why I will give you instructions as we go as to what you should do.

Marie: You are actually capable of this, baby-faced as you are?

Jason: What?! Yeah. It interests me that you keep saying that. Who, what were you expecting?

Marie: You know, it's funny … but I find you attractive and I find you completely out of the realm as to what I expected … There's nothing rough or hard about you.

Jason: And there shouldn't be …

Marie: But, you're a, you're a … baby.

Jason: But I'm here, aren't I … So, we move on to the next stage. OK? …

Alan: Marie, are you comfortable with Jason now?

Marie: Do you trust him?

Alan: I trust him with all my heart.

After the hour and a half 'meeting', Marie is dropped off at her car about 9.30. Alan then tells Jason why he refused Marie's request for him to kill her husband.

Alan: Oh, I could do it – that's not a problem – but I've done enough time, mate. You know what I mean. I've done 10 years' jail. I don't need another fuckin' 25 … How did you get stuck in this game, is it something you joined up with or … ?'

Jason: No, no, no. I've done a couple of fuckin' bad things.

Alan: Yeah?

Jason: And the last thing I did, I got given up.

Alan: Yeah?

Jason: And it was either go back inside, or give 'em a favour and as far as I know this should be the last and that's it, I'm out.

Alan gives his assessment of the situation.

Alan: There's this spastic fuckin' sheila … She's got a decent husband – doesn't slap her, doesn't slap her daughter – and she wants him knocked. All I worry about – because I've got kids, mate – is the 12-year-old daughter. If she knocks him and then she gets busted, where's the 12-year-old left?

Insanely Homesick

353

The next day – Wednesday 5 March 2003 – Jason and Marie meet at a coffee shop about 1pm. Jason checks whether, now sober, Marie is still keen to go ahead with the killing of her husband.

> *Jason*: There's no going back …
> *Marie*: Yep.

He demands a $2000 deposit, another $1400 the next day to top up the $600 Alan got out with her card at the pub, and $23,000 after the 'job'.

> *Marie*: I can get you the 23 within 48 hours …
> *Jason*: I just don't understand why you can't just leave him and go back.
> *Marie*: 'Cause I won't get my life back … The only way to get my life back as I had it … and that's the way I want it. Call it greed if you want, but I want my life back the way I had it … What I actually would like to do is buy a pub back home.
> *Jason*: So the thought of just taking off and just leaving him here in Australia?
> *Marie*: It doesn't work. I mean first of all, it means we'd have to sell our house back in Canada … I'd only get – if I'm lucky – 15 per cent of that, maybe less …
> The other thing is that one of the things I had to do when I came over here, in order to get a visa, was to give him joint custody of Lexi, which makes for a real hassle because he can actually, when I choose to go, fight me and try and keep Alexa here … I can't have any more children, she is the one and only, and I am not prepared to take that risk to go into a legal battle … So, I mean, the idea of just leaving him, I mean it does have its merits, but I could lose so bad … If there was an alternative I would take it.
> *Jason*: So, he has actually done nothing directly to make you do this apart from moving to Australia? …
> *Marie*: Exactly.

Jason: What are you going to say to the police, if they do speak to you down the track?

Marie: Nothing. I don't know anything.

Jason: How's she [Alexa] going to react?

Marie: She's going to be very upset and I am going to have to put her through counselling to deal with it – which is fine ... but my daughter last night was in tears, hysterical, wanting to go home. She wanted me to put her on a plane last night by herself because she wanted to go home so desperately.

Jason: So, what do you reckon would happen had you told him that she really wanted to go and you wanted to go?

Marie: It wouldn't make any difference. He'd sit there and think he would talk her out of it ... I understand the finality of it. Unfortunately, I do not feel that I have an option. If I had an option I would do it.

The next day – while her husband is at the Grand Prix – Jason and Marie meet at another coffee shop just after 12.30pm.

Jason: So if I do it tonight, still happy?

Marie: Yeah.

They talk about her alibi and Marie tells Jason of her husband's movements.

Jason: Do you want me to shoot him?

Marie: Can't you push him in front of a train?

Jason: They got cameras at train stations ... Do you want it brutal? Do you want him to feel pain?

Marie: Yeah, some way [inaudible].

Jason: You want him dead tonight?

Marie: Yes [inaudible] ...

Jason: You're clear on how much money you owe me after tonight?

Marie: Yeah, $23,000.

Jason: Twenty-three cash but it's got to be within 48 hours.

Marie: I know that.

Insanely Homesick

355

Jason: All right. Give me the $1400 …

Marie: I'm OK. Just like I said, I'm nervous. I'm committed to having it done … but don't like the idea of making Gerry hurt … I just don't want to get caught.

Marie hands $1400 cash to Jason. He counts it out in hundreds.

Marie: OK, I mean my preference is really [inaudible] without hurting him. Like I said, if there is some way that you can get into the [Grand Prix] function tonight and slip something in his drink that will just drop him.

Jason: What if someone else gets his drink?

Marie: They're not going to. I mean, quite frankly, Gerry doesn't put his drink down. He likes his drink too much.

Jason: You're paying me to kill him, not to kill anyone else, though. Remember that.

Marie: Yep, I know.

Jason: What about the robbery idea: I shoot him.

Marie: That's fine as long as it looks like a robbery gone bad, you know.

Jason: All right.

Marie: As soon as this is done, I will go – first thing in the morning – right across the street, to sell my car and I'm sure they can arrange payment for me that day.

***

As she was leaving the coffee shop, Marie was arrested. She had been right to suspect the 'baby-faced' Jason was no contract killer – he was a wired-for-sound undercover policeman. In her interview with police about an hour and a half after her arrest, Marie said she just had 'general chitchat' with Jason.

Police: And you didn't ask Jason to kill your husband and make it look like a … robbery gone wrong?

Marie: No.

356   **REASONABLE DOUBT**

She agreed she had given Jason $1400, but only to get Alan food.

> *Police*: Are you in the habit of giving people large sums of money?
> *Marie*: I try to help them, yes …
> *Police*: To be fair and really frank with you, I'll inform you that the person you know as Jason is a policeman, an undercover operative. As I said, all the conversations you had with him have been recorded with audio and video. So that doesn't change any of your replies?
> *Marie*: No.
> *Police*: So, you deny trying to incite Jason to murder your husband?
> *Marie*: Yes.

After being told she would be charged with incitement to murder, Marie was asked it she had anything to say.

> *Marie*: No. I mean, this is ridiculous. This is so far out of the realm of reality for me that I am floored.

***

Marie eventually confessed to trying to hire men to kill her husband.

Then came another astonishing twist in the Skura family's down-under odyssey, a twist that would surprise and test the judicial system: Gerry Skura forgave the woman who he had suspected of trying to poison him, and burn him alive, and who had admitted to trying to hire a hitman to murder him. Three months after his wife's arrest, he told a bail application that he still loved the self-described 'cold-hearted bitch'; the woman who hadn't cared if others had died in the car crash that killed him. His main message to his imprisoned wife was: 'Come home, we miss you.' He wept as he told the court: 'My wife has said she loves me and I know she loves my daughter. We'd like her to come home … She knows she has done some wrong things and needs help to change.' Despite this tearful plea, Justice Bernard Teague refused the bail application, saying there was too great a risk that Marie Skura would flee the country.

Insanely Homesick

On Thursday 24 July 2003 – nearly five months after her arrest – Dorothy Marie Skura pleaded guilty in the Victorian Supreme Court to incitement to murder.

Prosecutor Bill Morgan-Payler QC called for a 'substantial sentence of imprisonment … regardless of the attitude of the victim'.

Marie Skura's barrister Lex Lasry QC made the extraordinary plea that his client not only be set free but that she be set free in less than six days – in time to join her husband and daughter on a plane to Canada. Mr Lasry said that because of work commitments, Gerry Skura could not delay his flight home and hoped his wife could join him. He said the 140 days Marie Skura had served in jail was enough; that the rest of her sentence should be suspended.

Mr Lasry said Marie Skura had been suffering a significant mental disorder when she tried to have her husband murdered. He said the mental disorder that had been caused by the sexual, mental and physical abuse of her as a child had triggered her obsessive homesickness.

> *Mr Lasry*: I'm sure she means no offence to our country, but she simply felt totally isolated.

He said Marie Skura's psychological fragility had also helped cause – and been exacerbated by – her alcoholism. She now realised that she could never have another alcoholic drink, Mr Lasry said.

The barrister said his client had lied when she told Jason and Alan that she was not a gambler, that she had just made that up to fool her husband. She had, Mr Lasry said, put $60,000 through Australian poker machines.

He said that being in an Australian jail – away from her loving, forgiving family in Canada and away from much-needed intensive psychological counselling – would not only delay her treatment but be much harsher punishment for her than for other prisoners.

> *Mr Lasry*: It is the worst result – from her point of view – the worst possible result that could be imagined. For her, it is a nightmare.

358   REASONABLE DOUBT

***

Justice Bernard Bongiorno handed down his sentence the day before the Skuras were due to fly out, but their hopes that she would be on that long-dreamed-of flight to Canada looked doubtful when the judge said her attempts to hire someone to kill her husband were 'voluntary acts directed towards a logical and rational if wickedly criminal end'.

The Skuras' hopes were raised, however, when the judge said he accepted Marie Skura was remorseful, had suffered an appalling childhood, had a 12-year-old daughter to care for; would suffer more than other inmates because she would be isolated from her family, and had been forgiven by her victim.

But it all ended in tears. Justice Bongiorno said the victim's forgiveness was of doubtful relevance to sentencing her for trying to kill 'another human being' for the basest of all motives: greed.

> *Justice Bongiorno*: You wanted to rid yourself of your husband and Australia, and contemporaneously acquire substantial assets as a consequence.

As he sentenced Marie Skura to seven years' jail, her victim gasped, dropped his head and wiped away tears. Marie looked over at him and silently mouthed: 'I'm so, so sorry,' and broke down sobbing. Through the bars of the dock, her weeping daughter tried to wipe away her mother's tears and whispered to her.

Through all the crying, Justice Bongiorno ploughed on: setting a minimum term of four and a half years and making other technical orders. Finally, he ordered the weeping prisoner be removed.

***

Eight months after Marie Skura's tearful sentencing, she had some joy when the Victorian Court of Appeal cut her minimum sentence from four and a half years to three, and her maximum term from seven to six years. That meant Skura would be able to apply for parole 18 months earlier.

Insanely Homesick

The reason for the sentence cut? Mr Skura's forgiveness of the woman who had tried to have him killed. The judges ruled that although Justice Bongiorno was right that it was not up to victims to decide how to punish perpetrators, he should have taken more notice of Mr Skura's continuing support of his wife.

About seven months later, Marie Skura was still trying to get back to Canada. She wrote a letter from prison to the *Herald Sun* begging to be transferred to a Canadian jail. She said Australians were needlessly paying for her imprisonment.

Marie Skura: You house me, feed me, clothe me, provide me an income, medical attention and medication, you educate me, provide me with counselling, psychiatric care, dentistry and optometrist – even massages when necessary.

***

After flying home to Canada without his wife, Gerry Skura told *New Idea* magazine they would reunite after she was released from jail.

Gerry Skura: The future is a clean slate for us. We want to renew our vows. We want to re-pledge our love and start our lives all over again. I still don't believe that she ever really set out to hurt me. I believe these actions were an extraordinary cry for help and Marie thought this was the only means to an end for her.

He said they had even managed to laugh through the trauma.

Gerry Skura: I have used a lot of humour to get me through this. In fact, I've often joked that when Marie is released from prison, we'll have a 'How to Host a Murder' dinner party.

More true crime from Wayne Howell

Killer Excuses

Killer Excuses is a courtroom-drama collection of some of the extraordinary defences tried in Australian manslaughter and murder trials.

- **Fighting demons with Gladwrap** A woman dies while her God-fearing husband and two others pin her to a chair on a 40°C day and force her to watch a Bible-wielding 22-year-old 'exorcist' exhort the demon in her to go to the foot of the cross.
- **Repulsive sex** Millionaire James Ramage strangles his wife Julie, bundles her body into the boot of his Jaguar, drives to where she used to like horse riding, and buries her. He denies murdering his wife, saying she provoked him into losing control by telling him sex with him was repulsive.
- **A blond wig and a meat tenderiser** A policeman comes upon a man in the bush beside a shallow grave wearing a blond wig. The man says he's been abducted and his abductors have forced him to wear the wig.
- **Embrace of the sea** A woman dies while performing fellatio on a man in the sea. When he lifts her up and finds her not breathing he flees leaving her, as the judge puts it, to 'the embrace of the sea'.
- **Maniac behind the door** A man says he only shot a member of his robbery gang because a maniacal gangster was hiding behind a nearby door threatening to shoot him if he didn't.
- **Blame the espresso** A man says a Sambuca-laced espresso made him act like a robot and attack his father and stepmother with a kitchen knife – even crashing through a glass door and chasing them down the street.
- **A very bad game** The 13-year-old and the 14-year-old think it's fun to throw rocks off a freeway overpass … until a 1.8kg rock crashes through a windscreen and kills a man.
- **Drum of tragedy** For over three years a woman's body – dressed in matching black bra, crotchless panties, suspenders and stockings – with a rope tied round her ankles slowly mummifies in a 44-gallon drum of garden lime. Her father's dogged determination ends in police discovering the body, extraditing her boyfriend from the US and charging him with murder.

More true crime from The Five Mile Press

Forensics
True Stories from Australian Police Files
Vikki Petraitis

Vikki Petraitis is one of Australia's most popular true crime writers. In this collection she tells stories from the police files in which forensics, as well as dogged determination, have played a major part in their resolution. They make for riveting reading.

More true crime from The Five Mile Press

The Beat
A True Account of the Bondi Gay Muders
IJ Fenn

In June 2001, 12 years after television newsreader, Ross Warren, disappeared after an evening out with friends in Sydney, a police operation was set up to reinvestigate the disappearance. What this new investigation uncovered was to prove far more interesting than the anticipated 'missing person' case. This was only the start of Operation Taradale, which quickly turned into a horrifying saga of multiple murders committed mostly within a few hundred metres of each other – in Marks Park, the beat, the scrubby, rocky headland between Bondi and Tamarama.

IJ Fenn moves the story along with the pace of a detective thriller. Telephones are tapped, surveillance operations put in place, crime scenes re-enacted to ignite media interest and arrests are made. *The Beat* is an ugly story about ugly people committing ugly crimes. This is a disturbing book, but you will not be able to put it down.

'Meticulously researched, *The Beat* highlights that justice is blind and rarely meted out equally.'

Robin Bowles

More true crime from The Five Mile Press

The Australian Crime File 2
More Stories From Australia's Best True Crime Collection
Paul B. Kidd

One of Australia's best storytellers, and a renowned authority on true crime, Paul B. Kidd, is back with more from his famous collection of infamous stories. Murder, the macabre and the mysterious – it's all here in spades and is definitely not for the faint at heart.